AALTO, UTZC

This book examines the work of three seminal Nordic architects – Alvar Aalto, Jørn Utzon and Sverre Fehn – from a phenomenological perspective, utilising the methodology of 'paradigm' (or 'in the manner of'). Roger Tyrrell explains how the approach of each architect is defined by the three sub-frames of the paradigm: that of the 'origin' (*arche*), that of 'revealing' (*techne*), and that of 'the poetic conjunction', in order to gain a holistic understanding of the experiential or phenomenological predisposition of the three architects. Using this method the author describes the commonalties and distinctive qualities of the architecture and design methods of Aalto, Utzon and Fehn. The final chapter projects the intellectual heritage of the three protagonists into the contemporary world, examining the work of practices from the UK, Norway and the USA that each extend this particular way of making place.

Roger Tyrrell is a principal lecturer in architecture at the University of Portsmouth, School of Architecture, UK, an adjunct associate professor in architecture at the University of Aalborg in Denmark, and co-director of the Jørn Utzon Research Network. Roger is also the director of CHORA (www.chora.uk.com), an international consultancy company that strives to reconnect academia with creative practice.

AALTO, UTZON, FEHN

Three Paradigms of Phenomenological Architecture

Roger Tyrrell

Routledge
Taylor & Francis Group
NEW YORK AND LONDON

First published 2018
by Routledge
711 Third Avenue, New York, NY 10017

and by Routledge
2 Park Square, Milton Park, Abingdon, Oxon, OX14 4RN

Routledge is an imprint of the Taylor & Francis Group, an informa business

Library of Congress Cataloging-in-Publication Data
Names: Tyrrell, Roger, author.
Title: Aalto, Utzon, Fehn : three paradigms of phenomenological architecture / Roger Tyrrell.
Description: New York : Routledge, 2017. | Includes bibliographical references and index.
Identifiers: LCCN 2017020542 | ISBN 9781138960992 (hb : alk. paper) | ISBN 9781138961005 (pb : alk. paper) | ISBN 9781315660059 (ebook)
Subjects: LCSH: Architecture—Philosophy. | Aalto, Alvar, 1898-1976—Criticism and interpretation. | Utzon, Jørn, 1918-2008—Criticism and interpretation. | Fehn, Sverre, 1924-2009—Criticism and interpretation.
Classification: LCC NA2500. T975 2017 | DDC 720.1—dc23
LC record available at https://lccn.loc.gov/2017020542

ISBN: 978-1-138-96099-2 (hbk)
ISBN: 978-1-138-96100-5 (pbk)
ISBN: 978-1-315-66005-9 (ebk)

Typeset in Bembo
by Keystroke, Neville Lodge, Tettenhall, Wolverhampton

MIX
Paper from responsible sources
FSC
www.fsc.org
FSC™ C013985

Printed in the United Kingdom
by Henry Ling Limited

For Hazel, who tirelessly encouraged me 'to be' throughout the process of this book. With love.

CONTENTS

FIGURES

ACKNOWLEDGEMENTS

My parents, John and Elsie Tyrrell, provided my compass; any periods of floundering and beaching were entirely due to my predisposition to alter course without good reason.

My teachers: as a student at what was then Portsmouth Polytechnic School of Architecture (1979–1985; now the University of Portsmouth), under the tutelage of inspiring academics such as Barry Russell, Dr Ranulph Glanville, Nigel Mills, Millutin Tripkovitch, Tomas Llorens, the then Head of School, Professor Geoffrey Broadbent and my erstwhile teacher and now dear friend, Dr Richard (Dick) Bunt, to whom I extend particular thanks in supporting the theoretical discourse in this book in particular, but also for his mentorship in all things.

To all those I have taught, who have taught me more: my students, some of whom have become close friends and collaborators.

My academic colleagues at Portsmouth and across the world: in particular, Line Norskov-Eriksen, Belinda Mitchell, Tod Wakefield, Rachel Brown, Nicola Crowson, Greg Bailey, Nick Timms, Kate Baker, El Montacir Bensaid and Abdelghani Tayyibi (Morocco), Mathew Hinds, Poppy Taylor, Richard Leplastrier and Adrian Carter (Australia).

My co-conspirators at PAD, SAAW and PCA who contributed so generously, to both the form and content of this book.

Juhani Pallasmaa, who, despite the significant pressures upon his time, generously gave his time and spirit to provide a Foreword to this offering.

My sincere thanks to the custodians and guardians of buildings designed by Aalto, Utzon and Fehn who permitted my trespass; you are all generous spirits.

My publishing team at Routledge, New York, and in particular my commissioning editor Wendy Fuller, and Trudy Varcianna, editorial assistant, for unstinting support and professionalism.

And finally my sincere thanks to Hazel, for the encouragement, harrying and providing the space that is necessary in the delivery of a project such as this.

FOREWORD

Crafting Experience and Meaning: Three Alchemists of the North

Juhani Pallasmaa

Most architects would probably agree that Alvar Aalto, Jørn Utzon and Sverre Fehn are the most significant architects of the three Nordic countries, Finland, Denmark, and Norway, respectively, or perhaps of the Nordic countries altogether.[1] Roger Tyrrell's choice of the protagonists for his book is thus well motivated, particularly considering the heightened experiential quality, intuitive design methodology, and the material and contextual sensibilities of their works, on the one hand, and the phenomenological framework of the writer's investigation, on the other. In many ways, these three architects are ideal subjects for a phenomenological study.

In case a Swedish architect would also have been included, who would be the master architect from Sweden, Aalto's early role model Erik Gunnar Asplund (1885–1940), or Asplund's former collaborator Sigurd Lewerentz (1885–1975), perhaps? Both would qualify well to be studied within the phenomenological paradigm, as they expanded the modern architectural sensibility to materiality, hapticity, emotionality and deep historical resonance, and also their works emphasise the experiential dimension rather than rationality or theory.

Obviously, the three architects in this book have not been chosen because of their cultural and national backgrounds, but because of their personal philosophical and practical design approaches, and idiosyncratic design paradigms.[2] Yet Aalto, Utzon and Fehn unavoidably also represent their specific cultural realms, backgrounds and traditions, and exactly due to their crucial mental connections with their backgrounds, they can be presented as the ultimate Nordic architects. Democratic principles, the ideals of welfare state and socially orientated architecture and design, are areas where the five countries are usually seen to constitute a unity. There are certainly critics today, who argue that in the contemporary world of physical, ideological and mental mobility, regionally, culturally and historically grounded identities, such as 'Nordic', do not have relevance any longer, as we are now all subjects of a globalised, uniform, and technologised consumer culture.

However, I wish to disagree with the view that human character could be detached from its fundamental geographic, historical and cultural grounds. Even our mother tongues structure the world in distinct ways, and these pre-conscious processes condition our views of the world in specific ways. 'A change in language changes our view of the universe', the linguist B. L. Whorf argued dramatically (Whorf 1956), but the theories of Edward Sapir and Whorf were rejected too hurriedly.[3] There is no doubt in my mind of the fundamental impact of the natural landscapes and cultural conditions of life on our sensibilities and growth, as well as on our ways of thinking and feeling.

Consequently, although a devoted cosmopolitan, Alvar Aalto is a product of the Finnish regional reality of the early decades of the twentieth century, especially of the prevailing Finnish forest context. As Aalto himself confessed:

> We Northerners, especially the Finns, are very prone to 'forest dreaming', for which we have had ample opportunities up to now.
>
> *Alvar Aalto in Schildt 1984: 207*

Siegfried Giedion, the ideologist of modernism, argued in his influential book *Space, Time and Architecture* that Aalto's architecture always resonates with the site and terrain, and he even built the landscape when there were no distinctive natural land forms on the site:

> Finland is with Aalto wherever he goes. It provides him with that inner source of energy, which always flows through his work. It is as Spain is to Picasso or Ireland to James Joyce. Part of the essence of present day art is that its true representatives originate in a definite human environment and their work is not created in vacuum.
>
> *Giedion 1952: 455*

Aalto's buildings outside of Finland, from his unbuilt projects in Iran through his buildings in Germany, Italy and France, all the way to the West Coast of the United States, project a strong atmosphere of 'Finnishness', although they also respond sensitively to the characteristics of their local sites. His buildings abroad seem to express a 'double nationality' of sorts.

Similarly, Jørn Utzon's architecture reflects the flat, cultivated lands of Denmark, the high skies, and the presence of the sea and sailing, of his entire life. Also, Utzon was more interested in constructed, architectural landscapes, such as platforms and terraces as mediating elements between the building and the larger environment, than actual existing landscapes. Although he travelled extensively and studied architectural traditions of remote cultures, China and Japan, as well as Morocco and Mexico, his artistic syntheses in Kuwait, Australia and Spain are unquestionably products of Nordic, and specifically Danish, sensibilities which combine rational clarity with a sense of tactility and intimacy.

Sverre Fehn's mental and emotional world , likewise, is that of the dramatic landscapes of Norwegian mountains and fjords, as well as of ancient myths of the North. He was inspired by poetic as well as formal motifs, and his special fascination was the stunningly beautiful Viking boat. But, like Aalto and Utzon, Fehn fused images of his native settings with those from his travels to other countries, including Morocco. Fehn was an archaeologist–architect, who was always fascinated in the secrets of the earth. In his projects, he usually accepted the site or landscape as given, and placed his building and its parts to take advantage of the special features and qualities of the site. For him, landscape was primarily a source of stories and potential remains of former human occupation – actual or products of his imagination.

My view of the shared Nordic soul of the three masters can easily be seen as romanticism, but I myself rather see it as cultural realism, which I have felt in my own bones through decades of extensive travelling around the world. These travels have only strengthened my identification with my background. Edward T. Hall, the anthropologist who made seminal studies in the hidden connections of the environment and human spatial behaviour, writes:

> The most pervasive and important assumption, a cornerstone in the edifice of Western thought, is one that lies hidden from our consciousness and has to do with a person's relationship to his or her environment. Quite simply, the Western view is that human processes, particularly behavior, are independent of environmental controls and influence.
>
> *Hall and Hall 1975: 8*

In his book *Ecological Psychology* Roger G. Barker argues that some attributes of human behaviour vary less from person to person within a given setting, than the behaviour of any single individual in different settings (Barker 1968). We are, indeed, products of our worlds, more than we tend to believe, and on the other hand, the world is largely our own creation and mental construction. The three Nordic master architects are, of course, unique individuals and exceptional creative talents, but they also reflect the deep essences of their local cultures, as well as the shared characteristics of the Nordic world.

Architecture has traditionally been seen as material buildings, judged primarily by the sense of vision. Yet, already in 1934, the pragmatist philosopher John Dewey argued in his seminal book *Art as Experience*:

> In common conception, the work of art is often identified with the building, book, painting, or statue in its existence apart from human experience. Since the actual work of art is what the product does with and in experience, the result is not favorable to understanding … When artistic objects are separated from both conditions of origin and operation in experience, a wall is built around them that renders almost opaque their general significance, with which esthetic theory deals.
>
> *Dewey 1980: 3*

The currently expanding experiential and phenomenological view of architecture has made it evident that architectural and artistic dimensions are fundamentally mental, experiential and emotive qualities, and that they are identified in actual encounters with them. Roger Tyrrell's book is essentially a study of the design paradigms of the three architects in the light of phenomenological thinking.[4] Aalto and Utzon would probably not have known the notion of phenomenology, whereas it is likely that Fehn was familiar with this philosophical orientation due to his deep personal interest in the concept of place, and because his professor colleague at the Oslo School of Architecture and Design for nearly two decades, Christian Norberg-Schulz, was one of the earliest promoters of architectural phenomenology, largely based on Heidegger's philosophical writings.

Whether the three architects were versed in phenomenological thinking is practically irrelevant in this context, as their approaches and designs can be relevantly studied from this perspective, due to the openness of their paradigmatic thinking, as mentioned earlier. Tyrrell uncovers the complex and subtle experiential and emotive qualities and hidden mental meanings that make these architects rare and significant in the world of modern and contemporary architecture. They are all designers who could also be characterised as epic architects, because of the inclusiveness of their approach and the feeling of life and sense of internalised culture, projected by their works, instead of mere personal aesthetic preferences.

An interest in the mental significance of light and its architectural articulation, unites the three architects perhaps more than any other aspect of their architectures. This sensitised interest arises naturally from the amazingly differing qualitative conditions of illumination in the North, through the seasons and the hours of the day. The total absence of sunlight in mid-winter, and the continuous daylight at mid-summer mark the polarities of natural illumination in the North. But also the temperature, colour and angle of light vary dramatically all the way to the horizontal light, or light from below, reflected by surfaces of water and snow. Illumination and materiality are the two most powerful means of creating atmospheres, and these are mastered by the three architects. Their works could relevantly be studied also from the point of atmosphere, mood and tuning alone.

Although, after having entered the modernist ideology in the late 1920s, Alvar Aalto became so involved in radical rationalism that he planned to write a book on 'non-synthetic aspirations in architecture' and called the architect a 'social administrator' (in Schildt 1986: 195–196).

He soon turned against simplistic theorisation and kept emphasising the lived and emotional qualities of architecture. Within a couple of years, he developed his organicist, multi-thematic and emotive architecture. In all the scales of his design, as well as in his writings, he relied on his intuition, and he questioned the generally assumed conflict between rationality, intuition and emotional engagement. Early on, he also saw the connections between biology and architecture: 'I would like to add my personal, emotional view, that architecture and its details are in some way all part of biology' (Alvar Aalto in Schildt 1997: 108).

Jørn Utzon, who worked with Aalto for a short period at the age of 29 in 1947, was also orientated towards experientially and emotively rich architecture.

His approach was grounded in additive structural and thematic systems with rich variations, fusing a tectonic approach with contextually varying cellular, additive processes echoing biological principles. Even Utzon's small-scale works, such as his houses, project a monumental and epic image in the way they embrace the landscape and elements of nature as well as human movement and action. His buildings are designed for mobile and actively perceiving individuals, and their meanings transcend utilitarian issues of dwelling. Utzon's architecture has clearly a more southern and urbane feel, and his buildings suggest more lively social interactions than do those of Aalto and Fehn, which also express the coldness, darkness, silence and solitude of the North. At the same time that we acknowledge the Nordic similarities, we need to identify the subtle differences.

Sverre Fehn's architectural thinking is based on poetic metaphors, both verbal and formal. He aspired to reconnect architecture with its deep ontological origins in ancient myths and tales. He was a storyteller, mystic and philosopher both in his architecture and writings; his pronouncements often make one think of Louis Kahn's enigmatic, but poetic statements.[5] In Fehn's poetic metaphors, both narrated and sketched, earth, horizon, sky and fire have central roles. For him, the earth is not so much the condition of fertility and growth, the Mother Earth, as it is the medium and depository of accumulated human history. Fehn's designs are tectonic rather than moulded (he used plastic units as accents and foci in his designs), but he succeeded in engaging touching feelings of historicity, time, materiality, and an expressive, almost ritualistic sense of structure, and the inherent rituality of the act of constructing. He had the open-minded innocence of a child, combined with the mythic wisdom of a bard. Knowing that I had been intensely engaged in studies of animal building behaviour, Sverre suddenly said in a conversation between the two of us in the Villa Mairea: 'The bird's nest is absolute Functionalism, because the bird is not aware of its death'.[6] His thought implies that the utilitarian rationality of human construction is bound to be compromised by our unconscious need to attach our edifices to metaphysical concerns. The impact of our unconscious fear of death is fundamental in architecture, but largely censored from the modern consciousness.

The causalities of artistic expression are still largely unknown, but a sensitive architect, designer and artist is able to intuit and simulate imaginatively the full sensory and mental impact of complex entities. This skill could be called 'embodied and empathic imagination', the architect's most valuable gift. Aalto pointed out the extraordinary capacity of poetic thinking in creating a synthesis of irreconcilable and even conflicting elements:

> Almost every formal assignment involves dozens, often hundreds, sometimes thousands of conflicting elements that can be forced into functional harmony only by an act of will. This harmony cannot be achieved by any other means than art.
>
> *Alvar Aalto in Schildt 1997: 174*

Vittorio Gallese, one of the discoverers of the mirror neurons, supports Aalto's view of the supremacy of artistic thinking:

> From a certain point of view, art is more powerful that science. With much less expensive tools and with greater power for synthesis, artistic intuitions show us who we are, probably in a much more exhaustive way with respect to the objectifying approach of the natural sciences. Being human square with the ability to ask ourselves who we are. Since the beginning of mankind, artistic creativity has expressed such ability in its purest and highest form.
>
> *Gallese and Di Dio 2012: 693*

The thinking and design work of the three master architects surely tell us convincingly and comfortingly about both the world and ourselves.

I was fortunate enough to meet Alvar Aalto a number of times from 1960 onwards, and occasionally even argue with him. In his lifetime, his towering figure also evoked critical attitudes. However, the more I have studied his incredibly profuse oeuvre, the more I have been amazed by his productivity and ingenuity in all scales of design, as well as the intuitive and intellectual grasp of the complexities and mental dimensions of architecture expressed in his writings.

I met Sverre Fehn for the first time also in 1961 in Stockholm, where I was accompanying architect and professor Aulis Blomstedt, Aalto's counterpoint in the Finnish architectural discourse during the 1950s and 1960s. I immediately sensed the poetic character of the outwardly shy Norwegian architect, whose pavilion at the Brussels World Fair of 1958 I deeply admired. Gradually, we became friends and kept meeting at various events, such as 'The Modern Tradition' Symposium in Venice, organised in 1981 by the Venice Biennial and the Museum of Finnish Architecture.

I never had the chance to meet Jorn Utzon, but he and his work was strongly present in my architectural world ever since his legendary competition project for the Sydney Opera in 1957. In 2008, I was one of the eleven architects whom the Danish architectural journal *Arkitekten* invited to greet Utzon through a personal letter for his 90th birthday on 8 April 2008. Regrettably, Utzon passed away only a few months after the letters had been delivered to him.

I ended my letter to Utzon with the following paragraph:

> All profound work arises from a dialogue between actuality and dream. Imagination fuses observation and fantasy, memory and desire, past and future. Your images traverse space and time, unite traditions of distant cultures and merge natural phenomena with geometry, and history with Utopia. You have shown how to turn motion into form, matter into luminance, and gravity into flight. I can touch the chiaroscuro on the ceiling folds of the Bagsvaerd Church, and feel the moist wind when looking at the sails of the Opera House. Your poetic alchemy enriches the imagination of all of us. Thank you for your generosity.
>
> *Arkitektens Forlag 2008: 24*

I could have well sent the same letter of gratitude to all the three Nordic alchemists of architecture, who turned physical matter into immaterial experiences of beauty.

Notes

1 The notion of 'Nordic' includes the five countries of Denmark, Sweden, Finland, Norway and Iceland, whereas the notion 'Scandinavia' excludes Finland.
2 In the sciences and philosophy, paradigm is defined as a distinct set of concepts and patterns of thought, including theoretical assumptions, research methods, postulates and standards that give rise to legitimate contributions in a given field. The notion of paradigm does not impose a rigid or closed mechanically followed approach, as the concept can be taken flexibly and creatively. In the context of the three architects in Roger Tyrrell's study, the word refers to a design approach as a mixture of intellectual assumptions, beliefs, sensibilities, intuitions, and practical methods of design.
3 See also the role of language in perception of space and movement, and patterns of thinking in Strömnes (1976, 1981, 2006).
4 The application of the phenomenological approach in architecture has a strong Nordic component. See, for instance, Rasmussen (1964) and Norberg-Schulz (1980).
5 It is often forgotten that Louis Kahn was born in the Baltic Sea area on the island of Saarenmaa in Estonia.
6 The private conversation in Villa Mairea took place during the preliminary seminar before the 3rd International Alvar Aalto Symposium 'Modernity and Popular Culture' in 1985.

References

Arkitektens Forlag. 2008. *A Tribute to Jørn Utzon*. Copenhagen: Arkitektens Forlag.

Barker, R. C. 1968. *Ecological Psychology*. Redwood City, CA: Stanford University Press.

Dewey, J. 1980. *Art as Experience*. New York: Pedigee Books.

Gallese, V. and Di Dio, C. 2012. Neuroesthetics: The Body in Esthetic Experience. In *The Encyclopedia of Human Behaviour*, vol 2, ed. V. S. Ramachandran. Amsterdam: Elsevier.

Giedion, S. 1952. *Space, Time and Architecture: The Growth of a New Tradition*. Cambridge, MA: Harvard University Press.

Hall, M. R. and Hall, E. T. 1975. *The Fourth Dimension in Architecture: The Impact of Building on Behaviour*. Santa Fe, NM: Sunstone Press.

Norberg-Schulz, C. 1980. *Genius Loci: Towards a Phenomenology of Architecture*. New York: Rizzoli International Publishers.

Rasmussen, S. E. 1964. *Experiencing Architecture*. Cambridge, MA: MIT Press.

Schildt, G. 1984. *Alvar Aalto: The Early Years*. New York: Rizzoli International Publications.

Schildt, G. 1986. *Alvar Aalto: Decisive Years*. New York: Rizzoli International Publishers.

Schildt, G. 1997. *Alvar Aalto in His Own Words*. Helsinki: Otava Publishing Company.

Strömnes, F. 1976. *A New Physics of the Inner Worlds*. Tromsö: Institute of Social Science, University of Tromsö.

Strömnes, F. 1981. On the Architecture of Thought. In *Abacus: Yearbook 2*. Helsinki: The Museum of Finnish Architecture.

Strömnes, F. 2006. *The Fall of the Word and the Rise of the Mental Model*. Frankfurt: Peter Lang.

Whorf, B. L. 1956. *Language, Thought and Reality*, ed. John B. Carroll. Cambridge, MA: MIT Press.

PREFACE

The Shaman, the Theōroi and the Storyteller

> We have maintained that the Nordic world and Nordic Architecture have an essential affinity to our time. Both are characterised by openness, interplay, and dynamism, and modern architecture has sought to get rid of the dogma of the past ... The new freedom was not understood as something absolute but as the recovery of the origins: only in this way may we resist the devaluation of values.
>
> *Norberg-Schulz 1996: 197*

This is a study of the design methods and architecture of the Finn, Alvar Aalto (1898–1976), the Dane, Jørn Utzon (1918–2008) and the Norwegian, Sverre Fehn (1924–2009). Both the threads that bind them together and their unique qualities are considered, as is the intellectual heritage that each built-upon. In order to discover the essence of each I characterise them within the process of authorship, and it is hoped that such characterisation, exposed from the outset, may assist the reader in entering the realm of our three protagonists.

Alvar Aalto was the Shaman; albeit a very sophisticated shaman. Shamans are apparently able to transmute (change substances) and shape-shift (the ability to change living forms), which leads to the ability to transfigure. Transfiguration provides the ability to transmute. Yet, Aalto brought to those transmutations a level of sophistication previously unimaginable within his zeitgeist. Writing of the Great Stockholm Exhibition of 1930:

> Despite all the criticism [of the Exhibition], Sweden is well-prepared for change; I am thinking primarily of the country's social climate and industrial development, but also of the favourable spirit among intellectual circles. I therefore believe that we are on the threshold of something new here.
>
> *Schildt 1998: 72*

Aalto followed Erik Gunnar Asplund's example of being open to new influences, new ways; that provided a progressive and incremental set of transmutations through the movements of National Romanticism, to neo-classicism and to functionalism. That is a significant curriculum vitae. These transmutations were of course informed by the shifting cultural, social, political and economic contexts, but nonetheless represent a considerable contribution to architecture in the expression of our collective cultural soul. The sophisticated Shaman was also a traveller.

As was the Theōroi, Jørn Utzon. In the manner of the ambassadors of ancient Greek city-states, he travelled to observe and upon observation, to speculate upon and after speculation, absorb: bringing back experiences that were subsequently reinterpreted within his own context. He moved fleet of foot across landscapes to places of cultural density, uncovering ancient sources; constantly collecting. It was the Theōroi that advised the Shaman to travel to Morocco to rediscover that which had been lost.

> I saw that it was in my travels that I really got something. I went on a 500km hike – was it 500km? That probably isn't right ... but I went on a very long walk in Morocco, from Ourzazate around the southern side of the Atlas Mountains, and there I experienced a building tradition that was completely in harmony with the place and the materials. They built – now and then – and they sang while they built, stamped out mud houses, you know, in many stories from clay and grass ...
>
> *Holm et al. 2008: 10*

In Morocco sat the Storyteller, who, like the Shaman and Theōroi, had travelled: constantly seeking to discover tales of place and in doing so, striving to leave his own identity behind. He collected tales of the origins of things. The Jamal el Fna in Marrakech is the place of stories. As day gives way to night, people gather around the Storyteller to listen, and he told tales of conscience, mythology and imagination. Sverre Fehn is that Storyteller, engaging with the deep-rooted phenomena of mythology and essence that characterised him. He is the one of narrative.

> A long time ago, when the earth was very young, it was one huge garden covered in tall palm trees and perfumed jasmine and the songs of the nightingales flooded the landscape with their gentle melodies. At this time all men were loyal, trustworthy and honest. In fact, the word 'lie' did not even exist ...
>
> But one day someone told a lie. It was a very small lie, and of no importance, but it was the end of man's childhood and the age of innocence ...
>
> So God summoned all the men on earth together and said to them, 'each time one of you lies I shall throw a grain of sand onto the earth ...'
>
> And so lie after lie, little after little, the Sahara gradually came into existence as God threw grains of sand onto the Earth from the heavens above. But here and there, the odd oasis can still be seen. These are the traces of the original gardens, because not all men lie.
>
> *Hamilton 2001: 61*

References

Hamilton, R. 2001. *The Last Storytellers: Tales from the Heart of Morocco*. London: Tauris.

Holm, M. J., Kjeldsen, K. and Marcus, M. (eds). 2008. *Jørn Utzon: The Architect's Universe*. Humlebæk: Louisiana Museum of Modern Art.

Norberg-Schulz, C. 1996. *Nightlands: Nordic Building*. Cambridge, MA: MIT Press.

Schildt, G. (ed.). 1998. *Alvar Aalto: In His Own Words*. New York: Rizzoli International Publications.

1

OF BENEATH THE TABLE

> ... that music begins to atrophy when it departs too far from dance; that poetry begins to atrophy when it gets too far from music; but this must not be taken as implying that all good music is dance music or all poetry lyric. Bach and Mozart are never too far away from physical movement.
>
> *Pound 1934: 14*

The origins of this book lie under a dining room table in my parents' house. The year was 1959. I was three years old. This was not just any old table, however. This was a table designed by Alvar Aalto (1898–1976). To be specific: Finmar Reference 82/8-3, size 3′ 11¾″ × 2′ 5¾″, with a black top.

I often retreated under that table in my formative years. It was my cave, a world where imagination flourished; a territory largely impenetrable to adults and that, in that my innocence, I thought to be a secret place. It was my window on life. From that safe harbour, I could ponder upon my tiny world, as domesticity rumbled on. It was here that I made my first drawings. Much later I noticed crayon marks on the underside of the tabletop. My earliest scribbles according to my mother, hardly comparable to the cave paintings of Lascaux, but my first forays into representing thoughts. Under that table was a place 'to be'. A place that provided all that I later understood to be the primal essences of what it is to dwell: *retreat, prospect* and *reason*. It was my first, and to date, only Aalto dwelling.

Given this personal history, imagine my surprise to much later read that Alvar Aalto and I had shared a formative experience. Aalto wrote of *his* father's table – 'The White Table':

> The White table is big. Possibly the biggest table in the world, at least in the world and among the tables that I know ... in the lower story, I lived from the moment I learned to crawl on all fours. It was like a large market

> place where I ruled all by myself, until I was ready to be moved up to the upper story, the white table-top itself.
>
> *Schildt 1997: 11*

Serendipity aside, it is perhaps inevitable that having been surrounded by Nordic influences such as Aalto's furniture from a young age, my later academic interests might intuitively veer towards the realm of that we might term 'the Nordic world'; a territory that is central to the narrative of our three protagonists, Aalto, Utzon and Fehn.

In defining the physical territory of this exploration I turn to the words of Christian Norberg-Schulz in his articulation of the nature of conditions in the 'North'.

> In that the North is composed of several and differing countries, it may appear pointless to speak of a 'Nordic world'. But while it is true that the Nordic lands are distinct, we can nonetheless group them under the common heading 'the North'. That this term is something more than a collective noun is evident; we have already suggested that it encompasses a region of character and identity.
>
> *Norberg-Schulz 1996: 1*

These words represent precisely my own experience. While some speak of 'Scandinavia' (that excludes Finland), this term is predicated only upon a shared linguistic heritage and in that sense may be judged as a mono-dimensional classification. Given the complex historical inter-relationships between Denmark, Norway, Sweden and Finland, one has a sense that current nation-state boundaries are of relatively little significance. My own experience suggests that a series of subtle thresholds exist within the North where the presence of 'otherness' becomes evident. This is not merely a physical phenomenon that encompasses tangible characteristics such as landscape but extends to more existential dimensions such as the particular qualities of light that, while measurable and quantifiable, exhibit very particular experiential qualities, leading us perhaps almost inevitably towards a phenomenological interrogation of this particular place.

In his book *Nightlands*, Norberg-Schulz explores North and South from such a phenomenological perspective and suggests that while the South may be characterised by sharp direct sunlight and shadow, the nature of light in the Nordic world is profoundly different:

> Here in the North, the sun does not rise to the zenith, but grazes things obliquely and dissolves in an interplay of light and shadow.
>
> *Norberg-Schulz 1996: 1*

It is of course somewhat paradoxical that the focus of this book upon 'humane Nordic modernism', examines a movement of architecture that has its origins in the

South. The shadow bearing whiteness of Le Corbusier's modernism I would argue is born of Mediterranean conditions where shadow is actively sought by man, rather than speaking of the soft grey skies so characteristic of the world of Aalto, Utzon and Fehn.

However, the origins of modernism were reinterpreted and redefined in the North, as the significance of a sense of the humane attitudes and an ethos of collective responsibility bore weight; the modern movement was transformed and became particular to the Nordic world. For these reasons, the text will use two terms, the *North* and the *Nordic,* interchangeably in describing our territory.

Yet the distinct qualities of each place remain. To draw a place is often a good way of understanding 'place' a little more. Figure 1.1 shows what, for me, a parti landscape sketch of Denmark would be. Drawn purposely in landscape format, with the low horizon giving way to the overwhelming skies, any dwelling would hunker down within the slightest hollow like a fox in a hedge asleep. Here, the only elements that lift far above the horizon are places of significance; Church spires and places of civic activity.

In Demark the sky is all, perhaps best exemplified in big spaces such as that experienced in Skagen, Northern Jutland, where the Baltic and North seas meet across a sand-spit. The horizon is apparently compressed and diminished by the weight of the sky; itself in a state of constant flux as weather patterns roll-in, adding to a sense of insignificance of the human scale that shrinks within the greater measure of the landscape. Skagen also exemplifies the particular act of dwelling where the traditional summerhouses and fishermen's cottages hunker down in the dunes. Here is the home of the Skagen School of Artists that captured so beautifully the very particular qualities of light and landscape that drew them here.

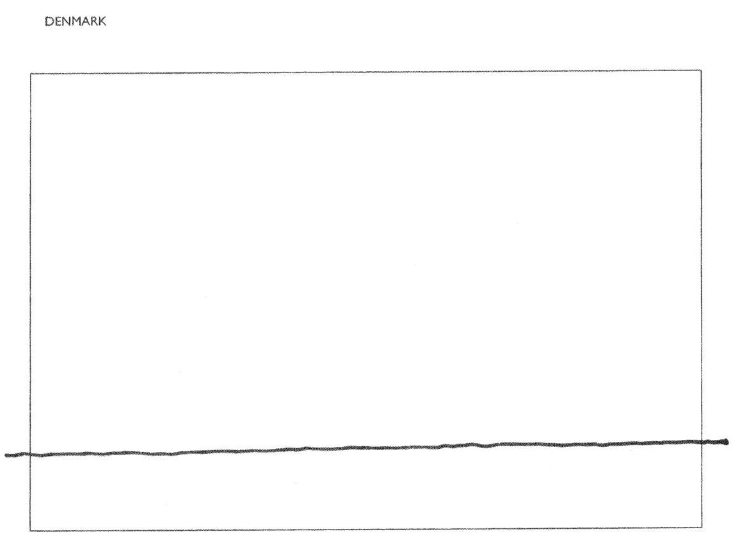

FIGURE 1.1 Danish Landscape Parti Diagram.

In Finland we switch the landscape parti sketch to portrait format (Figure 1.2). The orientation of the sheet is turned through 90° by the seemingly endless forests of pine and birch that lift our eyes from the horizon towards the skies. Colours of silver and green are only interrupted by slithers of glistening blue lakes. The forests are the territory of mythologies; a world of the spirits of the forest, some good, some bad and some benign. Within the forest the imagination gathers pace and perception is changed where the magnitude of sound is raised to that of sight, as the sheer density of the trees that surround us compresses our visual acuity.

These forests are equally significant within the landscape of Norway (Figure 1.3); however, there they conjoin with mountains that appear to possess the sky, tumbling down to meet the unseen depths of the Fjords. Of course, the format is portrait as required by these conditions.

Norway too is the place of mythologies and legends that of course are embedded within the Nordic psyche. Fehn has written extensively of such conditions, providing us with ready conduit to these existential conditions that inform our understanding of place.

The development of this book resides within ten years of consistent interrogation of the oeuvre of Jørn Utzon, in collaboration with my colleague Adrian Carter.[1] Utzon is now widely acknowledged as one of the most original, innovative and socially responsive of modern architects. He was the architect of what is perhaps the most noble and civilised housing built in Denmark; a simple, yet transcendent modern church at Bagsværd; and the most iconic and popular building of the

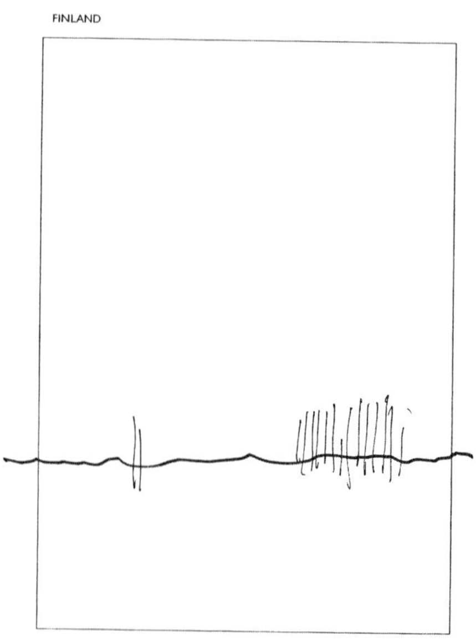

FIGURE 1.2 Finnish Landscape Parti Diagram.

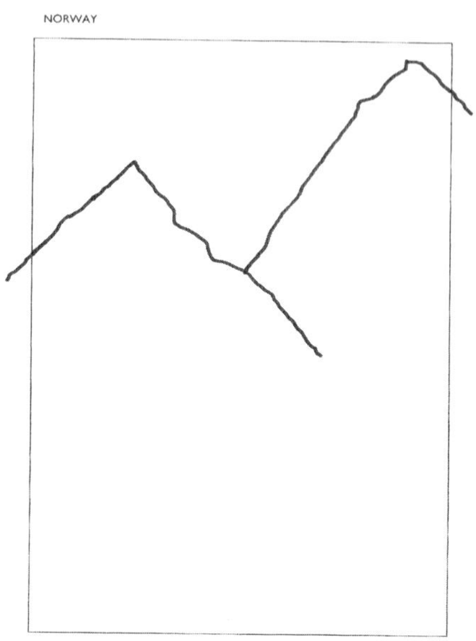

FIGURE 1.3 Norwegian Landscape Parti Diagram.

twentieth century, his great unfinished masterpiece, the Sydney Opera House, which became the symbol of not just a city, but also a nation.

The challenge when examining Utzon's work and methods, was that he never subscribed to, or indeed was ascribed, a particular theoretical position. Indeed, he actively rejected an overly theoretical or academic approach to architecture; instead he consistently drew from a diverse range of influences and experiences. Such a position is clearly challenging for those of us wanting to explore Utzon's ideas within the context of what we call architectural theory within our contemporary academic milieu.

If we seek the etymology of the word *theory*, we discover it is drawn from the Ancient Greek words *thēros* (meaning to spectate) and *thēoria* (meaning contemplation of, or speculation upon). It is this original meaning of *theory* that provides the intellectual positioning of this book, in the invitation to observe, speculate and reflect upon that which we observe. This is, in essence, a pragmatic position; it is the act of reflection upon experience.

In that sense this book is the antithesis of much of contemporary theoretical discourse within architecture; providing a counterpoint to theoretical models founded upon the Scientific Method. Such methods have their genesis within the period of the eighteenth-century Enlightenment that began to dissect, analyse and categorise; that provides a reductivist view of the world. As my former Professor Geoffrey Broadbent suggested to me in a conversation in 2013: 'The objective of the pure sciences is to explain the world. The objective of the architect is to change the world.'

Recourse to the origins of the term theory as a process of *observation and speculation-upon*, in turn led to the philosophical platform that underpins this book that draws upon the tradition of phenomenology. The etymology of the word is the study of or branch of knowledge of (*logy* or *logos*), drawing upon Ancient Greek *phainomenon*, 'that which appears or is seen'.

Thus, phenomenology is to return to the study of *'the things themselves'* and the manner of such study is a way of seeing. Assuming that the reader might not be acquainted with this area of philosophy, this intellectual heritage and application in architecture is explored in greater depth within the chapter that follows.

Given the conundrum that Utzon was, in a contemporary theoretical sense, 'beyond classification', it was necessary to find an alternative method of exploring his work, ideas and influences. It quickly became evident that innovative frames of examination were required that were inclusive rather than exclusive and appropriate to the particularity of Utzon's approach.

Adrian Carter and I were both educated at Portsmouth School of Architecture that has a long and rich tradition of encouraging students to study the work of great architects using the pedagogic methodology of 'paradigm'. The objective of this methodology is not only to uncover design methods, devices and theoretical positioning, but also to understand the lineage of such ideas, personal influences and the zeitgeist within which the architect worked. In this context, the word paradigm means '*in the manner of*'. Being an inclusive rather than exclusive technique, this paradigmatic methodology appeared to be an appropriate intellectual tactic in understanding Utzon and encouraged observation of and reflection upon his work, influences, ideas and zeitgeist. Carter and I utilised this process consistently in our exploration of Utzon's oeuvre. However, this inclusive framework demanded areas of focus if it were not to remain at best generic and at worst misleading. Returning to the etymology of the word *architect* and *architecture* provided appropriate sub-frames.

Architecture is drawn from the coalescence of two Ancient Greek words: *arche* (meaning 'of the origin') and *techne* (meaning a 'drawing forth' or 'revealing'), which provide distinct but overlapping frames of enquiry. Clearly in the realm of architecture *arche* devoid of *techne* represents only ideas about architecture; equally, *techne* without *arche* is mere building. However, alone these terms did not capture the poetic and metaphysical dimensions of Utzon's work and thus a third element was added: the '*poetic conjunction*' that in association with the elements of *arche* and *techne* provided a holistic and appropriate vehicle of interrogation (Figure 1.4). These terms are also extensively explored with the chapter that follows.

This model was tested within a diverse range of academic forums such as the Third and Fourth International Utzon Symposiums in Morocco (2012) and Sydney, Australia (2014), respectively, and through academic publication, gained broad acceptance as an appropriate methodological lens. This frame was subsequently populated as Utzon's particular paradigm emerged and this is discussed in detail within Chapter 4.

The exploration of Utzon's oeuvre using this paradigmatic methodology, perhaps inevitably led to speculation upon extending the study to those of a similar intellectual, cultural and geographical lineage. Moving chronologically back and forwards centred upon Utzon, it seemed appropriate to identify Alvar Aalto as Utzon's predecessor, and Sverre Fehn as inheritor of the mantle. Intuitively, it appeared that threads of commonality ran through the work of these three seminal architects, yet each held distinct and unique qualities.

So, in summation, this book is situated within the particular conditions of the Nordic world, the philosophical platform is within the tradition of phenomenology,

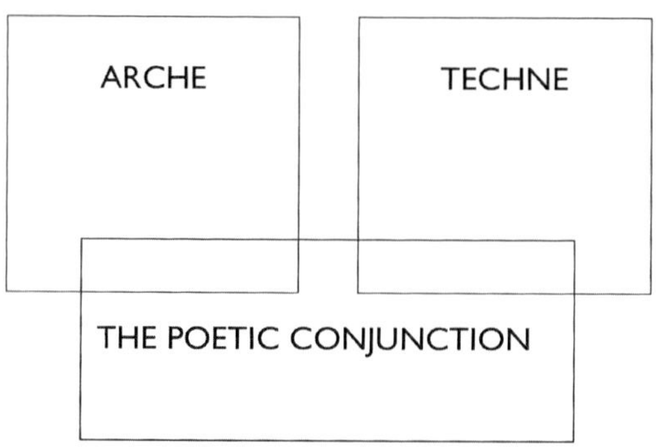

FIGURE 1.4 The Utzon Paradigm Framework.

and the methodology employed to interrogate our three protagonists is that of paradigm.

Aalto, Utzon and Fehn are of course part of a very specific architectural heritage that we may term '*humane Nordic modernism*' and it is important, at the outset of this study, that this heritage should be explored. The objective here is not to provide a historiography, but rather provide an understanding of the wider context and lineage of our three protagonists.

Many commentators suggest that the origins of humane Nordic modernism are initially identified within the work of the Swedish architect Erik Gunnar Asplund (1885–1940) and that Asplund's career exhibits a transition from the movement we identify as National Romanticism, through neo-classicism to modernism. Yet to understand Asplund's contribution we must first explore his zeitgeist, beginning with his education.

Asplund began his architectural education at Kungliga Tekniska Högskolan (KTH) that was largely focused upon the technical dimensions of architecture, and in 1910 progressed to the Kungliga Konsthögskolans Arkitekskola (the School of Architecture of the Royal College of Fine Arts), where his peers included Osvald Almquist (1884–1950) and his soon to be collaborator Sigurd Lewerentz (1885–1975). The School at that time was of a Beaux Arts tradition, classical in style and was seemingly untroubled by emerging issues of the time such as context, place and modernity.

In reaction to this atmosphere, Asplund and others took a decision that proved to be seminal; to set up their own School of Architecture inviting teachers such as Carl Bergsten (1879–1935), Ragnar Östberg (1866–1945), Ivar Tengbom (1878–1968) and Carl Westman (1866–1936), who led classes that were held in the evening. Named after its location in Oslo, the Klara School did not last even a year, but the influence of these significant Swedish architects proved a potent force for Asplund.

Bergsten and Tengbom were later to be responsible for leading the revival of neo-classicism in Sweden and produced significant works in the 1920s. In contrast, Westman, influenced by Louis Sullivan after a period in the USA, was a central figure in the material realism movement: 'The sheer concentration of talent among these teachers is remarkable, and leaves little doubt that here the baton was handed from one generation to the next' (Blundell-Jones 2006: 13).

This epoch was a time of significant change. New ideas were emerging particularly within fine art and architecture that were largely generated within Europe: 'A general upheaval took place in society in the latter half of the nineteenth century. So let us review what happened then …' (Asplund 2008: 328).

Asplund goes on to identify within this lecture delivered in 1931, the range of influences that shaped this 'general upheaval'; rapid expansion in population, increasing urbanisation and industrialisation, developments in communication and increasing democratisation that in combination resulted in a new epoch that characterised Asplund's zeitgeist – an age of emerging modernity. Within a wider context we must also be conscious of specific significant events; the two great wars of the twentieth century wreaked havoc throughout Europe and although Sweden remained neutral in both wars, the impact of large-scale destruction and subsequent reconstruction, resonated across Scandinavia. In Sweden this was manifested in the genesis of the *Folkhemmett* (literally 'peoples home'), a concept that considered Swedes as 'one family' and is widely considered to be an economic, social and political model that mediated between the Soviet Marxist system and Western capitalism.

It never fails to resonate when I visit the Nordic lands that a sense of the 'civic' remains, that is founded upon notions such as the *Folkhemmett*, that inculcates attitudes of collective responsibility. This atmosphere permeates architecture and resonates in a sense of striving for collective betterment, social responsibility and humane attitudes towards design. Such an atmosphere is represented not only through consistent investment in infrastructure and social services, but also within a spirit of reticence for the elevation of individuals, that presents itself as a sense of 'collective modesty'.

Nordic architecture of the period reflected these significant cultural and social shifts. In the late nineteenth and early twentieth century, National Romantic architecture spread throughout the Nordic countries in parallel to the Art Nouveau movement of Europe. While Art Nouveau sought to harmonise with nature in reinterpreting nature's forms, the distinct qualities of the National Romantic movement were rooted within the Nordic sagas and sought to give expression to new social and cultural constructs. The movement found precedent in medieval and prehistoric architecture that sought a return to the 'origins of things' in signifying this new, more egalitarian, world.

Yet, other influences were emerging that were to impact significantly upon Scandinavian Architecture in general and Asplund in particular. In Russia and Germany we see the reinterpretation of classical architecture. In Germany such work later became a symbol of Nazi rule in the work of Albert Speer (1905–1981), while in Russia, neo-classicism was used by architects such as Ivan Fomin (1872–1936) to signify the post-Revolution epoch.

Proximity to Russia and Germany fused with developments in communication ensured that the transition from National Romanticism to neo-classicism resonated in Scandinavia. In Sweden this movement was characterised as 'Swedish Grace', and adopted by Asplund for a period, as an appropriate model to signify the new age.

Perhaps the exemplar within this period of Asplund's work was Stockholm Public Library (1924–1928), which was apparently influential upon Alvar Aalto and served as a precedent for his design for the Viipuri Library Competition of 1927.

However, the fluvial influences of northern Europe continued and increasingly Asplund became aware of the emergence of modernism exemplified in the teachings of the Bauhaus that opened in 1919 and the new conceptualisations of art, graphic design, product design and, of course, architecture. In addition was the influence of modernist theoretical theses, given expression by Le Corbusier, Ozenfant, Mies van der Rohe and Picasso, among others.

In his 1931 lecture 'Our Architectonic Perception of Space' Asplund references the philosopher Oswald Spengler (1880–1936), who described the concept of 'cultural souls' that arise, flourish, wither and die, each epoch having its own particular expression of 'its own distinctive characteristic view of the world'. Such a position aligns precisely with the culture of *Folkhemmett* emerging within Sweden, concurrent to Asplund's essay. What interested Asplund were the architectural consequences of these 'cultural souls', and how epochs manifested themselves as architectonic entities: 'The architectonic signature of our era is the dissolution of architectonic space' (Asplund 2008: 329).

The conceptualisation of 'dissolved architectonic space' is the articulation of Asplund's shift from neo-classicism to functionalism epitomised by his design, in collaboration with Sigurd Lewerentz, for the Great Exhibition in Stockholm of 1930. It was this exhibition, which Jørn Utzon's parents visited, that had such an impact upon them that they returned to Denmark, disposed of their heavy traditional furniture and replaced it with items of modernity. Utzon was twelve years old.

The exhibition was a significant event that extended beyond the Utzon family. It signified a 'new way' of being, a post-First World War declaration of collective betterment that was to be so ironically interrupted by the events of the Second World War.

Nonetheless, as Asplund contended:

> Dissolution has an unpleasant ring, rather like decay. Is that what it means? No, it is merely the dissolution of architectonic and rather narrow and petrified forms in connection with a change of the nature of our lives and our society itself. It is not degeneration but regeneration.
>
> *Asplund 2008: 333*

Asplund was, as were his peers, of an internationalist disposition and travelled extensively as his reputation spread as a result of the Stockholm Exhibition. He visited the UK in 1930, Germany, Czechoslovakia, Austria, Italy and Switzerland in 1932, and Denmark in 1934. In the same year he travelled to Germany, Czechoslovakia, Austria, France and the UK, in 1938 embarked upon a lecture tour of the USA and in 1939 visited Germany, Switzerland, France and the UK. He was also acquainted with such Nordic luminaries as the Danes Kay Fisker (1893–1965) and Arne Jacobsen (1902–1971), who were visitors to Asplund's office.

This predilection for travel held by Asplund was to become an important constituent of the threads that tie our protagonists together. Aalto, Utzon and Fehn also travelled extensively and particularly sought places of what we might term 'cultural density and significance', where elements of the origin of things resonated. It was in these places that 'essences' were exposed that became inculcated within their work.

Alvar Aalto applied to work in Asplund's office but the application was rejected. Aalto contacted Asplund again after qualifying, and was invited to visit the Scandia Cinema Project with Asplund as his guide. This was the beginning of a lasting friendship; each inspiring the other to new heights. In the way in which Asplund's teachers handed the baton over, he in turn passed the baton to Aalto. Although presented here for reasons of clarity as a linear path, this actually represents a complex pattern of networks and inter-relationships, within which influences were mutual and progressive.

Indeed some of these influences and connections were perhaps subliminal and are perhaps most poetically exposed within Asplund and Lewerentz's Woodland Cemetery project. Here Asplund and Lewerentz strove to amplify the mystery, mythology and symbolism of the forest in a manner that was to be later described by the American academic Caroline Constant as 'eluding typological classification' (cited in Blundell-Jones 2006: 36).

> The forest is a pervasive symbol of the wild and primitive, sublime in its vastness, and through shared stories it has become part of every European's cultural heritage.
>
> *Blundell-Jones 2006: 37*

Aalto's father was a man of the forest; a Surveyor of forests. It was on Aalto's 'white table' that his father plotted the Finnish Forests with up to twelve apprentice surveyors working in parallel. Aalto grew up in Jyväskylä in the central Lakeland of Finland. This is a landscape of lakes and forests. He writes: 'The Northerners, especially we Finns, are prone to "Forest Dreaming", for which we have had ample opportunity up to now' (Blundell-Jones 2006: 37).

The forest both in terms of a tangible physical resource and a territory of mystery and mythology resonates strongly across the Nordic world. Imagine the hunter-gatherer moving through the forest and as day evaporates and night emerges he lights a fire:

> The night gains an incredible value in that it erases space. The fire invents light and heat, and through this light darkness gains new importance: it creates the story, it entertains. The fire invents a room where there is light. The fire is a producer of space, and in the shadow, mystery is born.
>
> *Schildt 1997: 21*

And we might imagine the significance of the throw of the light from the fire, outside of which sit the spirits of the forest, some good, some benign, and some evil.

This Nordic sensibility towards primal essences of fire, water, the earth, light (and the absence of light), horizon, sky and sea, conjoined with elements of the landscape such as mountain, forest and plain, holds a universal resonance for us providing another consistent thread that binds our protagonists together. I offer the view that while these primacies hold universal understanding they are somehow explicit in the work of our three, Aalto, Utzon and Fehn.

> The house as protection was dependent upon maximising the potential of the place. There is an almost religious respect for Nature's power that sets Scandinavia and Finland slightly apart from central Europe. The farther north

> one goes, whether in Finland, Sweden or Norway; the stronger a sense one finds of nature's immensity and power.
>
> *Fjeld 2009: 73*

This physical context promotes specific contextualised responses. Fehn, for example, was mystified by the Southern obsession with view. The light (and the absence of light) in the North holds particular qualities, and thus, as Fehn suggests, 'the architect deems catching light and bring it into interior spatial presence more important than focussing on the view out' (Fjeld 2009: 11).

The particular contexts of climate and landscape make the Nordic world often a difficult place for man to dwell and perhaps that is why the primal elements such as fire and water sit high within the human consciousness there. They both constitute essential elements of survival yet, at a deeper subconscious level, fire represents a place of safety and protection, a 'here-ness' as opposed to a 'there-ness'; embodied concepts within the Nordic psyche.

All of these particular conditions of this particular place fuse and within the zeitgeist of our protagonists were manifested within architecture as 'humane Nordic modernism'. As Kenneth Frampton wrote:

> Utzon belongs to that generation of Architects who still believed that the primary responsibility of the profession was not only to meet the building needs of society on an ad-hoc, daily basis but to evolve generic types and modes of practice that were appropriate to the unprecedented conditions of modern life.
>
> *Frampton 2003: 10*

Inevitably as this movement gained momentum, it became the subject of critical scholarly examination that strove to position the phenomenon intellectually. At the vanguard of this commentary were the Danish architect, urban designer and academic Steen Eiler Rasmussen (1898–1990), and the Norwegian architect and theorist Christian Norberg-Schulz (1926–2000), who each incrementally developed an increasingly phenomenological perspective in the discourse surrounding architecture that represents this distinctive heritage of thought. This heritage and territory of phenomenological thought are explored in detail within the following chapter.

Rasmussen's influential text *Experiencing Architecture* (1959) drew upon the implicit phenomenological traditions of Nordic place-making and made such elements explicit. He exposed and articulated an understanding of place that was rooted in human experience and thus by implication, humane in character. Rasmussen proposed a clear thesis that fused human senses with our perceptions of and understanding of place.

In 1971, Norberg-Schulz developed these themes in his book *Existence, Space and Architecture*, positing concepts such as 'Existential Space' that engaged with a phenomenological understanding of our world. This position was subsequently developed in his 1980 text *Genius Loci*, which more precisely articulated a phenomenological understanding of place:

> A place is therefore a qualitative 'total' phenomenon, which we cannot reduce to any properties such as spatial relationships, without losing its concrete nature out of sight.
>
> *Norberg-Schulz 1980: 8*

Within this book, Norberg-Schulz makes reference to the writing of the philosopher Martin Heidegger (1889–1976), and shares with his readers the poem used by Heidegger to analyse language and proffers it as a means by which place is concretised. The poem is 'A Winter Evening' by George Trakl. Both literally and metaphorically, it exposes us to the poetics of space. In *Nightlands* (1996), Norberg-Schulz takes a clearly articulated phenomenological position in the interrogations of particularity of place and the heritage of built form.

In his final book, *Architecture: Presence, Language Place* (2000), published in the year of his death, Norberg-Schulz develops his phenomenological treatise further and more densely. He illuminates explicitly the writings of Edmund Husserl (1858–1938), Martin Heidegger (1889–1976) and Maurice Merleau-Ponty (1908–1961) in providing an intellectual platform upon which he constructs a phenomenology of place, and the narrative consistently references places that in differing ways represent the origin of things:

> I have indicated that the environment is the everyday world of life, and that in order to understand it, one cannot rely upon scientific investigation. In this context I have adopted the phenomenological method, inasmuch as it is designed to provide access to the 'things themselves'.
>
> *Norberg-Schulz 2000: 125*

This intellectual tradition leads us in turn to the Finnish architect, writer and thinker Juhani Pallasmaa (1936–), who generously provided the Foreword for this book:

> To me architecture is an existential expression; buildings structure, express and articulate my being-in-the-world. In this respect I have learned much from the two French philosophers, Maurice Merleau-Ponty and Gaston Bachelard.
>
> *Pallasmaa 2002: 5*

This acknowledgement of the lineage of philosophical underpinning from the realm of phenomenology builds upon the writings of Norberg-Schulz and develops a critical polemic upon the condition of much contemporary architecture. He illuminates a sense of loss of meaning and substance within much contemporary architecture, which he posits are the essential elements of architecture. Pallasmaa also acts as a nexus into a wider world, engaging with contemporary exponents of this attitude to architecture, such as the Americans Steven Holl (1947–) and Rick Joy (1958–), and the Australians Richard Leplastrier (1939–),[2] Glen Murcutt (1936–) and Peter Stutchbury (1954–). These inter-relationships have ensured that the adoption of a phenomenological approach to architecture is brought to a wider constituency.

In his writing Pallasmaa questions adopted orthodoxies such as the 'hegemony of the eye' in the book *The Eyes of the Skin* (2005b), the role of the virtual and the visual within architecture in *The Thinking Hand* (2009) and focuses upon the evocation of the image in *The Embodied Image* (2011). However, it is the collection of essays contained within *Encounters* (2005a) which provides a comprehensive oversight of Pallasmaa's contribution. Under a series of verbs that define chapters, Pallasmaa explores 'being-in-the-world' from a number of diverse perspectives. In the essay 'Geometry of Feeling' (first published in 1985), he quotes from Ludwig Wittgenstein (1889–1951): 'Architecture glorifies and eternalises something. When there is nothing to glorify there is no architecture' (Pallasmaa 2005a: 87).

This returns us to the attitudes exemplified within the spirit of *Folkhemmett* that emerged in Sweden within Asplund's epoch, providing a sense that the discipline of architecture holds the potential of collective betterment and furthermore has responsibility outside itself. These values were clearly deeply embedded within each of our three protagonists.

Within this phenomenological position, sit two concepts that are a central dimension of this study that should be made explicit to the reader: *spatial archaeology* and *immersion*.

Spatial archaeology is a term used to explain the *process* of understanding space and place. It was a phrase adopted by myself and my erstwhile student and now colleague, Line Nørskov-Eriksen, in the interrogation of Can Lis, Utzon's family home on the island of Mallorca, in 2016.

The word archaeology is drawn from the ancient Greek: *arche-* meaning 'of the origin', and *ology* 'the study of', thus in conjunction 'the study of the origin', which in contemporary culture has evolved to describe the study of ancient things.

By archaeology, I of course meant the revealing of something; in the context of this book, the essence of both the artefacts and methodologies of our protagonists allowing us to observe and to speculate upon their purpose. The archaeologist cannot discover or reveal something from the office. There he may speculate upon where to dig based upon information available. But to actually reveal, the archaeologist needs to be at the end of the shovel, the trowel or the brush. Furthermore, the *act* of archaeology draws our attention to the origins of architecture and illuminates the *process* adopted that allows revelation to occur.

Archaeology holds another potential dimension in the understanding of place. By nature, archaeological praxis is formative rather than summative, speculative rather than absolute. Archaeology can only uncover and reveal that which remains, and then speculate upon the authorship, values and zeitgeist of the antiquities. That speculation is of course underpinned by comparative knowledge, but in essence it allows space for the 'as yet undiscovered' and as such defies absolute conclusion.

> Do you agree that there is a difference between looking at the girls on the beach and to study the human anatomy? Are you sure that when you look at the buildings you also discover the architecture?
>
> *Prip-Buus undated*

Looking beyond 'the girls on the beach' proved to be a fruitful pursuit: at Can Lis, Mallorca, the anatomy of place was revealed; in Fehn's Villa Busk, Norway, the stories of the house were exposed; at Aalto's Experimental House, Finland, the nature of dwelling, play, reverie and experiment was laid bare.

However, spatial archaeology is not a rapid process but is gentle and time-laden and requires *immersion*. I was privileged to live in Can Lis for one week, and that level of immersion revealed much. To experience day and night, firelight and shadow, sharp sunlight, rain, gathering and solitude, conversations and silence, allowed the stories and the anatomy of the house to emerge.

To engage with the concept of immersion demands a shift in attitude from the tourist to the traveller, from the photographer to the drawer of and from, the 'things themselves'; and for the architect it demands a meditative and speculative attitude that is active rather than passive, yet, reveals; almost through an osmotic process.

Fehn's stories emerged through immersive conversations with generous souls who now occupy his buildings. Stories emerged of delightful childhood memories (Villa Spare and Skagestad House), stories of process, communication and landscape (Villa Busk) and stories of children's laughter and tears (Skådalen School). Hearing those stories told in the places they were set, was a profound experience.

I first encountered Aalto as a student in 1979 and he has been a constant companion on my journey, striving to understand the nature of architecture. Like all good friends, there were periods of distance and periods of intensity but his works and methods (as my students will confirm) have become a central element of my thoughts upon architecture.

These themes are explored consistently throughout this book, providing a warp and weft that hopefully weaves the text together. Each theme provides 'ways of seeing'; ways of understanding the complexity of the architectural endeavour exhibited within the works and methodologies of Aalto, Utzon and Fehn.

This introductory chapter strives to set out the principles of the theoretical platform of the book, the methodology of interrogation and the themes that sit within that methodology, and more broadly describes a context for the study that is particular to the Nordic world.

Chapter 2 develops the intellectual premise of phenomenology and the methodology of paradigm in greater detail within the broader context of the Nordic world and the specific contexts of Aalto, Utzon and Fehn.

Chapters 3–5 focus upon the work and methodologies of Aalto, Utzon and Fehn respectively, each chapter commencing with relevant biographical information that places each within their zeitgeist, and going on to examine individual paradigm elements in the context of their canon of work.

Within each of these chapters, the oeuvre of each architect is explored and is further supported by a narrative focused upon a particular example of their work that best exemplifies particular ways of working. In each case this is a dwelling; for Aalto, the Experimental House, for Utzon, Can Lis and for Fehn, Villa Busk. The choice of dwelling as a consistent typology is purposeful; the dwelling sits at the very core of architectural endeavour; it was the reason that man first built.

As Gaston Bachelard suggests:

> The house, quite obviously is a privileged entity for phenomenological study of the intimate values of inside space, provided of course, that we take it with its unity and complexity, and endeavour to integrate all the special values in one fundamental value.
>
> *Bachelard 1969: 3*

He continues:

> In every dwelling, even the richest, the first task of the phenomenologist is to find the original shell.
>
> *Bachelard 1969: 3*

Bachelard ascribes a maternal quality to the house, he talks of it as a vessel; our first universe, our first position in the world, supporting the primal, visceral and essential nature of what it is to dwell within space and time. In this sense, the dwelling provides the archetype of architecture.

What is common to these three houses is that each is, in some way, a *retreat.* In the way in which Heidegger retreated to his Black Forest hut to think and write, the Experimental House is an archetype of the Nordic summer house, a place in which one retreats from the everyday and constructs an alternative way of being-in-the-world. Here the Aaltos could ruminate and as the name of the house suggests, experiment with the fundamental nature of architecture, without the encumbrances of client and other constraints.

For the Utzons, Can Lis became their cave, a place to retreat from perhaps the embodied pain and disappointment of the Sydney Opera House project and return to the essential qualities of architecture.

In commissioning Fehn to make Villa Busk, Terje and Astrid Welle Busk asked simply for a 'place to be'. Such a distilled request produced a place of retreat and the opportunity for the Welle Busks to create an 'everyday' of their choosing. In Villa Busk, one has a real sense of refuge yet we remain intimately connected with the forests, and the stone within which it nestles.

In each of the three houses, the mundane nature of the everyday evaporates and we are invited to construct a new reality; prescribed and informed by place.

Chapter 6 draws together commonalities and distinctions of the paradigms of Aalto, Utzon and Fehn, and speculates upon the legacy of such ways of architecture upon contemporary praxis with the Nordic world, the UK and the USA, concluding with further speculations that project into the future of architecture.

However, there is an additional polemical thread that runs through this work that should be revealed. I have become increasingly concerned with tendencies within discourse around contemporary architecture to be concerned predominantly with the *objects* of architecture (the buildings) rather than engaging with the *acts* of our discipline. It appears within that debate that the *objects of architecture* increasingly subjugate the *acts* of architecture. Much contemporary architecture has become obsessed with the *object* of its praxis, and, as a consequence, that the *act* (the verb) of architecture has been sacrificed at the high altar of these objects (the nouns). In our increasingly homogenised, fluid, horizontal, globalised world, images are transported across space and time eroding a sense of particularity of place, climate and culture.

In part, this tendency is perhaps born of the immediacy of digital communication, where the image of the object has apparent hegemony over the more protracted and difficult discussions about the *content* of the work involving the *acts* of architecture. Perhaps a renewed engagement with the verb and a re-balancing of the verb/noun relationship would provide a route into the core of existence and, indeed, a model for mediating between existential and pragmatic components of being, and thus architecture. Implicit within such an ambition is the potential to reclaim ideas of particularity of place, context and humanity, in counterpoint to the Universalist and homogenising ambitions of globalisation. 'Being active confrontations and encounters, all basic architectural events have a verb-form rather than noun-form. Architecture is essentially an art of actions not forms' (Pallasmaa 2005a: 319).

The noun objectivises architecture, and through the seductive image, concretises that objectification. As Pallasmaa suggests, the image provides a perceptual immediacy; but in semiotic terms, that immediacy is all too often an empty sign. Our contemporary world is increasingly dominated by the power of the image and nowhere is that clearer than in architecture. Magazines, websites and TV set the image in front of us, providing a seeming immediacy of understanding. Yet both literally and metaphorically, all those images are filtered through many lenses, each lens having a particular intent.

The sheer volume of such visual exposure ascribes an apparent absolute authority to the image, to the extent where our desire to understand what informed what we see, evaporates. This encourages a level of superficial understanding that resides only within the image of the object and encourages ever more, again literally and metaphorically, retouching; in search of a perceived perfection. This trend is of course a self-perpetuating mythology but, in turn, encourages a shift towards the superlative domain of architecture; biggest, tallest, longest.

Our three protagonists were all preoccupied within the *acts* of architecture. The *nouns* emerged as a consequence. The objective of this book is through Aalto, Utzon and Fehn to return to the origins of things, and as Fehn suggested, rediscover what has been forgotten. To rebalance the verb/noun relationship, offered within this book is a grammatical shift in architectural discourse, towards the fertile potential of the verb.

Hopefully, this introduction has provided the reader with a sense of the particular heritage that Aalto, Utzon and Fehn sat within, the intellectual methodology employed, and the philosophical tradition that the book draws upon, and, in addition, the inter-relationship between these elements.

Notes

1 Adrian Carter, colleague at the Department of Architecture, Design and Media Technology at the University of Aalborg, Denmark, currently Professor at Abedian School of Architecture, Bond University, Australia.

2 Leplastrier worked for Utzon on the Sydney Opera House and Bayview projects, and has consistently acknowledged his seminal role as teacher.

References

Asplund, E. G. 2008. Our Architectonic Perception of Space. In *Nordic Architects Write*, ed. M. A. Andersen. New York: Routledge.

Bachelard, G. 1969. *The Poetics of Space*. Boston, MA: Beacon Press.

Blundell-Jones, P. 2006. *Gunnar Asplund*. London: Phaidon Press.

Fjeld, P. O. 2009. *Sverre Fehn: The Patterns of Thought*. New York: Monacelli Press.

Frampton, K. 2003. *Proceedings of the First International Utzon Symposium*, ed. M. Mullins and A. Carter. Aalborg: Aalborg University.

Norberg-Schulz, C. 1971. *Existence, Space and Architecture*. London: Praeger.

Norberg-Schulz, C. 1980. *Genius Loci: Towards a Phenomenology of Architecture*. New York: Rizzoli International Publications.

Norberg-Schulz, C. 1996. *Nightlands*. Cambridge, MA: MIT Press.

Norberg-Schulz, C. 2000. *Architecture: Presence, Language Place*. Milan: Skira Editore.

Pallasmaa, J. 2002. *Sensuous Minimalism*. China Architecture and Building Press.

Pallasmaa, J. 2005a. *Encounters: Juhani Pallasmaa Architectural Essays*, ed. P. MacKeith. Helsinki: Rakennustieto Oy.

Pallasmaa, J. 2005b. *The Eyes of the Skin: Architecture and the Senses*. New York: John Wiley.

Pallasmaa, J. 2009. *The Thinking Hand*. New York: John Wiley.

Pound, E. 1934. *The ABC of Reading*. New York: New Directions Books.

Prip-Buus, M. Undated. *Tiden Med Utzon, I: Ideerne* [*The Time with Utzon, I: Ideas*]. Unpublished.

Rasmussen, S. E. 1959. *Experiencing Architecture*. Cambridge, MA: MIT Press.

Schildt, G. 1997. *Alvar Aalto: In his Own Words*. New York: Rizzoli International Publications.

2

OF PHENOMENOLOGY AND PARADIGM

Of Phenomenology

> Philosophy teaches us how to think deeply and broadly, and phenomenology grants architects this potentiality. It provides architects with a powerful and reliable ground from which they can establish their unique way of perceiving the built environment and develop their individual ways of thinking.
>
> *Reza Shirazi 2014: 3*

FIGURE 2.1 Aalto Chair Components, Artek Showroom, Helsinki.

At the outset, it is important to be explicit as to the purpose of this chapter. The objective is to expose and articulate a heritage of thinking, a stream of philosophical consciousness, that has been drawn upon in the development of this book. It is not intended as an exhaustive philosophical commentary upon any of those philosophers identified; reference to the plethora of writing that surrounds any one of them is testament to the fact that such an endeavour would demand far more space than this project affords, and this is not the purpose of this work.

Within this chapter, I have strived to weave fragments of the thoughts and acts of each of the three protagonists through the philosophical narrative, in order to construct a direct relationship between the intellectual concepts explored, and the processes and architecture of Aalto, Utzon and Fehn.

From the time of Vitruvius (first century BCE) onwards, people have sought to classify what is architecture, and of course, by implication, what isn't architecture. In his text *De Architecture* (*The Ten Books*), Vitruvius proposed that all architecture should comprise three components: *firmitas, utilitas* and *venustas* (solid, useful, and beautiful). That is itself an exclusive frame in all that it excludes, and is also loaded with judgement; for example, in what is considered beautiful. As an academic and praxis-based discipline, architecture does not sit easily within most of the contemporary interpretations of theory within academia that largely have their genesis within the concept of 'scientific method', born of the period of the Enlightenment. By their very nature, these methods are reductionist in manner, and when applied to architecture, seek to dissect architectural endeavour into constituent parts that all too often has the consequence of losing sight of the totality of the work.

As Colin Davies suggests:

> In the 1950s, architectural theory in Europe and America was a makeshift affair, a mixture of old ideas about composition, surviving from the time when architecture students were expected to know about the classical orders, newer ideas about form and function derived from the modernist manifestos of the 1910s and 20s, and a body of research aimed at making the process of design more rational and scientific. The discipline was intellectually rather unambitious.
>
> *Davies 2011: 6*

Within this 'intellectually unambitious' context, opposing philosophical tendencies emerged within the twentieth century that have drawn from cognate disciplines, particularly within fields of social theory:

> Yet the 'theory' referred to by Nesbitt and Hayes relates to a specific movement that began in the 1960s and strives to reconstitute the architectural discipline through mediatory concepts – derived from fields such as philosophy, linguistics, psychology and anthropology – that simultaneously connect architecture to other social realms and (attempt to) claim for architecture its own unique territory.
>
> *Krista Sykes 2010: 14*

Davies and Krista Sykes identify if not a theoretical vacuum, surely a lack of confidence regarding the intellectual foundations upon which the praxis of contemporary architecture is founded. This is problematic in presenting a lack of intellectual rigour and purpose, from which the artefacts of our discipline are currently derived.

As Aalto suggests:

> Architectural methods sometimes resemble scientific ones, and a process of research, such as science employs, can be adopted also in architecture. Architectural research can be more and more methodical, but the substance of it can never be solely analytical. Always there will be more of instinct and art in architectural research.
>
> *Schildt 1998: 13*

In Chapter 1, the etymology of the word *theory* was discussed, notably the sense of 'speculation upon that which we observe'. Such a definition provides in my opinion a far more inclusive way of understanding our world. However, perhaps for observation and speculation to have meaning and consequence, we need to introduce an a priori structure to those acts of understanding.

As M. Reza Shirazi suggests above, phenomenology provides such potential for the architect as a 'way of seeing'. In this we strive to occupy the intellectual void present within architectural theory, in returning to the origins of the word theory, in a process of observation of and speculation upon the 'things themselves', through the lens of phenomenology. This 'way of seeing' is the theoretical premise of this book.

The etymology of the word *phenomenology* is the study of, or branch of knowledge of (*logy* or *logos*), *phainomenon*, 'that which appears or is seen'. However, there are in all probability an equal number of phenomenologies as there are phenomenologists, and as Reza Shirazi suggests when citing Herbert Spiegelberg, suggesting the discipline occupies a fluid philosophical position:

> Phenomenology is a moving, in contrast to a stationary philosophy, with a dynamic momentum, whose development is determined by its intrinsic properties as well as by the 'things', the structure of the territory that it encounters.
>
> *Reza Shirazi 2014: 3*

Such a statement does not diminish the realm of phenomenology as a mediator in our understanding of the world, but rather it acknowledges its intrinsic nature as being affected by both the 'things' and the context of the 'things'. If we were to examine the 'wall-ness of wall' in Morocco, and perhaps Norway, our phenomenological 'seeing' of the wall would differentiate in each case, due to the context (or the territory, as Spiegelberg suggests) in which they exist.

Any discussion of Western Philosophy is of course in some way founded within the influence of Plato (427–347 BCE[1]), his teacher Socrates and his pupil Aristotle.

FIGURE 2.2 Sandbag Stepping Stone Bridge, Morocco.

At its core, philosophy is the pursuit of knowledge or wisdom utilising a systematic model of investigation. The etymology of the term is from the Greek *philosophia*, meaning 'love of knowledge', 'pursuit of wisdom', 'systematic investigation', from *philo* 'loving' and from *sophia* 'knowledge', or 'wisdom' from *sophis* 'wise or 'learned'.

Plato sought to understand and explain our being-in-the-world and introduced some important concepts that are central to the narrative of this book. Plato's contribution encompassed ethical, political, legal, metaphysical and epistemological[2] realms, utilising the vehicles of dialogue, metaphor and dialectic, that provided the foundation of what we now term 'Western thought'. Indeed, the British mathematician and philosopher Alfred North Whitehead (1861–1947) famously once remarked: 'The safest general characterisation of the European philosophical tradition is that it consists of a series of footnotes to Plato' (Whitehead 1978: 39).

In an exploration of the realm of phenomenology we turn first to Plato's metaphor of the cave in his text *The Republic*. Presented as a dialogue between Socrates, Cephalus, Polemarchus and Thrasymachus, the discourse seeks to firstly describe the limits of our 'knowing of the world' as being confined by particular circumstances and our consequential limited understanding of truth.

Plato's cave is dark; the only light emanates from the fire. The occupants are shackled with their backs to the fire and all they can observe is the shadows that fall upon the cave-wall that they face. As these shadows are the extent of perception the occupants assume that these flickering images are reality and represent their being-in-the-world. As Plato explains: 'And so in every way they would believe that the shadows of the objects we mentioned were the whole truth' (Plato 1974: 318).

He suggests a remedy. The prisoners are unshackled and led from the cave (albeit protesting), and move into the sunlight. And while being dragged from the darkness of the cave may involve significant pain, and furthermore, be a process to which we might object, once accustomed to the light man would 'find it easier to look at the shadows, next at the reflections of men and other objects in water and later on at the objects themselves' (Plato 1974: 319).

The dialogue goes on to suggest that such a liberation from the cave and its illusions would encourage further 'seeings of existence' that would include the sky, the night sky and heavenly bodies, and speculations would be made upon the nature of these 'things' themselves, their role within the cosmic order, and conclusions subsequently drawn.

Here Plato suggests differing degrees of being-in-the-world. Those in the cave are only able to react to the shadows as they are presented, and assume that the shadows, being the extent of their perception, are considered to be 'the thing' rather than a representation of 'the thing' produced by light falling and the shadow cast. Plato, through the metaphor of the cave is alluding to a rather 'unconscious' and disconnected manner of being-in-the-world.

In describing his childhood conversations with his brothers in 'A Fireside Story', Aalto articulates the dangers involved in applying logic to appearances and, indeed, the consequences of our limits of understanding:

> But as I said, we were seriously discussing the gossip of the day or other more important problems. A frequent subject was a little sister's sudden appearance in our cold climate, and our logic brought us to wonderful conclusions.
>
> *Schildt 1998: 13*

While, as Plato suggests emergence from the cave into light may be an uncomfortable process, the transition from the unconsciousness frame of the cave towards the light is transformational and encourages speculation upon the world, through a conscious level of being.

In *Timaeus* and *Critias*, which Perez-Gomez (2006) suggests contains the first systemisation of the Universe, Plato describes the different 'worlds' of *forms*, *ideas* and the *receptacle*. The world of forms (*eidos*) is a world of the immutable and unchanging, the world of ideas is a world of the sensible (*topoi*), that cannot be understood through the application of logic, and the receptacle is the receptacle of becoming: *chora*.

The concept of *chora*, is an essential element of understanding our existence that Plato suggests is a space or interval that sits between 'being' and 'non-being'. Timaeus admits within the text that this concept of 'receptacle' is of the three concepts of being, the hardest to understand as the inability to imagine the receptacle is itself implicit within the concept.

Chora is the feminine article of the word *choros* which has been variously translated as room, territory or land (specifically native land or homeland), that later came to denote in its feminine form *chora* (within the context of Athenian urban design), a place or receptacle that was revealed through the act of dance. The concept of a vessel or space in which something is revealed or becomes, is the essence of *chora*.

Some commentators have ascribed a maternal dimension to *chora*, it being the feminine form of *choros*, suggesting it to be as a womb; a place for something to come into being. Jacques Derrida, utilising all of his deconstructivist tendencies, suggested that *chora* hesitates between the order of the 'revealed' and the order of the 'revealable' and went on, in collaboration with Peter Eisenmann, to symbolise a revealing within *chora* in the Parc de la Vilette Project (1984). Here we may conceptualise the idea of architectonic territory as chora; the receptacle of becoming for the architect.

For the architect these two concepts of the metaphor of the cave and the idea of *chora* provide a substantive platform for our endeavour, in that we should emerge from the darkness of 'appearances' into the light of the 'things themselves' and acknowledge that the role of architecture is of that of *chora*: to make place that allows a 'revealing' of the 'things themselves'.

If we leap forward some 2,000 years, the philosopher Immanuel Kant (1724–1804) articulated two concepts that develop our narrative. '*Noumenon*', drawn from the Ancient Greek, was defined by Kant as an object or power that exists, that transcends experience and is, in the sense of perception, unknowable. In contrast, for Kant '*phenomenon*' was describing that which can be perceived and was thus the subject of sensibility. Within the Kantian paradigm, noumenon is of the essence, phenomenon is that which appears or is revealed to us.

Our next philosophical destination is the poet and playwright Jonathan Wolfgang von Goethe (1749–1832). Most famed for his fictional writing, Goethe made significant contributions within the fields of the applied sciences that were founded upon a particular philosophical position.

> In its time, Goethe's way of Science was highly unusual as it moved away from a quantitative, materialist approach to things in nature, and emphasised instead, an intimate, first-hand, encounter between the student and the thing studied. Direct experiential contact became the basis for scientific generalisation and understanding.
>
> *Seamon 1998: 1*

Here, Seamon argues that with hindsight, Goethe's approach to scientific enquiry is in counterpoint to the adopted authority of his period; in that he rejected the Cartesian paradigm of the Enlightenment in favour of an experiential paradigm; extolling a phenomenological understanding of the nature of the 'things themselves', predicated upon direct experience.

Of particular interest in this regard is Goethe's concept of '*Ur-phänonmenon*' (Ur-phenomenon) that Seamon suggests is 'primordial, basic, elemental and archetypal; the "*Ur-phänonmenon*" may be thought of as deep-down phenomenon' (Seamon 1998: 4).

Such a position may provide an antidote to our post-modern life in suggesting that beyond the ephemeral surfaces of contemporary existence there may be substance that lies below, worthy of interrogation.

Goethe's approach to the understanding of natural phenomenon predates that of Edmund Husserl (1859–1938) by a century yet it is Husserl that is widely acclaimed as the 'father of phenomenology'.[3]

Husserl's adoption of the term *phenomenological* was not original in that the term had been used previously by both Kant (1724–1804) and Hegel (1770–1830), among others. However, for Husserl, phenomenology provided a vehicle for a 'new way' of understanding the world through philosophical enquiry.

Husserl defined phenomenology as a 'science of the essences' (Husserl 1982: 34). These essences are not understood by pre-ordained philosophical knowledge, but rather we return to the 'things themselves'. Thus we see in Husserl's thought a clear rejection of previously held philosophical positions in the creation of a new, radical way of seeing and understanding our world:

> In Husserl's hands, then, phenomenology – the study of the essence of consciousness as it is lived – is centrally concerned with the structures of intentionality: in perception, imagination, judgement, emotion, evaluation, volition, consciousness of time and space, experience of other people and so on. So phenomenology is largely focused on how perception, thought, emotion and action are directed towards things in the world, how things are 'intended' in these forms of experience, and thus the meaning things have for us in different forms of experience.
>
> *Smith 2007: 193*

Within this commentary Smith introduces an important element of Husserl's thought: that the *things* do not exist within a vacuum; they are contextualised by that in which they themselves exist. For the architect this opens us to the potential that context holds in informing our response to the things themselves that is a fundamental element of the approach to the understanding of place in Aalto, Utzon and Fehn's work.

A second element of Husserl's thinking that is important to the architect is the idea of returning to 'what is given'. Implicit within this process is the idea of 'essence' and to understand that essence, Husserl suggests that we must suspend all understanding that may lead us to pre-ordain values for the 'thing' we are seeking to understand. Thus Husserl is suggesting that we divest ourselves of pre-conditioning in returning to the things themselves. This is an important component of the narrative of this text that is a pre-disposition on the part of the architect to engage in a deeper level of engagement with our world, looking beyond superficial appearances in the understanding of our being-in-the-world. It suggests that we should enter the process as unencumbered by pre-disposition as possible.

This resonates of Goethe's concept '*Ur-phänonmenon*', in the acknowledgement that there are primordial essences to be discovered through a process of 'going back'.

Husserl, through the introduction of the concepts of *Körber* (the physical body) and *Leib* (the living body in lived life) opens the discourse of the body in space: 'Thus we experience the things around us in relation to our body, that is in a spatial, spatiotemporal relation to our Leib' (Reza Shirazi 2014: 3).

This concept of the 'body in space', provides the nexus of our perception of the world and leads Husserl to another idea that would resonate particularly with Sverre Fehn, the relationship between the body-in-space and our fields of perception defined by the horizon. This idea reinforces Husserl's position that all things exist within particular contexts, and those contexts support our understanding of the thing itself, and the contextual territory in which the thing sits.

Fehn writes:

> How shall we respond to man and his objects affixed to the surface of the earth? Everything we build must be adjusted in relation to the ground, thus the horizon becomes an important aspect of architecture.
>
> *Fjeld 2009: 108*

He continues: 'Once the room exists and an object is placed inside, all decisions yield to the horizon. At least it was so a long time ago. When the earth was perceived as round, the horizon disappeared as a mystery' (Fjeld 2009: 108).

Within the later period of Husserl's canon we note the emergence of the concept of *regression* (*Rückfrage*): 'The direction of the other, more original (ontological) regression is the *archaeological* direction of accentuate concreteness' (Macann 1993: 51; emphasis added).

This term 'archaeological' aligns to my own conceptualisation of spatial archaeology described in the previous chapter as a core methodology within this book in facilitating a 'going-back', a 'dusting-off' of that which appears to us; an embodied mechanism of systematic doubt and systematic enquiry.

Husserl therefore provides a range of investigations that we might summarise as:

- *A return to the things themselves.* That we should seek to interrogate the things themselves, rather than that which superficially appears to us. We might strive to eliminate the white noise of everyday contemporary existence and instead focus upon the things of our being-in-the-world that in turn encourages …
- *A return to the essence of the things themselves.* We may strive to seek beyond the things themselves as they appear to us. In Chapter 1 Mogens Prip-Buus's phrase is used that articulates this principle perfectly suggesting that if we are interested in studying anatomy, we must look beyond 'the girls on the beach'.
- *The body as the nexus of the experience of the things.* Our 'being-in-the-world' is our potential nexus of understanding through experience. In this context, the essence of the things themselves.
- *The potential held in archaeology in understanding the things themselves.* We should not underestimate the value of 'going back' to allow the essence of things to be revealed. Aalto, Utzon and Fehn were each occupied by this sense of archaeology;

visits to the ancient hill villages of the High Atlas Mountains of Morocco (for example), allowed the essences of what it is to dwell to be revealed. This revealing was facilitated by returning to the essences of the things themselves, filtered through the inner-self.

If we were to seek the embodied essence of Husserl's contribution to the philosophical narrative that supports this book, I concur with Macann's summation: 'Indeed, if a single phrase were required as an epitaph for Husserl's thought, it might be like this: Truth dwells in the inner-man' (Macann 1993: 54).

Such a concept aligns with Fehn's own position:

> Every artist has an internal vocabulary, words forced into being by the desire to express. I believe the articulation of subliminal thought is one of the most authentic acts of the creative process. The internal vocabulary follows the artist like a shadow; it is an instrument or tool of the creative process. How the artist formulates his or her expressions is singular, since they are a reflection of the individual's personality; but common to all is the manipulation of intuition. These subjective translations of thoughts are part of the internal vocabulary; and it is this vocabulary that the artist leaves behind in his or her creation.
>
> *Fjeld 2009: 108*

In the same way that Plato studied under Socrates, our next philosopher Martin Heidegger (1889–1976)[4] studied under the tutelage of Edmund Husserl. Of the

FIGURE 2.3 Ait Benhaddou, High Atlas Mountains, Morocco.

philosophers exposed within this chapter, it is Heidegger that provides a very direct and tangible connection between philosophy and architecture. He uses conceptualisation such as 'being', 'dwelling', 'building', 'bridging' and the 'room' as exemplars of philosophical discourse that are embodied within the domain of architecture. Within the phenomenological narrative, Heidegger's contribution represents a key element. In Dermot Moran's words: 'Any fair assessment of Heidegger's contribution must recognise that it changed the shape of twentieth-century philosophy' (Moran 2000: 193).

His life did, however, attract some controversy:

> He was (with the possible exception of Wittgenstein) the greatest philosopher of the twentieth century. He was (with the possible exception of Hegel) the greatest charlatan ever to have claimed the title of 'philosopher', a master of hollow verbiage masquerading as profundity. He was an irredeemable German redneck, and, for a time, a gullible and self-important Nazi. He was a pungent, if inevitably covert, critic of Nazism, a dis-concerning analyst of the ills of our age and our best hope for a cure for them. Each of these claims has been advanced, with greater of lesser plausibility on Heidegger's behalf.
>
> *Wood 1997: 1*

The central concept of Heidegger's thinking, in the context of this book, is *being*. He was specific in that the notion of being was focused exclusively upon the human condition, and to ensure precision, used the word *Dasein* that is derived from the linguistic root: *Da* (here or there) and *Sein* (to be). Thus we might suggest that the term *Dasein* articulates our being-in-the-world, or describing our 'presencing' in the world. So in short, Heidegger's quest is differentiated from epistemological realms of philosophy (theories of knowledge) that strove to understand what could be understood, through the concept of *Dasein* that sought to understand being-in-the-world by returning to focus upon the things themselves, viewed through the lens of our presencing in the world.

Heidegger suggests that this concept of *Dasein* is also embodied within each of us as being something at our very core of existence in the world; it is in that sense not applied, or indeed learnt behaviour. He also focuses upon the notion of *authenticity* and by implication, *in-authenticity* that is an essential value and helpful differentiation in making sense of our being-in-the-world. Again he draws from etymology in using the ancient German word *eigentlich*, which 'in ordinary German means "real" or "proper". From it he forms the word "Eigenlichkeit" – authenticity' (Wood 1997: 21).

Utzon articulated such being-in-the-world in describing the ideas that sat behind the design of his own house in Denmark:

> The simple, primitive life in the country, trips into the mountains with skis or guns, sailing trips, a few weeks together with the Arabs in the mountains or in the desert, a visit to North America and Mexico, the lifestyle of Indians – all

> this has formed the basis for the way of life my wife and I have wanted to lead, and thus for the design of the house.
>
> *Weston 2002: 61*

Heidegger suggests that authenticity is marked by truth-to-self and inauthenticity by the inhabitation of the truths of others. For us all this distinction holds significant resonance in the act of making place.

In *Poetry, Language, Thought* Heidegger provides us with an exemplar that on one hand could not be more ordinary and everyday in nature, but when considered from his particular perspective, unfolds in holding extraordinary qualities and potentials; the subject – the jug. He suggests that the jug supports itself and appears as a distinct entity, he discusses the process through which the potter brought the jug into being and the intentionality that sits behind that process in the making of a vessel. We can perceive the jug as object, but what in Heideggerian terms makes it a thing? 'What is in the thing that is thingly? What is the thing itself?' (Heidegger 1971: 167).

Heidegger suggests that to get to the thing, we first have to have conceived of the thing as a thing. He suggests that first came the need for the thing (the need for the vessel), then came the idea of the thing (a vessel), and then the potter made it. Thus the need was translated to the thing through the idea of the thing to become the thing, the vessel, in this case, characterised by the jug.

In the shaping of the jug, Heidegger suggests that the potter's real role is the shaping of the void that the jug contains as the void is the purpose of the jug, its shape allows the purpose to presence itself. Thus, in making the pot, the potter is bringing-forth or bringing-into-presence, the void; for it is the void that gave life and purpose to the jug. The jug-thing holds other potentials, filled with water or wine we might gather around it; the jug-ness providing a purpose or reason to gather, we might imagine conversations flowing, laughter, arguments or indeed philosophical silences. But perhaps the greatest purpose of the jug is its ability to sacrifice its contents through the act of pouring. Such is the potential held by the jug-thing born of the idea of vessel and void. This is an exemplar of looking beyond appearances in striving to understand the thingness of thing.

FIGURE 2.4 Utzon's House, Denmark.

In this same essay, Heidegger touches upon another concept that informs this book and that is *'nearness'*. He suggests that to perceive the thing as thing we need proximity to it, the kind of proximity that allows a measure of metaphorical immersion; that aligns with the ideas of spatial archaeology and immersion discussed in the previous chapter or as my former studio tutor Nigel Mills[5] (1944–2014) would say: 'be in it – not on it'.

My father's table (Chapter 1) was a thing. The idea that allowed it to come into being was a platform on which to lay food to eat. It was also a platform for drawing, model-making, painting, reading, writing, but as a young child the 'thing-potential' that I discovered was that under that platform was a place to dwell. Here was my retreat where I could play, imagine, watch, hide or just be. It was here apparently that I often slept and dreamt; of course I had my own bedroom but that was of an adult scale. The underside of the platform was my scale; my place, in the same way that Aalto's father's table was young Alvar's place to be.

Heidegger was critical of industrialised processes in that they move away from the needs that are a priori conditions to the process of making place and suggests that we have become increasingly overtaken by the consideration of 'things' as artefacts of technological or political production. In this he may be accused of promoting a particular romanticism that was informed by his own dwelling in his Black Forest hut in which he spent so much time. However, what is essential in Heidegger's critique is resonant today as the speeding-up of the world and the compression of space and time is even more evident and is discussed further in the final chapter.

Heidegger's thinking may appear as fascinating but somewhat abstract concepts, until we apply such ways of thinking to architecture. Let us consider the house. The reason for the thing we call house is the need to dwell; the idea of dwelling, and that need has its genesis in a number of existing conditions; perhaps the need to mediate climate, the need for protection, the primal need for spatial enclosure and definition and the need for 'hereness' and 'thereness'. Thus the 'thingness' of the 'thing' of house is born from the need to dwell. That takes the house beyond being merely an object in space and time through the evocation of what it is to dwell.

Heidegger is enormously kind to the architect in that he made as exemplars of his thinking the act of making place. In his essay 'Building–Dwelling–Thinking' he asks the fundamental and a priori questions of architecture:

> 1. What is it to dwell?
> 2. How does building belong to dwelling?
>
> *Heidegger 1971: 145*

He suggests:

> We attain to dwelling, so it seems, only by the means of building. The latter, building, has the former, dwelling, as its goal. Still every building is not a dwelling.
>
> *Heidegger 1971: 145*

The inference here is that the act of *dwelling* is at the very core of human existence, providing authority for the decision to focus upon the design of *dwellings* by each of our three protagonists as key exemplars of their respective paradigms. Heidegger of course acknowledges that there are a range of building typologies (power station, bridge and market hall as examples) within which one may be 'at home' but does not 'dwell'.

Again, Heidegger seeks understanding of this key act of human existence, through reversion to etymology; the origins of the words themselves. He reverts to the roots of the Old English and High German word *Bauen* (now meaning to build) that in original form meant in both languages to dwell and furthermore expressly, and by implication, to remain and stay in place. Thus, for the hunter-gatherer the *idea* of dwelling was accompanied by the implication of moving from foraging to cultivation and within that transition is an implicit duty of care for the place in which we dwell that extends to nurturing and tilling the soil and cultivating the vine. So that there, we might belong. As Heidegger suggests:

> But if we listen to what language says in the word 'Bauen' we hear three things:
>
> 1. Building is really dwelling.
> 2. Dwelling is the manner mortals are on the earth.
> 3. Building as dwelling unfolds into the building that cultivates growing things and the building that erects buildings.
>
> *Heidegger 1971: 148*

He continues: 'We do not dwell because we have built, but we build and have built because we dwell, that is, because we are dwellers' (Heidegger 1971: 148).

In this same essay, Heidegger introduces two further concepts that are of significant interest to the architect and by implication, central to the philosophical positioning of this book: 'the fourfold' and the concept of 'site' each considered through an phenomenal lens.

In the concept of the fourfold, Heidegger posits that while we might *be* on the surface of the earth, that surface is under the sky, the domain of the deities, and thus describes the four elements of our existence: earth, sky, divinities and man. He suggests that this is our *primal* condition of being-in-the-world and his use of that word is itself interesting. If we follow Heidegger's tendency to explore the etymology of words, given his precision in the use of language, we see that, in its earliest definition, the meaning is 'of original form' or 'primary' rather than the pejorative meaning ascribed to the word today.

Per Olaf Fjeld described Fehn thus:

> He built an intellectual connection between heaven and earth, and in this exploration, he found another important theme: the built structure's meeting with the earth. These two themes, the establishment of a new horizon and

> the meeting of the structure with the earth, almost independent of the project brief, set a challenge or signalled a method of attack.
>
> *Fjeld 2009: 22*

Using the example of the bridge, Heidegger illuminates the relationship between dwelling and place: 'The bridge gathers the earth as landscape around the stream' (Heidegger 1971: 152). In this description, Heidegger represents a way of building (and thus by implication, dwelling) that is relatively benign in impact in that the waters of the stream are allowed to flow, and that man is able to cross from one side to the other, but that in addition, the banks are revealed by the act of bridging. This of course raises such questions as:

- Do we need to cross the stream?
- If so, how?
- If so, where?

That exposes intentionality on the part of the builder. This intentionality is consistently exposed within the chapters that follow within the acts of making place conducted by our three protagonists.

Perhaps the real value of Heidegger's exemplar of bridge is that it reveals the place in which it sits to us, where such a revelation was not available to us prior to building. In Chapter 5 I suggest that Fehn's Villa Busk, coincidentally through the act of bridging, gathers and reveals to us the landscape in which it sits.

However, the most generous gift from Heidegger to the architect is perhaps his conceptualisation of space as '*Raum*' or '*Rum*'. Again he retreats to the etymology of the word and suggests Raum or Rum in its original form means: 'a place cleared or freed for settlement and lodging' (Heidegger 1971: 154).

He goes on to suggest that such a phenomenon is bounded and here uses the Greek word '*peras*' which proposes that the boundary is the point at which something begins 'its presencing in the world'. It is of significant interest how this concept transcends scales of existence; the boundary at one scale may define 'site', at another scale, define room. In 1946 Heidegger presented his text 'What are Poets For?' (see Heidegger 1975) apparently to a small audience, in memory of the death of the poet Rainer Maria Rilke some 20 years previously. He may have released conceptualisations for the later text 'Poetically Man Dwells'; the title of which was drawn from a poem by Friedrich Hölderlin (1770–1843): 'Full of merit, yet poetically, man / Dwells on this earth' (Heidegger 1971: 216).

Here Heidegger suggests that it is need that first calls us to dwell, and that poetry is implicit within the act of building itself; providing the potential for sublime existence within the condition of the fourfold. Within this text Heidegger writes of the concept of the '*measure*' not as a scientific phenomenon, but rather as a transcendental phenomenon that has its own metric, bridging between the elements of the fourfold and that measure informs the plan, and by implication the section and the elevation in the articulation of space. As he writes: 'In poetry there takes place what all measuring is in the ground of its being' (Heidegger 1971: 221).

In the preface of his seminal work *The Phenomenology of Perception*, Maurice Merleau-Ponty (1908–1961), Heidegger's pupil, takes up the baton and asks the fundamental question: 'What is phenomenology?' (Merleau-Ponty 1962: vii). Merleau-Ponty argues that it is the study of essences, but within the process of study those essences are returned to existence.

He continues:

> It is a transcendental philosophy which places in abeyance the assertions arising out of natural attitude, the better to understand them; but it also a philosophy for which the world is 'already there' before reflection begins – as an inalienable presence; and all of its efforts are concentrated upon re-achieving a direct and primitive contact with the world, and endowing that contact with a philosophical status.
>
> *Merleau-Ponty 1962: vii*

Within this text are a series of key words. Clearly, for Merleau-Ponty, as for Husserl, the process demands divestment of pre-conceived ideas and concepts. In addition that which we study is present before it is studied; Merleau-Ponty reinforces the position that the role of phenomenology is to reveal to us that which pre-existed. The words *direct* and *primitive* here are of fundamental importance. The word *direct* suggests a direct encounter with the essence is unencumbered by what we may term 'the white noise of everyday existence' and the word *primitive* in this context refers not to the pejorative sense inferred within contemporary meaning, but refers instead to 'going back to a different originating condition'. This draws upon Goethe's concept of '*Ur-phänonmenon*' (essential phenomenon) and Husserl's conceptualisation of '*rückfrage*' (regression).

While Husserl moved from the philosophy of science towards phenomenology, Merleau-Ponty was explicit in his rejection of the 'scientific method' in understanding of the world. He was of the view that this dualist (we would now argue binary) paradigm reduces everything to an object and suggests that the role of phenomenology is: 'a matter of describing, not of explaining or analysing' (Merleau-Ponty 1962: viii).

In establishing this position, by implication Merleau-Ponty rejected the Cartesian binary division of 'body' and 'soul' and in place, suggested a holistic paradigm of the body and soul being enmeshed and proposed that the body does not merely occupy space but inhabits space in our essence of being-in-the-world. As Reza Shirazi writes: 'The aim of Merleau-Ponty's phenomenology of perception can be understood as bringing human perception as the manifestation of consciousness into one's daily bodily engagement with the world' (Reza Shirazi 2014: 32).

Helpfully, given our subject, Merleau-Ponty reinforces the importance of context that Husserl earlier alluded to in the process of understanding the world. He refers to this condition as 'background' and that the boundary of our perception of this background represents the extent of our perceptual field. Such a conceptualisation is fundamental in the praxis of architecture, and central to the oeuvre of our three protagonists each of whom might ask fundamental questions such as 'where does the site end?' or 'where does the site begin?'.

Perhaps Merleau-Ponty's essential contribution was (in his own words):

> Imagine this: one of the greatest advances in twentieth-century Western philosophy consists of reminding the species designated as rational animal, as the significantly speaking animal, that it is flesh.
>
> *Dillon 1997: 246*

We cannot leave the subject of phenomenology, particularly given the context of this endeavour, without recourse to the French philosopher Gaston Bachelard (1884–1962). Mirroring the intellectual progression of both Husserl and Merleau-Ponty, Bachelard incrementally developed his philosophical position moving from scientific enquiry in his early career towards the realm of phenomenology. His seminal work (certainly in the context of architecture) *The Poetics of Space* sought to explore a diverse range of spatial typologies through the lens posited by Merleau-Ponty of conscious description. If Plato, Goethe, Husserl, Heidegger, and Merleau-Ponty were each articulating the value of returning to the 'things themselves' it was Gaston Bachelard that illuminated the poetic potential that constitutes the 'things'.

As did Husserl and Merleau-Ponty, Bachelard questioned the philosophical efficacy of (rational) scientific enquiry:

> A philosopher who has evolved his entire thinking from the fundamental themes of the philosophy of science, and followed the main line of the active growing rationalism of contemporary science as close as he could, must forget his learning and break with all his habits of philosophical research, if he wants to study the problems posed by the poetic imagination.
>
> *Bachelard 1969: 1*

Bachelard beautifully articulates the lived-body conceptualisation of Merleau-Ponty: 'And by remembering "houses" and "rooms" we learn to abide within ourselves' (Bachelard 1969: xxxiii), suggesting that houses and rooms are 'in us', just as we are 'in them', describing a condition of innate embodied memory.

Within the previous chapter, I described the reasoning behind the choice of the dwelling as an exemplar of the work of Aalto, Utzon and Fehn. This typological choice was in part founded with Bachelard's description of lived-body experience:

> Finding little to describe in the humble home, they spend little time there; so they describe it as it actually is, without really experiencing its primitiveness, a primitiveness which belongs to rich and poor alike, *if they are willing to dream.*
>
> *Bachelard 1969: 4; emphasis added*

Bachelard developed a particular methodology in exploring philosophy through fictional writing with explicit recourse to metaphor. He thus produced a prolific number of philosophical narratives; essays in the sense of wanderings of the mind.

In *The Poetics of Space* Bachelard focuses upon everyday 'things'; the house, drawers, chests and wardobes, nests, shells, etc., and through poetic description he takes us to the poetic qualities of the things themselves. In his chapter 1 ('The House-from Cellar to Garrett: The Significance of the House') he begins with a poem by Pierre Albert Birot taken from 'Les Amusements Naturels':

> At the door of the house who will come knocking?
> An open door we enter
> A closed door, a den
> The world pulse beats upon my door.
>
> *Bachelard 1969: 3*

With these few words Bachelard opens possibilities for the reader. The poem speaks of here and there, the threshold that illuminates the presencing of otherness: retreat, communality, privacy and gathering. Bachelard invites us to retreat within our own embodied memory and being-in-the-world in order to reveal the poetic qualities of all that which we encounter on a daily basis. Such a way of understanding the world conjoins precisely with my perception of what I would term 'architecture of significance'.

Our world clearly is populated with architecture. But, I would contend much of that architecture is mundane and lacks significance and holds little substantial ambition for itself. Yet there are examples of significant architecture designed by significant human beings, which arise above the morass of the inconsequential and in all dimensions, represent a zenith in architectural endeavour. These are the places where perhaps upon entry the little hairs on the back of our neck stand up, we might feel a temperature change in our body, perhaps a slight shiver, or a gasp. One such piece of architecture of significance is Utzon's Bagsvaerd Church in a small suburb of Copenhagen.

Approaching Utzon's Bagsvaerd Church on a field trip with students it began to rain. I ran ahead with one student and arrived at the church doors just as they were being closed in order for a wedding to take place. We snuck in and sat silently in the first floor gallery. The wedding was of little account to the student and I, and we gazed into the void of the cloud form roof studying the constant flux of light across the ceiling surface. When the wedding ended and the congregation had left, we continued to sit in silent contemplation. After a while we left the building and I asked the student what was his experience of that place. His response was simple: 'It has changed me forever'. Such is the power of architecture and when open to such an experience the poetic qualities of the 'things themselves' are revealed.

At this juncture having explored, albeit briefly, the theoretical platform provided by Plato, Goethe, Husserl, Heidegger, Merleau-Ponty and Bachelard, it may be helpful to provide direct connections from these philosophers to the Nordic context of our protagonists through the writings of Christian Norberg-Schulz (1926–2000) and Juhani Pallasmaa (1936–) that build upon these earlier philosophical positions within the context of architecture.

> At the same time, phenomenology appeared to me as a method well suited to penetrate the world of everyday existence, since architecture is in fact at the service of totality which the term 'world of life' implies, a totality that eludes scientific procedures.
>
> *Norberg-Schulz 2000: 15*

Drawing from and extending the earlier heritage of a Nordic phenomenological understanding of place articulated by Stein Eiler Rasmussen conjoined with concepts within Heidegger's writings, particularly in the conceptualisation of *Dasein* and *Raum*, Norberg-Schulz incrementally developed a phenomenological positioning that provided a platform for the *application* of phenomenological understanding within architectural endeavour. My sense is that in his early work, Norberg-Schulz's engagement with the phenomenological project was both tentative and intuitive as alluded to in the previous chapter. However, by 1996 in his book *Nightlands* he is absolutely explicit in the location of his thought within a phenomenological frame. In the preface he writes:

> The method employed is phenomenological; that is I do not seek to explain buildings as a result of their influences, nor do I arrange them within a chain of stylistic developments, though of course both influence and style are significant realities. Instead, I consider building as it occurs as part of a local context and attempt to see it as it actually is.
>
> *Norberg-Schulz 1996: 6*

Here the word *see* is of significance, suggesting that for Norberg-Schulz it is the ocular experience that holds authority within a phenomenological reading of place. This position is later reinforced within the same book:

> The phenomenological method is based upon 'seeing'. 'Seeing', means above all, recognising something 'as' something. When we visit a new place, we spontaneously recognise differences without being able to pinpoint what they consist.
>
> *Norberg-Schulz 1996: 8*

I am of course conscious that I may here do Norberg-Schultz a disservice in adopting such a literal position with regard to the word *seeing,* but within the context of his writing the authority of the eye appears clear.

It is particularly within this Nordic realm that the phenomenological project was adopted and significantly extended by the Finnish architect, thinker and writer Juhani Pallasmaa.

Pallasmaa, within the book *The Eyes of the Skin* (2005), questions the a priori assumption that it is the eye that holds absolute authority in our understanding of our world. He points us towards the pervasive authority of ocular experience within contemporary culture that in his view has occupied the praxis and theory of architecture. He provides points of resistance; counterpoints to such circumstances.

> Within the title *The Eyes of the Skin* I wish to express the significance of the tactile sense for our experiencing and understanding of the world, but also I intend to create a conceptual short circuit between the dominant sense of vision and the suppressed sense modality of touch.
>
> *Pallasmaa 2005: 10*

Pallasmaa's argument extends beyond touch, engaging with the temporal dimensions of architecture and all sensual modalities that include what he terms 'the haptic experience'. The word represents a 'sense of touch' but in relation to the thing being touched. Here Pallasmaa's purposeful use of this very specific term connects our presencing in the world to that which the world contains.

I have within the period of authorship of this project been unfortunate to suffer with lower back spasms and sought the services of a local osteopath, Oliver Curties, to resolve matters. He is an osteopath of a holistic demeanour, and has a somewhat existential disposition. In one of several conversations while being treated we discussed the (to me) astonishing possibility of altering the internal state of a human body through external manipulation. Oliver's response was that during the processes of treatment, he often 'saw through his fingers', supporting, should support be required, Pallasmaa's position.

However, Pallasmaa's contribution is not contained to the articulation of this all-sense experience potential. Perhaps his greatest contribution is in his consistent ability to challenge our individual and collective a priori assumptions. In his book *The Thinking Hand* (2009), he articulates the relationship between hand and imagination within the process of design:

> The pencil in an Architect's hand is a bridge between the imagining mind and the image that appears on the sheet of paper; in the ecstasy of the work, the drafts man forgets both his hand and the pencil, and the image emerges as it were an automatic projection of the imagining mind.
>
> *Pallasmaa 2009: 17*

He questions the apparent authority of the tendency of contemporary architects to revert to computer-generated images as a default position. In acknowledging the value of computers within a range of circumstances he suggests that the loss of the tactility in drawing with the hand distances us from the object of our endeavour: the artefact.

Pallasmaa also articulates very clearly the concept of embodied memory and thought; drawing upon the phenomenological heritage of Maurice Merleau-Ponty he writes: 'Buildings are not abstract, meaningless constructions, or aesthetic compositions, they are extensions and shelters of our bodies, memories, identities and minds' (Pallasmaa 2009: 117).

In these words we see reference to concepts of individual and collective memory that reside deeply within each of us. Perhaps we all hold subliminally the remnants of a farmer, a hunter, a gatherer, a maker of things, that we bring-to-bear consistently in our being-in-the-world. This concept of collective and individual embodied memory is a consistent theme of this book and is discussed variously in the work of Aalto, Utzon and Fehn.

When the history of this particular heritage of thinking and being is written, I sense that Pallasmaa's contribution will be seen as seminal; in the same way that Rasmussen articulated an experiential manifesto for understanding the world and Norberg-Schultz concretised that within the intellectual frame of phenomenology, the shift that Pallasmaa provides in challenging the hegemony of ocular experience and articulating an all-sense perception clearly provides a new paradigm for our presencing in, and understanding of the world.

The architecture and writing of the American architect Steven Holl bring this philosophical discourse into the present and simultaneously project it into the future. It is clear that for Holl, the return to the 'things themselves' is a transcendental act:

> Our experience and sensibilities can evolve through reflective and silent analysis. To open ourselves to perception we must transcend the mundane urgency of 'things to do'. We must try to access that inner life which reveals the luminous intensity of the world. Only through solitude can we begin to penetrate the secret around us. An awareness of one's unique existence in space is essential in developing a consciousness of perception.
>
> *Holl 2008: 40*

This insistence upon transcendence is of course somewhat at odds with our contemporary world that appears obsessed with immediacy of experience and as Pallasmaa suggests is governed by the absolute authority of the eye. The paradox of course here is that Holl suggests that a particular way of being-in-the-world is required as an a priori condition of returning to the 'things themselves' which is in close alignment with many Eastern ways of thought and being. This position of course does support a return to the original meaning of 'theory' (*thēoria*) as being a process of observation and speculation-upon, rather than a process that tests a predetermined hypothesis.

I have personally experienced only one of Steven Holl's buildings, the Kiasma Museum of Contemporary Art (1998) in Helsinki, Finland, that intertwines and enmeshes volumes articulated upon a processional (one could almost say ritualised) route punctuated with light in a manner reminiscent of the streets and alleys of Marrakech. Engagement with particularity of site is executed at a number of levels,

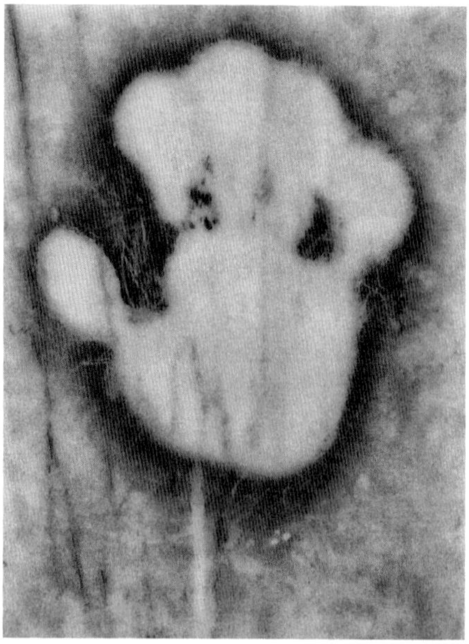

FIGURE 2.5 Kiasma, Helsinki, Steven Holl.

perhaps the subtlest being: 'implicit cultural line curves to link the building to Finlandia Hall' (Holl undated).

Finlandia was, of course, designed by Alvar Aalto. In the Kiasma project, the visitor was invited by Holl to leave a 'stain' of their presence in the building: a simple square plate that borders the ramping route at lower level is etched with the hand prints of all those that have offered themselves as memory.

Holl has a very particular and refreshing attitude to the phenomenological project, even engaging with concepts often avoided by most architects such as colour. If we examine the work of Aalto, Utzon and Fehn, there is much 'whiteness' present but Steven Holl wrestles with colour and harvests its potential in the heightening of human experience in space. Holl's D. E. Shaw Office Project (1991) in New York City exhibits sublime ambitions in harnessing of light and the consequence of colour: 'Yellow orange and brown autumn leaves seen along the upper Hudson River serve to illustrate the concept of variation and indeterminacy of color' (Holl 2008: 40).

In *Questions of Perception* Holl provides the reader with a number of frames of consideration of perception that include colour, light and shade, spatiality of night, time, duration and perception, water, sound, the haptic realm, proportion, scale and perception, and site circumstance, and idea, that provide fascinating spheres of potential enquiry if we project the phenomenological discourse into the unknown territory of the future.

It is fascinating to reflect upon how the phenomenological project, which has its genesis in Europe, has been developed and reinterpreted within the Nordic world and provides a philosophical context that surrounds our three protagonists. It is also interesting to reflect that this particular intellectual heritage now extends beyond the shores of our Nordic world and is now inhabited and extended in-turn in Australia by those such as Glen Murcutt, Richard Leplastrier and Peter Stutchbury and in America by Rick Joy and Steven Holl drawing simultaneously upon the influence of Frank Lloyd Wright and Louis Kahn.

In hoping that the first section of this chapter has articulated the philosophical underpinning of this book and has, in places, provided fragments of the relationship between such thought and the work of Aalto, Utzon and Fehn, we now turn to the application of phenomenology through the methodology used: that of paradigmatic enquiry.

Of Paradigm

The fundamental research methodology of this book is that of paradigm. This methodology was initially utilised to examine the design processes and work of Jørn Utzon; chosen because Utzon never subscribed to or indeed was ascribed a singular theoretical position; rather he drew inspiration from a diverse range of influences. The methodology of paradigm strives to capture these influences and was subsequently extended to the study of Aalto and Fehn, forwards and backwards chronologically, as it was clear that there were distinctions and similarities within each paradigm and that the methodology was appropriate to their shared Nordic heritage and design methods.

> Paradigm, par'a dim, noun. an example, a pattern.
>
> *Hayward and Sparkes 1968: 825*

The dictionary definition is helpful in that it provides the platform for the application of paradigmatic study in architecture: an *exemplar*. Thus in the study of Aalto, Utzon and Fehn, the paradigmatic methodology captures examples of their influences, thinking, design methodologies and output.

The etymology of *paradigm* draws upon the Latin '*paradigma*', a pattern or example, and from the ancient Greek '*paradeigma*', a pattern, model precedent or example, and from '*paradeiknynai*', to exhibit or represent.

McEwen provides a further perspective of the potential of paradigm:

> One might assert that Plato's notion of the heavenly craftsman and his eternal 'paradeigma' was 'nothing but' the projection of known, human way of building onto the unknown, divine or cosmic sphere.
>
> *McEwan 1993: 41*

Here McEwan suggests that in Ancient Greece, the idea of paradigm was the evolution and application of patterns or models that were subsequently applied to the world through the making of place. As she states:

> It is my contention that, with the dawn of Greek thought, the pattern discovered, or allowed to appear, through making was universalised to become

> the pattern that eventually came to be understood as the one embodied cosmos as we understand the word.
>
> *McEwan 1993: 42*

Within the field of Architecture paradigmatic methodology was first developed by the Swiss architect Bernard Hoesli, as a pedagogic model.[6] Hoesli moved to the USA in 1951, where he was appointed professor of architecture at the University of Austin School of Architecture, joining Colin Rowe, John Hedjuk and Walter Seligman and others, to form the Texas Rangers group of architects, who developed an innovative curriculum in the School that challenged extant notions of architectural education. What interested Hoesli and his colleagues, was how complex architectural ideas could be understood by students that were relatively unskilled in the consideration of such constructs. He developed a systematic and incremental programme of study that increased in complexity over time and with the study of seminal works of architecture (and the ideas of the architects) as a central element of the curriculum. Upon his return to ETH Zurich, this paradigmatic methodology was installed as a core element of Hoesli's innovative curriculum and became in itself a pedagogic paradigm.

Bernard Hoesli developed a pedagogic process that sought to:

> 1. Familiarise the student with what can be considered the classics of modern architecture.
> 2. To enlarge the student's repertoire of space concepts and to acquaint him with the possibilities of handling space.
> 3. To practice the reading of plans and sections.
> 4. To further his understanding of structure by simplifying the models to a presentation of load-bearing and non-loadbearing elements.
> 5. To demonstrate the relationship between structural concept and space concept.
>
> *Caragonne 1995: 268*

It is clear that Hoesli sought analysis of an extant 'classic work of modernism' to inform students' architectural vocabulary. However, this analysis was to be later conjoined with synthesis of a design proposition 'in the manner of…'. The vehicle was developed over time principally in the United States.

Alan Balfour introduced the idea of analysis of the ideas and strategies of architects to my own School, Portsmouth School of Architecture, in 1967. Supported by the then head of school, Professor Geoffrey Broadbent, Barry Russell and Peter Jenkins developed and variously reinterpreted Balfour's premise and in 1975 Ruslan Khalid (a former student at the AA under Peter Cook) brought the 'design in the style of' to Portsmouth School of Architecture. The heritage of this project lay with Phillipe Boudon from the Nantes School of Architecture who in 1970 had developed 'Le Project a la Maniere de' (Project in the Manner of) which provided students with a plural opportunity of analysis and synthesis 'a la maniere de'.

Barry Russell reports that Tomas Llorens was responsible in 1975 for its most precisely defined incarnation.

> It was clearly redefined and sharpened by Tomas Llorens (the Spanish philosopher and critic), when he taught with us, into the Paradigm Project, and with this title it has survived many transformations under different hands …
>
> *Russell 1995: 34*

The project has, since adoption at Portsmouth, run to this day; the content and nuance of interpretation being dependent upon subsequent authors.

Given Utzon's reticence to articulate a singular theoretical position, it was appropriate to use the methodology of paradigm to examine and explain his work and extend the methodology to Aalto and Fehn. The idea of paradigm, as indeed Utzon's work, transcends, but may also encapsulate theory, in analysing influences, methods and synthesis.

Initial analysis suggests that Utzon's oeuvre may be described as two distinct, but interconnected frameworks of consideration, *arche* and *techne*, both terms drawn from Ancient Greek and which of course provide the etymological root of the word *architect*.

Of Arche

> A spider conducts operations that resemble those of a weaver, and a bee puts to shame many an architect in the construction of her cells. But what distinguishes the worst architect from the best of bees is this, that the architect raises his structure in imagination before he erects it in reality.
>
> *Marx 2013: 121*

Arche is concerned with that which sits in front of the idea, in this case, the idea of architecture, that draws as Marx suggests, from the imagination. The term acknowledges that there is something at the very core of human existence that informs the *idea* of architecture and specifically Utzon's architecture. *Arche* encapsulates core phenomena such as 'dwelling' and 'room' that have been exposed within the philosophical narrative (above). Such intuitive engagement with primal phenomenon is encapsulated within the Nordic psyche and clearly underpins the canon of work of Aalto, Utzon and Fehn. The realm described by the term *arche* has been the subject of consistent interrogation within Nordic architecture, striving to reveal core conditions of human existence apropos the idea of architectural endeavour.

One example of *arche* is Utzon's a priori engagement with the concept of plateau in the context of the Sydney Opera House project. Utzon had experienced the power of the plateau as an archetypal typology in his visits to the Mayan temple ruins of Mexico. Here, through the process of ascension towards the realm of the deities we are removed from the everyday context of the ground and in the case of the temples, rise above the tree canopy of the jungle. We are thus

FIGURE 2.6 Sydney Opera House Plateau.

transported from the ordinary to the extraordinary through the process of ascending the plateau.

The decision to utilise the concept of plateau within the Opera House project had two significant advantages; one metaphysical, the other pragmatic. For the opera-goer the process of ascension allowed the everyday to be incrementally left behind and the extraordinary, the opera performance, to be anticipated. Here, rational belief had to be discarded, or at least temporarily suspended as one was enveloped within the world of theatre, an otherness, that demands suspension of our everyday beliefs.

The second, rather more prosaic advantage was that all of the 'stuff' of the opera house, workshops, parking, storage, goods handling could be installed within the underworld beneath the surface of the plateau, making the 'plateau of the extraordinary' even more extraordinary by the removal of all these serving spaces.

Perhaps also informing this decision was the embodied memory that within Danish culture, the only buildings that did not hunker down in the landscape were those of significance; civic and religious buildings were often raised on highpoints of the ground plane to signify their importance.

Thus 'the plateau' represents an archetypal precedent and exemplar of the concept of *arche* exemplified within the Sydney Opera House project.

Alvar Aalto, Jørn Utzon and Sverre Fehn represent exemplars of those who sought the core, the essence of architecture routing back towards primal sources of what it is 'to be', 'to dwell' and of course by implication, to make place. Examples of this tendency within our three protagonists are numerous but perhaps best encapsulated in Aalto's childhood tales such as 'The White Table' or 'A Fireside

Story' (Schildt 1998: 11, 12), which allude to the core qualities of what it is to dwell, seen through the eyes of a child.

For Utzon, the spirit is perhaps best articulated within his essay 'The Innermost Being of Architecture':

> It demands a good healthy common-sense understanding of life. An understanding of walking, standing, sitting and lying comfortably, of enjoying the sun, the shade, the water on our bodies, the earth and all the less easily defined sense impressions.
>
> *Weston 2002: 11*

This tendency to return to the things themselves is perhaps most explicit in Fehn's writings: 'Do you ever think of building a tree when you stand in front of a pile of wood planks?' (Fjeld 2009: 182). Here, Fehn in returning to the 'thing itself' is informed by that which is revealed to him (the planks), and thus there is something that is essential, particularly for the architect within this notion of 'revealing' or 'bringing forth'. The *arche* of Villa Busk was the client's request for a place *'to be'*.

Of Techne

As with the term *arche*, the use of word; *techne* is purposeful. I could of course have used the term *tectonic*, but in the purpose of this frame of enquiry that would be misleading. *Techne* as a concept sits ahead of the *tectonic*; *techne* is a frame of intention, knowledge and ability to act whereas the *tectonic* is the outcome of the act. The word *techne* is drawn from the ancient Greek τεχνη and Demetrei Porpherius provides an excellent definition: 'Craftsmen and artists alike were all thought of as "technites (τεχνιτες), that is men who had a "Techne" and knew how to practice it' (Porphyrios 2002: 129).

It is of note that within the use of this term the Greeks did not distinguish between craft and art, which suggests that there is an implicit suggestion within the use of the word that goes beyond merely a practical ability to make something. Porpherius continues:

> The essential meaning of 'Techne' as reasoned intelligence and knowledge put into practice can also be found in the old German 'kunst' or the Swedish 'konst' which today stand for art, but which originally meant knowledge and skill deriving from 'kennen' or 'können', to know with a sense of know-how.
>
> *Porphyrios 2002: 130*

Kenneth Frampton articulates a particular poetic quality implicit in the term when exploring the etymology of the word 'tectonic': 'In Greek it appears in Homer where it alludes to the art of construction in general. The poetic connotation of the term first appears in Sappho where the "Tekton", the carpenter assumes the role of poet' (Frampton 1995: 3).

Here we understand that within our context the term tectonic does not reside merely in the act of making, but rather in the act of making *poetically*, in the same manner that Heidegger invites us to *dwell poetically*.

McEwan argues that it is through the process of making (bringing-forth or revealing), that the cosmos (*kosmos*) is revealed, and thus the potential held by *techne* to bring-forth or reveal provides a core element of architecture.

> It has so far been my argument that the theoretical event, so called, of sixth-century Greece, hinged upon the emergent awareness of order whose 'genesis', whose coming-to-be, was rooted in the early Greek perception of craft as revelation of the 'kosmos'. The work of the carpenter revealed it through cutting and assembly, the textile embodied it through the rhythms of the shuttle moving over a loom, the dancing floor was its appearance in dance and the boat, which sped through the waves like a bird through the air, made it manifest in both its building and navigation. The first articulation of this order was Anaximander's, but the discovery was that of Daedalus, and if Daedalus was the mythical first architect, it is through the Daedalus legend that the architectural beginnings of Western thinking are understood.
>
> *McEwan 1993: 79*

The concept of *techne* focuses upon the 'bringing forth' or revealing of the idea, which in turn was, at its origin of course, informed by *arche*. Such a discourse at a fundamental level involves making the idea 'material'. Porphyrious extends his argument to suggests that the knowledge embedded within the *technites* includes an innate sense of the material used, its nature (for example, length) and its capacity (for example, structural capacity) and these 'knowings' are implicit within the process of making and thus reveal to us the very essence of the material used, exposing the 'ontology of constructing' (Porphyrios 2002: 129).

As an exemplar of this concept of *techne* we turn to Alvar Aalto's Experimental House. Here, Aalto revealed the essence of place through precise tectonic acts. The guest wing extension to the main house is founded upon tree-trunks that lay at 45° to the main house that bridge between the outcrops of rock that existed upon the site. The building itself is set parallel to the main house above this foundation; the juxtaposition between the two tectonic elements celebrating the potential of the site topography and geology to support the act of dwelling.

Similarly, Sverre Fehn used the topography and geology of the site to provide the measure of dwelling in the Villa Busk project. The two large rock outcrops on the promontory define the extent of the house and thus the extent of dwelling within the landscape.

Therefore the term *Techne* in the context of the paradigmatic method of this book, is concerned with the intentions, embodied knowledge and wisdom that inform the acts of revealing of Aalto, Utzon and Fehn within the process of the bringing-forth of the objectives of their respective realms of *Arche*.

FIGURE 2.7 Log Foundations, Aalto Experimental House.

Of Gathering

Although, for the sake of clarity, *arche* and *techne* are defined as distinct elements of the paradigm, it is Gottfried Semper[7] (1803–1879) that provides a Heideggerian bridge that gathers the concepts together yet allows the distinct nature of each to remain and resonate:

> At the risk of falling into the same error that I criticise (materialistic speculation) I see myself forced to go back to primitive conditions (Urzustände) of human society in order to come to that which I actually propose to set forth. I shall do it as succinctly as possible.
>
> *Semper 1989: 102*

Within these words we detect parallel tendencies to those of our three protagonists: a going back to primal circumstances in order to discover (as Aalto remarked) what has been forgotten.

In his text *The Four Elements of Architecture* (1851) Semper defined archetypal 'elements' that he believed represented the foundation of all architecture: *hearth, roof, enclosure, mound.* The term 'elements' here is somewhat misleading as it leads us to think of these as material forms. It was Semper's view that these words actually represented the idea of hearth, roof, enclosure and mound – the *Arche* of each primal typology. These archetypes, if we return to Heidegger's example of the jug, represent the *idea* of each *thing*; here, the *idea* being the need to dwell.

At this point, I would comment upon the precision and resonance of the particular terms that Semper uses. *Hearth,* for example, I believe to be simultaneously specific and generic. He could have used the term *fire* (generic) or *fireplace* (specific – as in place of fire) yet he used the word *hearth* that has a specific resonance in that we can all imagine an image of a known hearth, but it also evokes a sense of the idea of *hearth*: a place of gathering, a place of cooking, a place of warmth, light, conversations and silences. This precision in language is central to the descriptive dimension of phenomenology and to the limits of my ability I have striven for such precision wherever possible.

Returning to the things themselves, Semper was clear as to their chronological ordering. First came the hearth. We might imagine a group of humans in the landscape with a need for warmth and light; an opportunity to cook food and to gather. A particular place within the landscape reveals itself that is most suitable for the purpose, material is gathered and the fire is lit; dwelling exists in primal form. They sleep under the stars within the warmth provided by the hearth.

Semper also argues that it is around the hearth that the first alliances were made and that the first spiritual acts were performed. Hearth becomes Altar.

This primal description of dwelling resonates strongly and consistently within Heideggerian conceptualisations of dwelling and within our three protagonists. Fehn, for example, writes of such things but contextualises within his landscape conditions of mountain, fjord and forest. In Can Lis the primordial fire is the place of gathering, as it is in the Experimental House, as it is in Villa Busk.

Semper writes of the hearth:

> It is the first and most important, the 'moral' element of architecture. Around it grouped the three other elements; the 'roof', the 'enclosure' and the mound, the protecting negations or defenders of the hearth's flame against the three hostile elements of nature.
>
> *Semper 1989: 102*

Semper, through the examination of ancient cultures, moves on to the idea of enclosure, the wall, suggesting that the first walls were woven, of fabric or twigs, and the choice of material was determined by climate and the availability of material. Semper suggests that the practice of weaving is as old as the practice of the potter, and posits that in some instances the weaving of walls and mats pre-dates the weaving of clothing; such is the imperative of the enclosure. The purpose of the enclosure of course is to protect the hearth.

For Semper, the roof begets the hut. He suggests that the roof, whether in the form of a tent or a fixed structure, allows man to move from enclosure to hut. In primal states the family would share the hearth, the enclosure and the roof with their livestock; affording equal protection to man and beast.

In discussing the typology of mound Semper writes: 'Another great, unknown, perhaps older than any others referred to earlier, left behind powerful traces of their ancient work, which has almost no connection with the artistic trends just discussed' (Semper 1989: 102).

These are the dwellers in the mounds. Here we imagine the realm of the troglodytes drawing from prehistory but remaining in existence today. Here I am reminded of the Roman settlement of Bulla Regia in Tunisia; a whole underground complex of Roman artifice, hewn from rock in order that its inhabitants could retreat from the heat of the Tunisian sun. A glorious undertaking, informed by particular climatic conditions that Tunisia provides. There are many other examples, albeit less grand, in the Loire Valley of France, Southern Spain, the Greek island of Santorini, each providing examples of contemporary dwelling within the mound.

Semper argues that of course these archetypal typologies evolved and developed over time informed by social and cultural developments; communal enclosure became hut, huts became villages, villages towns and cities. Social order evolved and architecture responded; the leader built the tower and the huts gathered around its base basking in the warmth of symbolic protection.

Semper extended this argument in the bringing-forth or making of these 'elements' through defining two models of building: *framing* and *stereotomy*. 'Framing' is an act of repetition; lightweight elements forming structure. 'Stereotomy' (drawn from the Greek *stereos*, solid, mass, and *tomia*, to cut or carve) is to carve solid mass. In Villa Busk we see Semper's models conjoin: the massive (carved) concrete base gives way to the repetitive light timber frame seemingly draped in the fabric that is roof. Of course as Frampton illustrates, that notion of carving mass is not necessary literal – it has the material quality of mass – it may be stone, brick, concrete, rammed earth; the principle in actuality is the manipulation and bringing-forth of mass. What Semper does in this identification of mass is illuminate the distinction, and potential of heavy and light, stone and feather.

The architect Steven Holl subscribes to this mass/lightness duality: 'A phenomenological architecture calls for both stone and feather ... Architecture's materiality is likewise conveyed via the structure and material of optic and haptic spatial experience' (Holl 1995: 18–19).

In building the bridge that gathers *arche* and *techne*, Semper illuminates the way in which the 'things' are made manifest; processes such as weaving are informed by the material to be weaved, the later application of stucco to weaved form is another level of bringing forth of the things themselves. The burrowing and mining of the mound dwellers is equally informed by the material that is mined.

Gottfried Semper does not distinguish *arche* and *techne* as separate entities; rather he fuses them in a narrative that suggests that the idea of the thing is informed in the manner in which it is revealed and, in turn, that the process of bringing forth is an intrinsic quality of the thing itself.[8]

Of the Poetic Conjunction

> The Nordic art of building thus manifests what it is to 'live poetically' under Nordic conditions whereby the word 'poetic' acknowledges the qualitative identity of the environment.
>
> *Norberg-Schulz 1996: 6*

The term '*poetic conjunction*' signifies a poetic, metaphysical presencing within the work of each of our three protagonists that is somehow greater than the sum of the parts of their individual paradigm expressed through the elements of *arche* and *techne*. This of course begs the question: what is the nature of that conjunction?

Within the realm of *arche*, there is a clear theme emerging in this chapter which we might summarise as a 'going-back', and for all of the philosophers, critics and commentators discussed that 'going-back' is a central preoccupation and a core element of their method. Within the process of going-back we reveal the un-measurable, the inexpressible, the poetic.

Heidegger was absorbed by the idea of the poetic and the poet. He dwelt upon the question posed in Holderlin's elegy 'Bread and Wine': 'and what are poets for in a destitute time?' (Heidegger 1971: 91). He suggests (his) time is destitute due to 'God's failure to arrive' (Heidegger 1971: 91).

That failure of God to arrive has the consequence of extinguishing divine radiance from our existence; hence of the diminution and destitution of spirit. We may argue that *our* time is more destitute in these terms than that of Heidegger, and we now need, perhaps more than ever before, for the poets to gather us to ourselves.

Heidegger was an admirer of Rainer Maria Rilke (1875–1926), a poet and writer of prose. In his book *Letters to a Young Poet* he is contacted by the young poet Franz Xavier Kappus (1883–1966), who consistently sends examples of his work for Rilke to comment upon. Rilke is immediately clear in his first correspondence with Kappus that he will not undertake the role of critic:

> I cannot go into the nature of your verses, for any critical intention is too remote from me. There is nothing less apt to touch a work of art than critical words: all we end up with is more or less felicitous misunderstandings.
>
> *Rilke 2011: 5*

Nonetheless, Kappus continues to write to Rilke sending further examples of his work. Refusing to be drawn, Rilke consistently responds by suggesting to Kappus that: 'You are looking to the outside, and that above all you should not be doing now' (Rilke 2011: 6).

Rilke goes on to suggest that all Kappus needs actually already resides within himself, and it is that he should explore. In subsequent correspondence Rilke refers to the poetic potential of the everyday: time, relationships, sexual relationships, love, eating, solitude and childhood. Yet consistently within these narratives Rilke suggests to the young poet that he should seek depth rather than surface, the value of patience and tenacity and the poetic qualities that reside in each of us. In his final response to Kappus, Rilke writes:

> Art too is only a way of living, and it is possible, however one lives, to prepare oneself for it without knowing; in every real situation we are nearer to it, better neighbours, than in the unreal half-artistic professions which by pretending to be close to art in fact deny and hurt its very existence, as for

> example the case with the whole of journalism and almost all of criticism and three-quarters of what passes for literature.
>
> *Rilke 2011: 48*

Rilke exposes here the notion that poetry, or the poetic, is not an external force but resides deep within each of us. In the manner that Heidegger suggests that we identify need, we build and in the process of building poetry is released, we identify parallel processes in art, literature and of course poetry itself.

In this sense, Aalto, Utzon and Fehn are each in their way poets. Their work uplifts us, inspires us but more importantly exposes something of us to ourselves. Utzon's Bagsvaerd Church exposes the deity within us, Fehn's Villa Busk exposes our being-in-the-world through its primal quality, Aalto's Saynatsalo Town Hall reveals ritual and democracy to us. Providing of course that we allow it.

This chapter commenced with the proposition that there are probably as many phenomenologies as there are phenomenologists, and in examining the philosophical heritage of this book we identify nuanced differences within each of our philosophical protagonists. It is appropriate therefore that I clearly articulate what is drawn from each in developing the intellectual platform of this book.

Plato, through his metaphor of the cave, projects us to the core of what it is 'to be' and the dimensions that the act of being encompasses. He speaks of dark and light, of shadow and fire and of the cave; all primordial phenomena that sit deep within our embodied memories. He suggests that the task of being is to move from the facile nature of surface appearance and move out of the darkness into the light where we might speculate upon our being-in-the-world within a cosmic rather that constrained context.

In *Timaeus* and *Critias* he presents '*chora*', the 'receptacle of becoming'; that as a concept overflows with potential for the architect. At one level it imagines the possibility of *Arche* in the idea of 'making something become', at another level it suggests that the idea of the site is itself a 'receptacle of becoming'.

Goethe unlocks the potential held within the concept of '*Ur-phänonmenon*', suggesting the existence of primal typologies of phenomena that Seamon proposes are 'deep-down phenomena' that suggests a going-back and going-deep is required in perceiving such things.

Husserl provides a radical shift in thought. In the identification of and differentiation between our physical bodies and of lived in bodies in the world, he invites a transcendental attitude of being-in-the-world that seeks to return to the essence of the things themselves and the potential held by regressive archaeology in uncovering such essences; a position that clearly informed the emerging thought of Martin Heidegger.

Heidegger provides the fundamental element of the *arche* of architecture: *dwelling*. Yet, in parallel, Heidegger releases to us the *acts* of architecture, referred to in the previous chapter. Gathering, conjoining, bathing, retreating, exposing, cooking, abluting, sleeping and of course being, are all revealed as the core acts of human experience within the realm of dwelling (poetically).

To 'be' we need to dwell and Heidegger sets the project of dwelling (poetically) through the act of building (*Bauen*) and articulates the core dimensions of the project in defining space as '*Raum*'. Heidegger also suggests that the act of dwelling requires authenticity.

For me Heidegger's single most significant contribution to this book is his articulation of 'the thing' unfolded in his speculations upon the 'jug-ness (essence) of jug'. This led me to speculate upon the essence of architecture and following the Heideggerian (and Platonic) models, search beyond appearances. This is a process of archaeology that encourages us to go back and to observe (deeply) and speculate (intensely); the etymology of the term '*theory*' in '*theoria*'.

Heidegger also hints that we need to understand not just the thing, but also the context in which the thing resides that in his view has boundaries. My preference here is to use the term thresholds, which is less finite and suggests the presencing of otherness beyond the threshold. This concept facilitates the idea of the perceptual field; a territory of perception that is a consistent reference point for this book.

Heidegger also exposes the fourfold; on the *earth, man* dwells, under the *sky* and before the *deities* as mortals, which provides a sense of inter-connectedness and a cosmic dimension that I speculate may be drawn from his interest in Eastern thought and conceptualisations such as the Buddhist term '*sunyata*' that also suggests the idea of the cosmic inter-relationship between all things.

Finally, Heidegger's use of etymology as a means of 'going back to the origin' has provided a useful tool in informing the narrative of this text.

I am particularly drawn to Husserl's rejection of the dualist method of understanding the world prescribed by the scientific method, which holds the danger of ignoring complexity and inter-relationships. Also, his demand to describe rather than explain the world, provides the potential to 'read the book time and time again' and if indeed 'the book' is a great book, uncover more and more in each reading.

Semper is a seminal source in the fusion of *arche* and *techne* through his definition of the four 'elements' that is reinforced by his duality of mass and lightness. Similarly, Bachelard has significant resonance in this work through the articulation of the 'poetic' and providing tools through which it can be experienced.

I offer huge gratitude to Rasmussen, Norberg-Schulz and Pallasmaa in their powerful descriptions of the Nordic conditions and their each distinct interpretations of the heritage of philosophical thought described by phenomenology. In addition to my own research and personal experience of the Nordic world, these contributions have been essential in informing the structure and content of this book.

My sense is that Steven Holl projects phenomenology into the future with great potentials yet to be fully explored or indeed imagined. His 'frames of consideration of perception' unlock the opportunity for augmented examination of the phenomenological project that encapsulates potentials such as colour.

I agree with M. Reza Shirazi (above) that the project of phenomenology provides us with the potential to think deeply about architecture, and that is adopted as the intellectual platform for this study. Of course, due to the implicit dynamic and speculative nature of phenomenology, I have striven to extract from this heritage that which is appropriate to this work.

The concept of paradigm provides the primary mechanism for the application of phenomenological method and the subdivisions of *arche*, *techne* and the *poetic conjunction* provide frames through which the narrative of description and speculation (as opposed to analysis) is developed. The return to the original etymological meaning of the word *theory* allows, in my belief, for a much more speculative and observational approach to the things themselves; appropriate to the project.

In conclusion, this chapter is not presenting a *theory* of architecture; rather it presents a particular and individualised 'way of seeing' that leads to a 'speculation-upon' the things themselves. Therefore in no sense is this chapter intended as prescriptive in encouraging adoption of any particular theoretical methodology; the ambition is to simply describe the foundations upon which all that which follows rests upon.

Notes

1 Precise dates vary between sources – this is drawn from Betty Radice's edition of Plato's *Republic* (1974).
2 A branch of philosophy that is concerned with theories of knowledge.
3 Edmund Husserl, born of a Jewish family, in Prostějov, then in the Austrian Empire, now in the Czech Republic, that is located within the region of Morovia, initially studied mathematics and physics at the universities of Leipzig and Berlin, transferring to Vienna for postgraduate study where his academic interests focused upon philosophy. Upon graduation he taught variously at the universities of Halle, Göttingen and Freiburg.
4 Martin Heidegger was born into a relatively poor family in Messkirch, Baden, Germany, the son of a sexton, and studied theology at the University of Freiburg. Rejecting the Catholicism of his parents, he moved his attention to the realm of philosophy, and Husserl in particular influenced his early works.
5 Nigel Mills, studio tutor for 27 years at Portsmouth School of Architecture.
6 A member of the so-called 'Texas Rangers' group that included Colin Rowe, John Hejduk and Robert Slutzky; a group of academics at the University of Architecture in Austin, Texas, USA, between 1951 and 1957. They challenged the accepted orthodoxies of pedagogic methodology and sought to develop a pedagogic model supported by theoretical intellectual constructs.
7 Semper was a German architect, art critic and professor at Dresden and Zurich universities. He studied mathematics at Göttingen University before enrolling at Munich University to study civil engineering. In 1826, Semper moved to Paris to study architecture under the tutelage of the architect Franz Christian Gau, with whom Semper subsequently worked. Within France in this period was a significant debate within architecture that focused upon the issue of *polychromy*; a debate as to the colouration of ancient architecture. While in Paris, Semper was witness to the July uprising of 1830 that marked the abdication of Charles X. This period of political, social and economic turmoil heralded a new era and encouraged within the intellectual community radical re-thinking of accepted orthodoxies. Semper was clearly sympathetic to the uprising and aligned himself with such attitudes. Increasingly, and given his experiences in Paris, unsurprisingly, Semper sought a radical reconsideration of architecture and in doing so, went back to pre-history in order to establish the fundamental typological archetypes.
8 However, my critique of Semper's analysis is that it is devoid of reference to place as a core element of architecture. It is important to understand this critique in the context of his zeitgeist. Although he rejected the opportunity to enter the École des Beaux-Arts in

Paris, deciding to study under Gau instead, these formative years in Paris were clearly within the intellectual context of Enlightenment thought that is given expression within architecture through the neo-rationalist architecture of Boulee (1726–1799) and Ledoux (1736–1806). Within this period, the primary focus of architecture was on the object (noun) of architecture and the opportunity to express the potential contribution of site, rarely expressed. It is therefore unsurprising that this in my view essential component of architectural endeavour is absent from Semper's thinking.

References

Bachelard, G. 1969. *The Poetics of Space*, tr. M. Jolas. Boston, MA: Beacon Press.

Caragonne, A. 1995. *The Texas Rangers: Notes from an Architectural Underground*. Cambridge, MA: MIT Press.

Davies, C. 2011. *Thinking About Architecture: An Introduction to Architectural Theory*. London: Lawrence King Publishing.

Dillon, M. C. 1997. *Merleau-Ponty's Ontology*. Urbana, IL: Northwestern University Press.

Fjeld, P. O. 2009. *Sverre Fehn – The Patterns of Thoughts*. New York: Monacelli Press.

Frampton, K. 1995. *Studies in Tectonic Culture*. Cambridge, MA: MIT Press.

Hayward, A. L. and Sparkes, J. J. 1968. *The Concise English Dictionary*. London: New Orchard Editions.

Heidegger, M. 1971. *Poetry, Language, Thought*, tr. A. Hofstadter. New York: Harper & Row.

Heidegger, M. 1975. *Poetry, Language, Thought*, tr. A. Hofstadter. New York: Harper & Row.

Holl, S. 1995. The Matters of Architecture: A Note on Hariri and Hariri. In *Hariri and Hariri*, ed. K. Frampton, S. Holl and O. Reira Ojeda. New York: Monacelli Press.

Holl, S. 2008. Question of Perception – Phenomemology of Architecture. In *Questions of Perception: Phenomenology of Architecture*, ed. S. Holl, J. Pallasmaa and A. Pérez Gómez. Tokyo: A+U Publishing.

Holl, S. Undated. Kiasma Museum of Contemporary Art. Retrieved 20 August 2016 from www.stevenholl.com/projects/kiasma-museum.

Husserl, E. 1982. *Ideas Pertaining to a Pure Phenomenology and to a Phenomenological Philosophy: Book 1*. The Hague: Martinus Nijhoff.

Krista Sykes, A. (ed). 2010. *Constructing a New Agenda: Architectural Theory 1993–2009*. New York: Princetown Architectural Press.

Macann, C. 1993. *Four Phenomenological Philosophers: Husserl, Heidegger, Sartre, Merleau-Ponty*. London: Routledge.

Marx, K. 2013. *Das Capital*. Ware: Wordsworth Editions.

McEwan, I. K. 1993. *Socrates Ancestor*. Cambridge, MA: MIT Press.

Merleau-Ponty, M. 1962. *The Phenomenology of Perception*, tr. C. Smith. London: Routledge.

Moran, D. 2000. *Introduction to Phenomenology*. Abingdon, UK: Routledge.

Norberg-Schulz, C. 1996. *Nightlands*. Cambridge, MA: MIT Press.

Norberg-Schulz, C. 2000. *Architecture: Presence, Language Place*. Milan: Skira Editore.

Pallasmaa, J. 2005. *The Eyes of the Skin: Architecture and the Senses*. Chichester: John Wiley & Sons.

Pallasmaa, J. 2009. *The Thinking Hand: Existential and Embodied Wisdom in Architecture*. Chichester: John Wiley & Sons.

Perez-Gomez, A. 2006. *Questions of Perception: Phenomenology of Architecture*. San Francisco, CA: William Stout Publishers.

Plato. 1974. *The Republic*, ed. B. Radice. Harmondsworth: Penguin Books.

Porphyrios, D. 2002. From *Techne* to Tectonics. In *What is Architecture?*, ed. A. Ballantyne. New York: Routledge.

Reza Shirazi, M. 2014. *Towards an Articulated Phenomenological Understanding of Architecture*. New York: Routledge.

Rilke, R. M. 2011. *Letters to a Young Poet*. London: Penguin Books.

Russell, B. 1995. In *Educating Architects*, ed. M. Pearce and M. Toy. London: Academy Editions.

Schildt, G. 1998. *Alvar Aalto: In His own Words*. New York: Rizzoli Publications.

Seamon, D. 1998. Goethe, Nature and Phenomenology. In *Goethe's Way of Science: A Phenomenology of Nature*, ed. D. Seamon and A. Zajonc. New York: State University of New York Press.

Semper, G. 1989. *The Four Elements of Architecture*, ed. F. Pellizzi. Cambridge: Cambridge University Press.

Smith, D. W. 2007. *Husserl*. New York: Routledge Press.

Weston, R. 2002. *Utzon*. Hellerup: Edition Blondal.

Whitehead, A. N. 1978. *Process and Reality*. New York: Free Press.

Wood, M. 1997. *Heidegger*. Oxford: Oxford University Press.

3

ALVAR AALTO – THE SOPHISTICATED SHAMAN

> Building converts the community's cosmological view of the world into physical reality. Simultaneously, the temporal order is linked with the mythical order. In the end there is complete affinity between the individual and the community, between thinking and place.
>
> *Pallasmaa 2005: 73*

The characterisation of Aalto as the 'Sophisticated Shaman' within the Preface is reflective of the shifting political, cultural and social conditions that characterised his zeitgeist and the inherent permeability he displayed in being aware of such shifts, and responding to them.

Alvar Aalto (1898–1976) lived, as the Chinese proverb suggests, in 'interesting times'. The year of his birth was shared by the German author Bertolt Brecht, the Italian motor manufacturer Enzo Ferrari, the Spanish poet Federico García Lorca, the Dutch artist M. C. Escher, the American artist Alexander Calder, the American composer George Gershwin and the British author C. S. Lewis. To paraphrase Bob Dylan: 'The times, they were a-changing'.

> Finland is with Aalto wherever he goes. It provides him with that inner source of energy that flows through his work.
>
> *Gideon 1969: 620*

Finland was in a state of flux. Following centuries of Swedish rule, the territory we now recognise as Finland was occupied by Russia in the Swedish–Russian War (1808–1809) and was eventually established as the largely autonomous Grand Duchy of Finland within the Russian Empire. The period between 1863 and 1898 saw an increasing establishment of the Finnish identity that included the adoption of the Finnish language as the national language. From 1898 to the start of the Russian Revolution in 1917 the Finns witnessed a period of increasing Russification.

On 6 December 1917, Finland declared independence following the Russian October Revolution and in 1918 Finland was declared a republic after the defeat of Germany in the First World War.

Aalto's formative context was clearly within a period of political and economic flux with Finland's national identity emerging. In Chapter 1, I charted the parallel movements in architecture that reinforced national and regional identities within this period, represented within architecture by the National Romanticism movement exemplified by the Finnish National Theatre (1902), the Finnish National Museum (1905–1910), and Helsinki Railway Station designed by Eliel Saarinen which gave built expression to progressive social and political ideas.

Seeking perhaps a more sophisticated identity that was influenced by movements in Germany in the early twentieth century, the Nordic world increasingly sought to adopt the apparent authority of classicism expressed as the movement we identify as Nordic Neo-Classicism, as the signification of this new age. However, this movement halted almost overnight, stopped in its tracks by a single act of design: the Great Exhibition of Stockholm of 1930. Aalto was 32.

It was the Great Exhibition designed by Gunnar Asplund in collaboration with Sigurd Lewerentz that signalled the entry of modernism into the Nordic lexicon of architecture, influenced by earlier and parallel movements in northern Europe. We cannot underestimate the impact of this event, bringing lightness, light, permeability, functionalism and porosity to a context that had previously defined in all its stylistic interpretations in the concept of '*hygge*'.

Hugo Alvar Henrik Aalto was born in Kuortane, Finland, on 3 February 1898 to Johan Henrik Aalto, a land surveyor, and Selma Matilda Aalto, a Swedish-speaking

FIGURE 3.1 Helsinki Railway Station (1919).

postmistress. When Alvar was five years of age the family moved to Jyväskylä in central Finland, characterised by forests and lakes. It was in Jyväskylä that he spent his formative years and his Father worked as a forest surveyor. In 1916 Aalto began his studies of architecture at the Helsinki University of Technology; his studies were interrupted by the Finnish Civil War of 1918, within which he became a combatant, joining the White Army. He eventually graduated in 1921, and completed his National Service in 1923. Aalto returned to Jyväskylä to open his own studio, having already completed his first house design for his parents in Alajärvi while a student.

We should recognise that within his early years, Aalto was exceptionally productive and exhibited what we may even describe as qualities of a prodigy. In 1913, at the tender age of 15, Aalto was writing features and cultural articles for the regional newspaper, *Keski-Suomi*, and by 1915 contributed articles on such diverse subjects as sports, literature and art. This early engagement with the written word was to later re-emerge as he chronicled his views on architecture.

In October 1924 Aalto married his office assistant Aino Marsio. They visited Italy for their honeymoon for a period of six weeks. This trip was to have a significant impact upon the couple. Alvar and Aino worked closely together until her death in 1949, and the contribution she made should not be underestimated. Aalto subsequently remarried in 1952, to Elissa Mäkiniemi, also an office assistant, with whom he lived until his death in May 1976.

Aalto was a 'renaissance man'; he did not contain himself to architecture but was also a painter, furniture designer, designer in glass and ceramics, and within each of those disciplines was at the very edge of technical possibility, testing new ways of making. The bending of plywood and laminating of timber were two examples of his tectonic ambitions. It is this engagement with the conjunction of designing and making that is central within the narrative of our three protagonists. Aalto also demonstrates an exceptional ability to move seamlessly between scales of creative endeavour: from the macro-scale of urban and industrial planning to consideration of the door handle, the vase and the chair. We will see such qualities re-emerge in the examination of the work of Sverre Fehn in Chapter 5.

At this juncture Aalto's particular paradigm is exposed and will be examined and articulated (Figure 3.2).

I have chosen to structure this chapter alone chronologically, to amplify the sense of the shifts in Aalto's thinking over time in response to wider changes in the context in which he sat. The choice of projects is purposeful and is not intended to represent the full canon of Aalto's work, but rather focuses upon particular projects that best illustrate the thesis of this study.

Of Arche

We commence Aalto's narrative with two chronologically parallel projects located in his adopted hometown of Jyväskylä in central Finland: the Railway Workers Housing (1924–1926) and the Jyväskylä Workers Club (1924–1925).

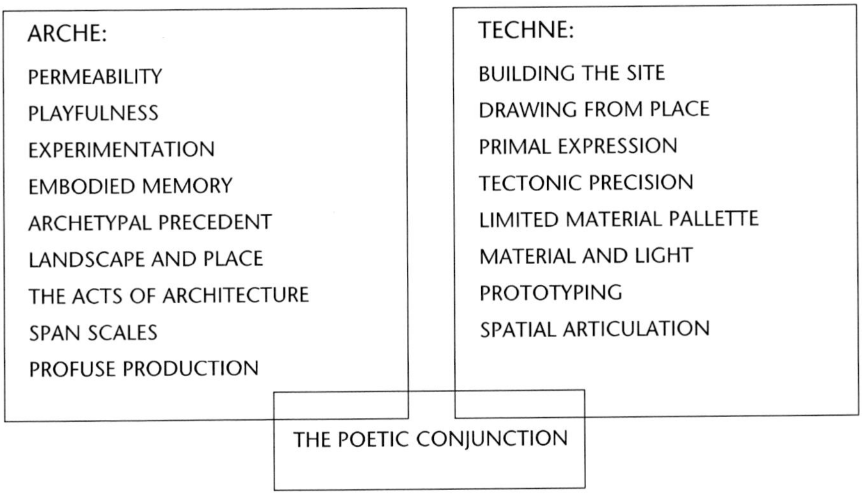

FIGURE 3.2 Aalto's Paradigm.

Both projects exhibit emerging social values of the provision of high quality housing for workers and leisure facilities for working people that represent one facet of Aalto's cultural attunement. Aalto manifested these values in a paired-back version of National Romanticism that was fused with neo-classical tendencies, exhibited within the work of Gunnar Asplund in the 1920s.

FIGURE 3.3 Railway Workers Housing.

FIGURE 3.4 Jyväskylä Workers Club.

The Workers Housing Project has faint resonances of Asplund's Snellmen House Project (1917–1918), which has been described as a seminal building within the neo-classicist period, in (for example) the precise disposition of fenestration providing a restrained and mannered façade. The Workers Club is somewhat resonant of Asplund's Lister Courthouse Project in Sölvesborg (1917–1921), again in the restraint of the façade, the highly articulated point of entry and even the form of the court-space articulated as a circular element in an otherwise largely orthogonal plan form. We see in Aalto's placement of the auditorium and vestibule below an effective counterpoint of fluid volumes 'held' by the otherwise orthogonal plan.

Yet in both projects elements of National Romanticism remain; the 'Piano Rustica' treatment of the plinth that mediates floor level and street level in the Workers Club project, and the projected rendered plinth of the Workers Housing Project speak of the language of National Romanticism exemplified by the National Museum of Finland by Saarinen, Lingren and Gesellius opened in 1917 that signified the emergence of new social and political values of the period. This represents attitudes of permeability in Aalto; in being aware of shifts in external circumstances, and reacting to such shifts with architectural responses that reflected such change. Permeability is about two-way flows; an awareness of changes in conditions flows in; responsive architectural solutions flow out.

> There are certain architects whose work develops almost of itself. Aalto's work is of a different kind. Each line tells of close contact with human destiny.
>
> *Gideon 1969: 666*

FIGURE 3.5 Workers Housing Plinth.

As Gideon suggests, in some senses due to his engagement with the seismic shifts within his zeitgeist, Aalto's oeuvre plots those shifts across space and time, embracing new ideas yet subtly reinterpreting them within his particular Nordic context.

In these two early projects we see the emergence of Aalto's capacity to span all scales of architectural endeavour; from design concept to door handle, Aalto gives a sense that no element of architecture is beneath his consideration, which was later reinforced by industrial scale production of furniture and glassware produced by Artek and Iitalla, respectively. This 'across-scale' disposition is a consistent element in all of Aalto's work; handrails, balustrades, door and window furniture and lighting are all of Aalto's hand, regardless of the scale of the project. In this sense Aalto stands as perhaps the most 'complete' architect of the twentieth century on the basis of his ability to span all scales in design.

In the Workers Club project we also uncover Aalto's reinterpretation of archetypal precedent. Aalto, like Utzon, travelled extensively to places that we might define as possessing 'cultural density'. Both Alvar and Aino were admirers of the ancient architecture of the South, as Alvar wrote:

> I do not wish to speak of any specific journey, for in my mind there is always a journey to Italy. It may be a past journey that still lives on in my memory; it may be a journey I am making or perhaps a journey I am planning. Such a journey is probably necessary, a 'conditio sine qua non'[1] for my work.
>
> *Schildt 1998: 38*

FIGURE 3.6 Portico and Plinth of the Workers Club.

FIGURE 3.7 Door Handle Detail, Workers Club.

This is of course a direct consequence of his embodied attitude of permeability; being open to external influences as they are revealed to him. In the classical architecture of Italy the Aaltos found the archetypal precedents that they were to consistently draw upon and reinterpret within their work in the same way that Utzon drew from his travel experiences in informing his work. The six weeks the Aaltos spent on honeymoon in Italy were to prove seminal in providing references to the ancient forms and intent of what we might term primal architecture: the term *primal* in this context meaning 'of the origin'.

However, in the space of only five years Aalto had, as a consequence of his permeability in being attuned to his zeitgeist, fundamentally shifted shape, reflecting the cultural, social and political changes around him. In the Paimio Tuberculosis Sanatorium Project (1929–1933) we see a significant move away from neo-classicism towards the emerging realm of modernism that was exposed with such impact in the Great Exhibition of Stockholm of 1930. In the period between 1926 and 1929, Aalto was increasingly exposed to the trends of modernism emerging from Europe. As Weston writes:

> He discussed developments (of modernism) with his fellow architect Sven Markelius (1889–1972) who undertook an extensive study tour of Europe in 1927, including the Weissenhof[2] Exhibition in Stuttgart and the new Bauhaus in Dessau. Once Aalto became familiar with the ideals and forms of the new architecture, he brought to them the same enthusiastic commitment hitherto expressed for his beloved Italy.
>
> *Weston 1995: 40*

In 1928 the Aaltos undertook a study tour, visiting several of Le Corbusier's houses in France, Hilversum in Holland to see housing by J. J. P. Oud and apparently Duiker's Sanatorium Project; timely in view of what was to transpire the following year. In the autumn of 1929, Aalto attended the second Congress Internationaux d'Architecture Moderne (CIAM) event and was exposed to such luminaries as Le Corbusier, Gropius, Gideon and Moholy-Nager. In addition, Aalto's friendship with Asplund and Markelius opened his view to the preparations being made by Asplund and Lewerentz for the seminal Great Exhibition in Stockholm of 1930:

> When I arrived at the official opening of the Stockholm Exhibition, I did not come as a foreigner who hopes to see something new. I had closely followed the work of the exhibition management, from the drawing of the very first guidelines to the final result. So I went around looking at things as a 'friend of the exhibition,' not admiring at random, but as one whose relationship with the subject is on a deeper level.
>
> *Schildt 1998: 71*

Of course, Aalto's awareness of, and engagement with, the cultural shifts of his age required serious endeavour, but it would be incorrect to characterise him in this mono-dimensional sense. For Aalto, a sense of playfulness was central to his approach to architecture.

Aalto cites the influence of his friend Yrjö Hirn (1870–1952), the Finnish professor of aesthetics at the University of Helsinki, in recognising the value of play and playfulness within the realm of creativity. Writing of the Experimental House, Aalto suggests:

> Whether it is due to Yrjö Hirn's influence or not, through the force of his personality, a conception or an instinctive feeling has taken root in me, that we, in the midst of our hard-working, calculating, utilitarian era, must regard play as of decisive importance when we build communities …
>
> *Aalto 2013: 11*

He continues:

> On the high-lying island of Muuratsalo in the middle of Lake Päijänne, stands an experimental house – still without a name – which was built to give the architect a chance to play purely for pleasure's sake. But it has also been done for serious experimental purposes, essentially to deal with problems that the architect cannot get involved with on ordinary building projects.
>
> *Aalto 2013: 13*

Within these words, Aalto suggests that this sense of playfulness is a necessary precursor to the imagining of realms of serious experimentation, suggesting a visceral relationship and resultant oscillation between the adult Aalto and the child within. Such oscillations resonate within Aalto's writings in stories such as 'The White Table' and 'A Fireside Story'; the latter we may speculate as being the subliminal inspiration for the dominant fire-pit in the centre of the patio at Muuratsalo. It is not the notion of playfulness that is important per se, but rather what was liberated by such an attitude.

While this notion of playfulness is perhaps most pronounced at the Experimental House, and discussed in more detail later within this chapter, it is evident in most of his work. This playful disposition allowed Aalto to reimagine what would otherwise be assumed orthodoxies that encouraged re-conceptualisations of space to emerge. One example of this playful demeanour and its consequence is the Paimio Tuberculosis Sanatorium (1928–1932) where Aalto reconsidered the idea of hospital ward from first principles and, one should accentuate, from the perspective of the patient. The project marked a significant stage in Aalto's narrative.

The spread of tuberculosis (TB) in Finland between the wars was met by the construction of a number of sanatoria throughout the country. The Paimio Tuberculosis Sanatorium project was supported financially by some 48 local municipalities, and the site chosen for its particular landscape qualities and woodland setting, that became the subject of an invited competition in which Aalto was placed first of the 13 entries. Aalto had previously studied the challenges that TB presents to the architect in his entry to the Central Finland Tuberculosis Sanatorium Competition of 1927 and was thus acquainted with contemporary medical theory on recovery from the disease that was focused upon rest, recuperation, and maximising exposure to fresh air and sunlight.

> Every part of a sanatorium should have abundant independent ventilation, and be readily cleansable without raising dust. The patients' quarters should be quiet, easily accessible from the grounds, and freely open to the sunshine while sheltered from wind.
>
> *Walters 1913: 20*

This paradigm for the treatment of tuberculosis aligned precisely with the vision of an architecture that is imbued with qualities of health and well-being as espoused by Le Corbusier, and this perhaps reinforced Aalto's alignment with these modernist, functionalist tendencies. The sanatorium is of course a place of dwelling; a place for people 'to be' and 'to heal', and Aalto's conceptualisation of such a condition was articulated within an article published in *Domus* in 1930:

> A home is an area that forms a sheltered space for eating, sleeping, working and playing. These biodynamic forms must serve as the basis for the internal divisions of the home, not obsolete symmetrical axis and standard rooms dictated by façade architecture.
>
> *Schildt 1998: 77*

FIGURE 3.8 Paimio Tuberculosis Sanatorium.

Within these words, Aalto exposes his functionalist tendencies striving to give expression to the purpose of space, rather than applying abstract systems of geometry. The sanatorium is an exemplar of such an approach, the three wings that it comprises specifically orientated to respond to the functions of the spaces within: the A wing is orientated south–southeast ensuring the sun balconies that terminate each floor face due south with the circulation spine running down the northern façade of the wing. The B wing that houses spaces of collective activity is orientated north/south across its short axis and the C wing, which is the only wing that disposes rooms to both major elevations, ensures that both primary facades receive direct sunlight.

Aalto, through the vehicle of playfulness, reimagined the accepted orthodoxy of 'hospital ward' to conceptualise such spaces as small individual apartments that facilitated the disposition of furniture and sanitary-ware within individual dedicated spaces, each with a view of the forest. These ideas were centred upon the needs of the patient and each room conceived of as a place to dwell and a place to heal. Furthermore, his subtle use of glowing colours used within the interior, which were designed in collaboration with the artist Eino Kauria, added to the vibrant colouration of the external solar blinds in orange and green, dissipating the sense of an austere clinical atmosphere painted white.

At Paimio we also witness Aalto's predilection for experimentation emerging. The design and placement of the radiant heating system within the ceiling was to ensure that appropriate levels of heat were delivered effectively to where that heat was required; in the case of the patient rooms, the surface of the bed.

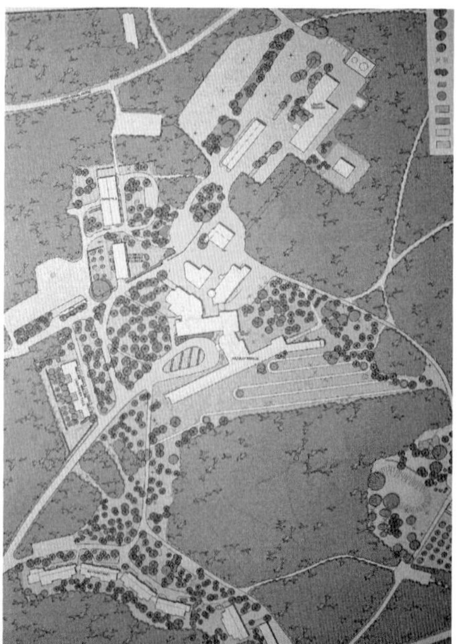

FIGURE 3.9 Paimio Site Plan.

> To examine how human beings react to forms and construction, it is useful to use for experimentation, especially sensitive persons, such as patients in a sanatorium.
>
> *Aalto in Schildt 1998: 103*

While such experimentation and innovations were perhaps rather constrained by budget and other factors within live projects such as Paimio Tuberculosis Sanatorium, in Aalto's Experimental House, we witness his tendency to experiment given free rein.

The structural system of Paimio facilitates such a functionalist approach; the brick clad and insulated reinforced concrete frame permits the placement of horizontal and vertical ducting that house the service systems that provide the environmental and sanitary qualities demanded by Aalto.

This framing, as Le Corbusier suggested, 'liberated the wall', allowing natural sunlight to be drawn deep into space effectively exposing residents to available light and heat and modelling interior space through shadow. This provides animation of space ensuring that supine patients would have some sense of time and orientation through the movement of light in space.

Here we see Aalto giving expression to such principles at every scale of design consideration, from the spatial disposition and orientation of the patient rooms, to the ventilation system, the radiant overhead heating system that ensures appropriate positioning of heat sources, through to the design of elements of iron-mongery, sanitary ware, furniture and lighting. These not only represent Aalto's

FIGURE 3.10 Paimio Staircase Detail.

FIGURE 3.11 Paimio Plumbing and Sanitary Ware.

ability to span across scales of design, but also exhibit tectonic precision in the execution of detail.

In this project, which is widely acclaimed as one of the most significant buildings of the twentieth century, Aalto clearly embraces the shape-shift of thought towards functionalism within this period that culminated in the Great Exhibition in Stockholm of 1930. Omnipresent within this functional approach is a clear sense of understanding the primal aspects of dwelling poetically that are manifested by Aalto in colour, materiality, textures and the play of light, that in symphony imbue the sanatorium with poetic existential qualities.

FIGURE 3.12 Paimio Chair.

FIGURE 3.13 Paimio Light.

The two aspects of Aalto's functionalist tendencies and understanding of the core components of what it is to dwell poetically conjoin in the relatively modest house that the Aaltos designed for themselves in the northeastern Helsinki suburb of Riihitie, completed in 1936. Until the completion of this project the Aaltos had lived in various properties including a house designed by the architect Wivi Lōnn, renowned particularly for her design of interior space, and it is generally acknowledged that this experience was influential in the Aaltos' design response to their own house.

Approaching the house from the road to the north, the façade reads as being very closed, rather reminiscent of the closed facades of Moroccan vernacular housing that Aalto had visited, which were also to be later reinterpreted by Utzon in the Kingo and Fredensborg housing projects. Yet it is within this apparently closed façade that Aalto's subtlety and attention to detail are evident. The house number cut into the shade of the external light over the entrance door is orientated not at right angles to the road and pavement as one might expect, but rather orientated to align with the curving stone path across which you enter the property.

The house combines the two functions of dwelling and working separated by the shoji-like screen sliding door and thus the workspace and living space have the potential to conjoin as required. The attention to detail is everywhere: from the

FIGURE 3.14 Riihitie House Entrance.

subtle nuance of the cutlery draw in the dining space that can be accessed equally by the maid from the kitchen side of the wall or from the dining space, to the exquisite light fittings that appear to shimmer like the pierced metal candleholders of Morocco.

The construction method is a hybrid of loadbearing masonry and steel frame that again, as in the sanatorium project, liberates the wall and allows Aalto's functionalist predilections to come forth. In the studio Aalto's worktable sits beneath a corner window that affords views to the garden to the south and west, and allows direct sunlight to fall upon his work surface.

In this house the hearths work hard. In the studio space the fire articulates a change in level and in spatial hierarchy, it being the point of elevation to Aalto's private room complete with private exit/entrance door. In the living space the hearth is the point of gathering; the disposition of furniture, including the grand piano, is defined by it. A third hearth articulates the upstairs hall or vestibule at first floor level that acts as a mediating space between the bedrooms to the east and the terrace to the west, beyond which lies the entrance to the gallery over the studio space. The subtlety of design intention is also informed by surface finishes, which range from painted face-brickwork to timber panelling and coir-matted wall surfaces.

In contrast to the northern façade, the south elevation fragments and becomes permeable and allows relationships to be constructed between internal space and the garden. The bedrooms to the southeastern corner of the south elevation float across and define an external terrace at ground level, providing an al fresco dining space and giving an additional threshold between inside and outside.

FIGURE 3.15 Living and Studio Space.

In the Riihitie project we can see a maturation and sophistication that extends the functionalist agenda of modernity into the territory of phenomenology, returning to the things themselves in exposing the fundamental acts of dwelling. The house is, in Semper's terms, in-part stereotomic, at least in its public face, and in-part woven as the form unravels and loosens, and provides clear precedent for the Villa Mairea project (1938–1939).

The Villa Mairea project should not be discussed without first acknowledging the role of the clients, Harry and Maire Gullichsen. He was a forestry magnate; she was educated in fine art in Helsinki and Paris, and subsequently founded the Free Art School in Helsinki in 1935, which was modelled on Ferdinand Léger's Academy in Paris where she had once studied.

Maire's father, Valter Ahlström, made his fortune in forestry and sawmills and ironworks and was somewhat of a philanthropic entrepreneur, commissioning projects such as workers housing from the architect Carl Lindahl and ambitious building programmes for his industrial facilities that included housing provision. Upon his graduation from business school, Harry Gullichsen was appointed as Ahlström's assistant, eventually taking control of the business upon Ahlström's death in 1932.

Harry Gullichsen was a liberal thinker by disposition and his social, cultural and political attitudes aligned with Maire's cultural radicalism. The couple married in 1928. As members of the Finnish bohemian community the Gullichsens moved in the same circles as the Aaltos, and Maire met Aalto in 1935 and subsequently co-founded the Artek company, and with her husband, the Aaltos and Nils Gustaf-Hahl, manufacturing and marketing furniture designed by Aalto and also exhibiting the artist output from Maire's Free School of Art.

The relationship between the Gullichsens and the Aaltos flourished; Harry commissioned Aalto to design master plans for his industrial operations in Varkaus and Karhula and this in turn led to several large-scale commissions from other industrial entrepreneurs. The significance of these initiatives should not be underestimated as they did represent substantial shifts of political and social values predicated upon attitudes of cultural radicalism and political liberalism. Maire, it is

FIGURE 3.16 Landscape Setting.

said without conscious intention, became a prolific collector of art and pieces by such luminaries as Kandinsky, Gris, Léger and Matisse populated her collection.

The Gullichsens commissioned Aalto to design a house on a heavily forested site in Noormarkku, in western Finland, which was to be:

> ... the ideal family home, with space for creative dialogue between friends from the worlds of culture and business. More than this, the house was intended as a demonstration of the potential of Modern architecture; it was to convince even narrow-minded sceptics about the purity of the ideals of a new age.
>
> *Pallasmaa 1998: 12*

The development of a brief for such a project represented significant ambition on the part of the clients and Aalto responded with a design process that comprised nine iterations – testament to his tenacity, exactitude and prolific output.

Set on a modest hill within a clearing of dense pine woodland, the house builds a seamless relationship with its forest context, apparently boundless; the territory considered as an inhabited extension of the forest floor. Here Aalto's biomorphic and ethnographic influences are concretised in what is now regarded as one of the most significant houses of the twentieth century.

In the Villa Mairea we see Aalto's engagement with landscape and place emerge. The project is clearly 'of the forest' and has a permeable boundary that ensures the threshold between dwelling and forest is virtually indistinguishable. Writing of Aalto's attunement to landscape, Schildt suggests:

> The organic, non-geometrical perception of space that he attained in the late 1930s was clearly connected to his experience of the northern forest, just as the wavy lines that characterise his architectural idiom were obviously related to the winding shorelines and meandering terrain contours on the maps of his father the surveyor.
>
> *Schildt 1998: 21*

The concept development sketches show an incremental progression towards this idea, moving from the courtyard configuration that was the genesis of the project. Here Aalto is 'dwelling in place'. We might imagine in Villa Mairea that we inhabit the forests of which Fehn writes, with all of the mythical and existential meanings encapsulated within such an idea.

In an article published in 1926 Aalto articulates the importance of the relationship of 'room' to landscape; in a study of and commentary upon Fra Angelico's painting *L'Annunziazione* (*The Annunciation*) he writes: 'Two things stand out plainly: the unity of the room, the external wall and the garden, and the formation of these elements as to give the human figure prominence, and expresses her state of mind' (Schildt 1998: 51).

The Villa Mairea, in that sense, represents a sophisticated domestication of the forest clearing yet, in its placement, orientation and shifts between porosity and density, constantly makes references to the origin of the idea: the mythical forest. The house has a spatial disposition that perceptually oscillates between inside and out: the 'forest stair' drawing the forest into the house, the purposeful articulation of openings allowing the interior to perceptually flow out into the landscape it sits within. Furthermore, subtle changes in level, for example between the entrance hall and living space, shift eye level and enhance the sense of relationship with the territory beyond the walls.

The development of the project moved from the original proposal of a courtyard house of several floors complete with a dedicated gallery space to house Maire's art collection, through a series of iterations that tested the relationship to site and landscape, issues of orientation, articulation of internal and external spaces, that increasingly become less formal, more asymmetrical, responding to the nuances of site introducing curvilinear forms that resonate within the final design. Iteration 8, which his biographer Gøran Schildt described as the 'proto Mairea', commenced on site in 1937, yet Aalto's clients challenged Aalto further and a final concept (iteration 9) was developed that articulated the spatially undivided nature of the living space, the final placement of the sauna and the courtyard space became more ambiguous as an element within the landscape.

The house is of L-shape plan form, formal entry made under the projecting canopy that appears as a horizontal incision of the verticality of the pines that surround the house. The front door leads to an entrance hall, which is the point of distribution, rising up four steps leading west to the library, the living space, and the 'flower room' and on the northern face, the forest stair. The vestibule also distributes to the northern wing of the house providing a more constricted route to the dining

FIGURE 3.17 Villa Mairea from the South.

FIGURE 3.18 Entrance Canopy.

space, and to the east the spaces that represent rigorous servant/served configuration of kitchen and servants quarters that serve the dining space.

The forest stairs lead up to the first floor comprising a studio located over the flower room with dedicated stair access, two master-bedrooms en-suite, three further bedrooms and within the projecting element to the north, a library and music room with a westerly facing terrace. The forest stairs are set against the glazed northerly façade and inevitably lead the eye to the forested landscape beyond.

In Villa Mairea we see Aalto's a priori engagement with the *acts* of architecture. The spatial disposition, spatial articulation, layering of space, the clear delineation between spaces that serve and the spaces that are served and the prominence of such primal elements as the hearths represent a primitive (in the context of the definition made in Chapter 1) understanding of the core human preoccupation of dwelling poetically. The house also represents a sophisticated layering of exposure and privacy. We can easily imagine gregarious events populating the living space and music room. We can equally imagine large dinner parties in the dining space yet

FIGURE 3.19 The 'Forest Stairs'.

Source: Alvar Aalto Archive

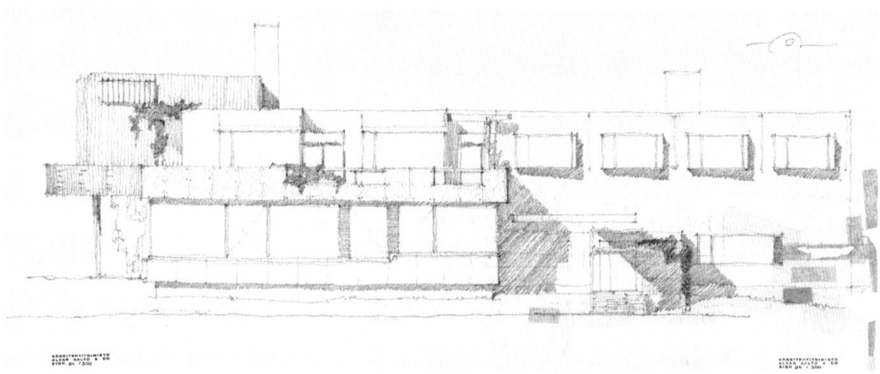

FIGURE 3.20 South Elevation Study.

Source: Alvar Aalto Archive

perhaps upon tiring of such events, Harry Gullichsen may have quietly taken his leave and retreated to the library and, in peace, perhaps smoked a cigar.

The L-shape configuration is extended from the northernmost limit of the house by a low stone wall that deflects west to form a northern limit to the territory that gradually falls in level, apparently dissipating to read as a ruin within a woodland setting. This wrapping wall holds both the swimming pool and sauna within its embrace, providing an unfettered relationship to the woodland to the west.

Villa Mairea also is evidence of Aalto's profuse production and tenacity. Having visited the Aalto archive, the proliferation of drawn material was astonishing; for example, a huge number of three-dimensional sketches that interrogated the 'forest stair' evidencing increasing finesse, simplicity and slenderness as the process advanced. A similar portfolio of studies exist for the hearth in the living space that move from the quite 'blocky' original form to the sophisticated three dimensional sculpture that was finally built. This sheer volume of production exhibits Aalto's resolve in not merely resting with the first iteration of a design, and is an object lesson to all aspiring architects.

Of Techne

In Villa Mairea Aalto 'builds the site', in a manner that 'draws from place'. The virtual dissolution of the threshold between forest and the domestic realm, the position of the swimming pool that reaches towards the forest as if it were searching for its origin, the grassed roof of the sauna that presents itself as an extruded clearing on high when viewed from the house and an apparent allowance for the forest to invade the domestic realm, all in conjunction reveal this place to us, bringing forth its essence.

In combination this is a primal expression of what it is to dwell poetically. As with the Riihitie house, the hearths again work hard in Villa Mairea. The fire that defines the northwestern extent of the living space is cavernous in scale, with a rough stone hearth and overly scaled lintel and mantle-shelf above mediated by the subtle curved indentation on the northeast corner that is simultaneously suggestive perhaps of melting ice and the receptacle of the burning wood shaving that gave light in traditional Finnish farmhouses. The fire to the dining room is positioned within a sculpted niche again redolent of the Finnish farmhouse, the fire to the bedroom hall at first floor a sumptuous curved form, while the fire in the studio space is an altogether simpler affair. The fire to the external sitting space under the covered walkway that leads north to the sauna is more rustic; set within the stone wall that supports the external stair to the terrace, the fire is suggestive of a point of gathering within a landscape condition. We can imagine long conversations deep into the night as the protagonists assemble around the fire keeping the cold of the night at bay, assisted perhaps by strong liquor and countless cigarettes. The spatial inter-relationship between sauna and pool of course reflects the Nordic traditions of oscillation between fire and water but simultaneously gives expression to primal human instincts that are so deeply embodied we may judge them to be universal. It would surely resonate with Utzon and Fehn.

Villa Mairea is an essay in Aalto's tectonic practice. The tectonic qualities are beautifully represented within early elevational studies (Figure 3.20) that precisely define a limited material palette carefully articulated against each other where textures and the layering of space are amplified through the throw of shadows.

Aalto tells the narrative of his biomorphic tendencies and counterpoint through his tectonic response. While we read the majority of façades as being of white functionalist tendencies, particular spaces are articulated in counterpoint by material and form; the curving studio space to the western extent of the house is curvilinear in form and clad externally in vertical timber, the library and piano space of the ground floor are held within a timber clad aedicule form that in its projection into the landscape of the south, effectively 'holds' the entrance canopy and terrace beyond. Similarly the windows to the three first floor bedrooms are pushed out from the wall at an oblique angle suggestive of the sleeping spaces beyond.

Internally his tectonic precision is consistent; the wrapping of columns either in rattan or beach slats provides tactility suggestive of a domestic condition, yet in counterpoint exposes the coldness of that material which they wrap. The rush mat

FIGURE 3.21 Bedroom Windows to South Façade.

FIGURE 3.22 Tectonic Exactitude in Biomorphic Expression.

FIGURE 3.23 Hearth.

Source: Alvar Aalto Archive

cladding of the stair enclosure to the flower room reinforces a sense of an oriental atmosphere when read together with the sub-screened windows of the northern glazed façade.

Villa Mairea is also an exemplar of the possibilities that unfold when architect and client share values, are determined and ambitious, and are both prepared to embrace risk and experiment. Aalto's friend, architect and critic Siegfried Gideon wrote:

> Mairea is a house poured as it were, from a single crucible, for architect and client worked together, as in the eighteenth century. They had the same will and inclinations, a rather rare coincidence in this period when the architect has to spend most of his energy convincing a hesitating client in whom the last century still lingers.
>
> *Gideon in Pallasmaa 1998: 70*

In the Villa Mairea project Aalto was consistently challenged by his clients and early proposals were apparently rejected as not being sufficiently experimental, yet in one iteration of the design process (sketch phase 2) we can detect some stereotomic forms that would later become manifest within the Saynatsalo Town Hall project (1949–1952).

Aalto won the government-commissioned competition for the design of a new town hall in Saynatsalo, an island settlement south of Jyväskylä that was founded upon the wood processing industry. The project is imbued with Aalto's values of democracy and the representation of that democratic process in built form. The stereotomic composition is focused upon a central open-air courtyard, one level higher than the street that is, in terms of morphology, resonant of the tradition of Finnish farms that cluster around courtyard spaces. The courtyard as a semiotic device is also suggestive of the places of gathering and civitas found in more southerly climates of the Mediterranean, so loved by Aalto. Indeed he named the project 'Curia' that referred to this precedent, which in Latin means 'Roman senate house' or 'courthouse'. These devices are the tectonic expression of the primal archetypal precedents explored above.

FIGURE 3.24 Saynatsalo Town Hall.

FIGURE 3.25 Elevated Council Chamber.

This illumination of democracy in built form extends to the council chamber itself where those represented sit at a slightly higher level than those that represent and one has the sense, given this configuration, that one could lean across from the public gallery, tap a councillor's shoulder and whisper; 'remember what you promised at the last election?'

The act of elevating both the external courtyard and the council chamber implicitly adds to the sense of hierarchy of both spaces that, as Utzon reflected, goes back to the origins of man exhibited by the plateaus of the ancient temples: the places of ritual made more significant by the promenade of ascension.

Here we see a further manifestation of Aalto's use of a limited material palette, used to great effect. The stereotomic mass is given expression through brick that provides a sense of mass from which the central courtyard appears to be carved from. The brick extends to the floor plane, stairs and windowsills/seats supporting the glazing to the courtyard, adding to this sense of stereotomic mass and gravitas. Timber is used to signal lightness, porosity and tactility. The stereotomic qualities are deftly reinforced externally; the granite plinth that serves to receive the snow of winter forms a subtle and sophisticated 'Piano Rustica' faintly resonant of the Worker's Club project from which the brickwork is lifted, and that brickwork is of such quality that Aalto was moved to write letters of thanks upon completion of the project, to each of the six bricklayers.

FIGURE 3.26 Elevated Courtyard.

FIGURE 3.27 Cloistered Circulation Route.

The plan is spread over three levels and public entry achieved by ascending one of two sets of steps that articulate the library to the west of the plan from the town hall to the east. Formal entry to the town hall is at first floor level with the courtyard set centrally to the building that wraps it. A cloister-like circulation route bounds the eastern and southern sides of the courtyard, which consistently reference the courtyard through the permeable glazed screen.

The council chamber is accessed directly from the entrance vestibule via brick paved steps and corridor that reinforce the stereotomic sense of place, matching as they do the internal wall finishes, and provide a sense of ritual through the act of ascension. The chamber is an expressive double storey-height volume with elegant fan-form trusses supporting the roof should one lift one's eyes skyward in disbelief perhaps of the political process.

It is within the council chamber particularly that Aalto's penchant to manipulate light to illuminate material is evident. The clerestory windows to the council chamber are set behind the public seating space, emitting shafts of light upon those represented rather than those that represent. The large panel window that lights the council chamber itself when read with the clerestory windows gives one a sense of being in a sacred space and one inevitably lifts one's eyes to the ceiling above articulated by fan-form timber trusses.

In previous projects we have observed Aalto's ability to design at a diverse range of scales and in the Saynatsalo project, this ability is again manifested. The stereotomic mass is carved gracefully; that carving informed by democratic ambition yet with equal ambition brass door handles are wrapped in rattan, harder than the hand but

FIGURE 3.28 Stair to the Council Chamber.

FIGURE 3.29 Clerestory Lighting of the Public Space.

softer than the brass ensuring that the 'handshake of the building' is mediated through tectonic intervention. It is the tectonic precision that Aalto exhibits in the design process that (for example) in the door handles, provides a beautiful and memorable tactile conjunction between hand and handle. We see again such ambitions extended across all scales of design consideration that include simple yet elegant light fixtures, shelving and furniture.

Despite its rather modest scale, Saynatsalo Town Hall has a monumental presence both externally and within the council chamber, internally. This monumentality is similarly recognisable in the House of Culture project (1952–1958) in Helsinki that, like Saynatsalo, is presented as a stereotomic mass of beautifully articulated brickwork. Commissioned by the Finnish Communist Party, Aalto designed the project on a pro bono basis and much of the construction work was executed by volunteers. The ownership passed to the government in 1990 when the Finnish Communist Party went into bankruptcy. Very much still a house of culture today, the 1,400-seat auditorium has been witness to concerts from such musical legends as Jimi Hendrix, Cream, Frank Zappa and Leonard Cohen.

On visiting this building I met with the resident chef who asked me if I had knowledge of what he termed the 'Aalto brick'. The chef, who could recite Aalto's back-catalogue with no prompting, showed me an example of the 'special bricks' Aalto designed and commissioned for the project that facilitated the fluid form of the building and those that were left over were now utilised by the chef to provide table decorations for the buffet table!

FIGURE 3.30 Aalto Light Fitting.

FIGURE 3.31 House of Culture.

Here is exposed Aalto's use of prototyping as a design method, which is inextricably bound to his sense of playfulness described earlier. Brick in its standard UK form (215mm × 65mm × 105mm) is essentially a construction component (usually) most effectively used within orthogonal building forms. However, Aalto's desire to use brick as a fluid stereotomic form within the House of Culture demanded 'rethinking of the brick' and through the process of prototyping, brick forms were developed that delivered such a possibility. These bricks are testament to Aalto's tectonic engagement within the endeavour of architecture. The intention was clearly to deliver a sense of stereotomic mass, and in this regard brick is a logical choice, yet the use of standard bricks would dissipate the biomorphic expression. In response, Aalto not only designed the form of the wall but also the brick; allowing the resolution of these conflicting challenges and the realisation of the design ambition that is, in itself, an object lesson in architecture.

We see Aalto's prototyping also evident within his furniture design; ever increasingly finessed interrogations of the relationship between material, structure and form in the development of laminated frames are exemplars of engagement with such a process.

Aalto's deft tectonic hand is seen throughout this project from the copper caps to the pergola timbers, to the texture of the handrails and the brass patina-covered door handles except where the acid of countless hands has made their presence obvious.

In the Studio Aalto (1955) in Helsinki this consistent attention to tectonic ambition that transcends scale is exhibited. Like the Riihitie House, the studio

FIGURE 3.32 Aalto's Brick.

FIGURE 3.33 Copper Pergola Caps.

presents a virtual blank northern façade to the street and shelters behind the boundary wall that mitigates between street and site. Entry is gained at right angles to the street by descending a steep driveway to the front door where, again, Aalto designs the 'handshake of the house'.

Within the studio project, we see Aalto's finesse in spatial articulation. The plan-form is of an 'L-shape' configuration, in part two-storey in part single-storey, that embraces the stepped external amphitheatre orientated towards the south and east to the rear of the site. The plan is ordered in two distinct parts, the orthogonal workspace within which individual desks are distributed, and the free studio space, with a curving substantially glazed wall that defines the edge of the auditorium.

FIGURE 3.34 Handrail Detail.

FIGURE 3.35 Wrapping Wall and Blind Façade.

FIGURE 3.36 Door Handle.

The toilet and the meeting room mediate these two spaces, with its top-lit glazing over the display table.

Within Aalto's archive there are numerous sketches that focus upon the glazed screen wall to the studio space that began as an obtuse angle that formed a shard-like space that developed through a number of iterations to become the curved wall that was built. This design development allows the external wall to become the holding element of the external amphitheatre within the garden, uniting studio and landscape. The amphitheatre of course represents another of Aalto's archetypal precedents, in this case drawing from the classical amphitheatres of southern Europe.

The Aalto Archive provides evidence of the sheer tenacity and extended iterative endeavour that characterise Aalto's design process. There are countless sketches that strive to articulate the precise geometry and alignment of the curved studio wall, the precise levels of the boundary wall to the north of the site in relation to the studio behind and a number of sketches testing the precise line of the studio roof that is lifted in height to follow the landscape it sits upon. Incrementally, we see the glazed

FIGURE 3.37 The Workspace.

FIGURE 3.38 The Studio Space.

FIGURE 3.39 External Amphitheatre.

wall turn from an angular almost shard-like form into the soft arcing curve that it became. Similarly we see the boundary wall to the north of the site shift from being stepped at several points to a single step that is articulated to be in alignment with the aedicule top-lit display space of the meeting room. As was evident in Villa Mairea, this tenacity produces increasing finesse and exactitude and is again, an object lesson to any aspiring architect. This tenacity is not widely acknowledged within the body of writing that surrounds Aalto, but is clearly central to his achievements across a diverse range of design activity.

The building was extended in 1962–1963 to form a new kitchen/dining area that Aalto named 'the Taverna', with a private office above. Angular in form that is in counterpoint to the curved wall of the studio it may perhaps be resonant of the original intention for the studio wall that resided within Aalto's embodied memory.

The studio was designed to facilitate a shift in scale of Aalto's practice as his work gained greater recognition and larger-scale works were commissioned. Such projects as the Jyväskylä University Campus projects (1954–1971), the Museum of Central Finland (1956–1961), Jyväskylä, the Academic Bookstore (1961–1965), Helsinki, and the Finlandia Concert Hall (1962), Helsinki, all took shape and form in this

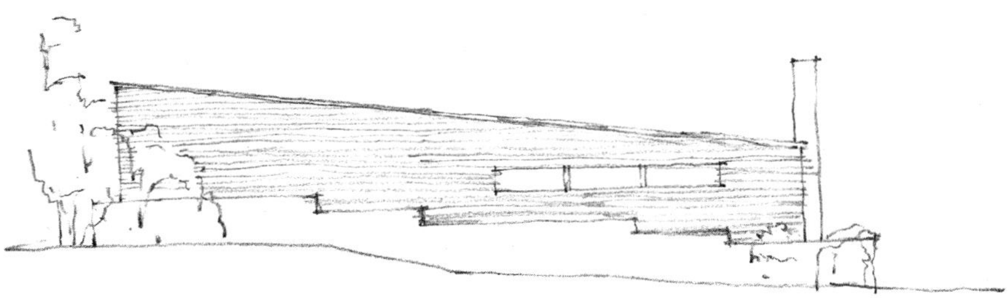

FIGURE 3.40 Early Front Wall Sketch.

Source: Alvar Aalto Archive

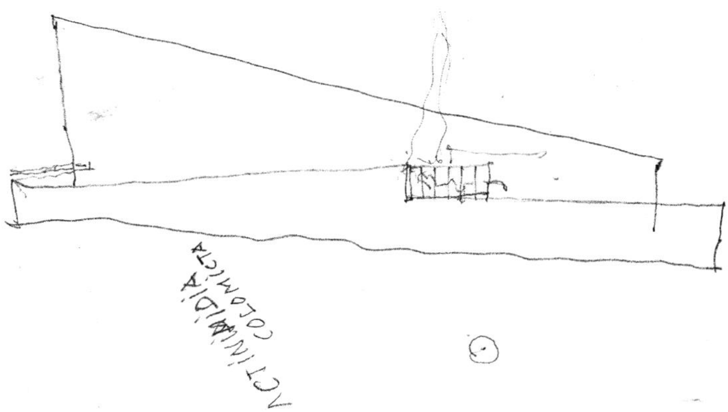

FIGURE 3.41 Later Front Wall Sketch.

Source: Alvar Aalto Archive

quite modest studio (when compared with contemporary trans-national practices). All of these projects have had significant exposure elsewhere, but it is to a lesser-known work that this narrative turns for the purpose of exposing some inter-relationships between our protagonists.

The Jyväskylä City Theatre project was an element designed within a 'Civic Block' master plan by Aalto in the 1960s and was completed in 1982 subsequent to Aalto's death in 1976. Utzon's Sydney Opera House Competition submission was made in 1957, pre-dating the City Theatre by some years.

Interestingly, both architects employed the same fundamental device to 'build the site' and mediate the level changes within the landscape with a plateau. For Utzon, the plateau provided the opportunity for ascension; from the predictability and ordinariness of everyday existence into the world of the exceptional experience that theatre provides, where belief has to be suspended. Aalto employed the same device differently. In the City Theatre public entry is made within the plateau, almost a descent from the everyday into the extraordinary. Both architects, however, articulate in form the auditoria upon the plateau, which in the case of Aalto's project also provides an external civic space from which to view the city from on high. The notion of plateau again references the archetypal precedents that both Aalto and Utzon drew from.

These archetypal precedents of plateau and amphitheatre were to emerge again in the Nordjyllands Kuntsmuseum project in Aalborg, Denmark, won in competition and the result of a collaboration between Alvar Aalto, Elissa Aalto and Jean-Jacques Baruël[3] in 1959 that was constructed between 1966 and 1972. The chosen site was a former quarry in the industrial region of Northern Jutland, by coincidence the town in which Jørn Utzon spent his formative years.

The museum is entered at street level upon the plateau, below which are housed the parking and service areas, as is the café which opens through a porous glazed screen to the external sculpture space and landscape beyond. Upon entry across the plateau, the visitor is received by the reception desk, from which the circulation routes pivot in a 'pin-wheel' configuration with galleries off. The major gallery space that is represented as a double storey-height element is 'held' within the plan by the circulation routes. Again here we see precise intention in the disposition

FIGURE 3.42 City Theatre Plateau.

FIGURE 3.43 Clerestory Lights to Gallery.

and articulation of space. The section is everything in the museum and is constantly manipulated in order to bring mediated natural light into this deep plan-form. This is, as Christopher Harlang observed, 'The Building of Light' (in Bak et al. 1999: 37).

The Aaltos and Baruël were clear from the outset as to the role of light within the typology of Art Museum. Within the written accompaniment to the competition entry they wrote: 'Light in an Exhibition Hall, an Art Gallery is just as important as acoustics within a Concert Hall' (Bak et al. 1999: 14).

Each gallery space is top-lit with sophisticatedly articulated projecting reflective elements that ensure direct sunlight never meets the artefacts being exhibited yet also houses the required service elements including artificial lighting. Within the major hall, once more light is brought into the space from above.

Again within this project we see Aalto's ability to design at all scales of architectural endeavour, as much consideration being given to the stair handrail as to the parti of the plan. Externally the archetypal precedent of the amphitheatre is again present, effectively closing the morphology of the plan-form to the landscape.

Aalto travelled extensively in the 1960s and 1970s, visiting variously the USA (staying at Lloyd Wright's Falling Waters project) in 1961, the Soviet Union, England and Italy (1962), Mexico (1963), Italian Alps (1965), Moscow, Italy and Sweden (1966), the USA (1967), Italy and Switzerland (1968), Germany and Iran (1969), and France and Denmark (for the opening of the Aalborg Kuntsmuseum) (1972). The importance of Aalto's travels cannot be underestimated in his consistent quest to see and to speculate upon all that he discovered upon these journeys.

In 1971, Aalto was commissioned to design a Museum in Jyväskylä that celebrated his contribution to design in all of its manifestations, located adjacent to the Museum of Central Finland designed by Aalto in 1957 that opened in 1962. Juxtaposed, these two civic buildings are testament to the development of Aalto's work across a period of just 14 years.

The Museum of Central Finland is clearly of a modernist style and functionalist in expression. It carries all the hallmarks of the international style and presents itself rather as an ocean liner form in the semiotic sense, when viewed from the valley below.

FIGURE 3.44 Clerestory Lighting to Major Gallery.

FIGURE 3.45 Handrail Detail.

FIGURE 3.46 Amphitheatre.

In contrast, the Aalto Museum is an altogether more sophisticated affair, the entrance door demarked by a subtle 'peeling away' of the façade, low-set openings to catch the reflected light from the snow and ceramic cladding that glistens in the sharp Finnish sunlight.

In many senses, the Aalto Museum represents a complete exposé of Aalto's paradigm, capturing his paradigms of *arche* and *techne*, but also, in the manipulation of light and material, exposes the poetic dimensions of his oeuvre.

FIGURE 3.47 Museums Juxtaposed.

FIGURE 3.48 Museum of Central Finland.

FIGURE 3.49 Aalto Museum Entrance Door.

FIGURE 3.50 Low-Set Window Openings and Ceramic Façade.

Of Poetic Conjunctions

Existential Conversations in a Cave 1: The Island of Reverie, Playfulness, Imaginings and Experiments

The Experimental House (1952–1953), Muuratsalo, Finland

The Aaltos found the Muuratsalo site during the construction of the Saynatsalo Town Hall project on the adjacent island and decided to build a summer house that from the outset was envisaged as a place of reverie, playfulness, imaginings and experimentation. Here the Aaltos were to dream the impossible and through serious playfulness, experiment with ways of making place without the encumbrance of the pragmatic pressures inculcated within a live project for a real client.

I have previously within this chapter made reference to the influence of Yrjö Hirn upon Aalto's embodiment of playfulness as an a priori condition in questioning orthodoxy, and the Experimental House due to the lack of constraints represents the zenith in some ways of approaching architecture. We should be clear, however: this is not playfulness in the sense of frippery and giggles; this is serious playfulness that is utilised in order to see 'the thingness of things'. It is a mechanism to look beyond the mere appearance of that which confronts us and to ask, through the voice of the embodied child: why? Aalto suggests to us that this sense of playfulness is a necessary precursor to the imagining of realms of serious experimentation, suggesting a visceral relationship and resultant oscillation between the adult Aalto and the child within. Such oscillations resonate within Aalto's writings in stories such as 'The White Table' and 'A Fireside Story'; the latter, we may speculate, being the subliminal inspiration for the dominant fire-pit in the centre of the courtyard at Muuratsalo.

The Experimental House represents Aalto's response to the long tradition within the Nordic world of the summer house typology. The significance of the typology of summer house should not be underestimated within this culture. As society became increasingly urbanised and the deep-rooted sense of connectivity with nature

FIGURE 3.51 Experimental House Fire Pit.

dissipated, the urge to return to cultural origins became stronger and the phenomena of the summer house became increasingly widespread. These places of retreat, often passed down through families, became foci of gathering, communing with nature and in many senses represented a return to the origin through the expression of humans' fundamental relationship with the natural world.

In built form, the Nordic summer house is usually a simple affair, some might judge even utilitarian, in that it contains the essential ingredients to sustain life, but holds little that is not useful. Typically such houses are located at the threshold of forest and water, whether it be sea, lake or river, reinforcing, were such reinforcement required, the deep-rooted cultural relationship between the Nordic landscape, the inhabitants and the mythologies and spirituality developed that mediate the two, and thus make sense of place.

Originally, the only means of access to the Experimental House was by boat. This fact is significant within the Nordic context in several ways. The nature of departure and arrival by boat, the travelling across water; both describe a state of 'otherness' that contrasts to our everyday existence with our feet firmly planted on the earth. The nature of 'otherness' recognises this change of state, of being, and we might imagine Elissa and Alvar's sense of anticipation as they left shore for their next adventure at the summer house. Landing was effected by a short timber peer that projected into the lake, with timber steps cut to the forms of the rock outcrops they are defined by, leading up to the house. One can imagine the Aaltos ascending from boat to peer to step to solid ground with an increasing sense of anticipation of all that was to come. A sense of ritual is evoked.

Given the exquisite nature of this site, within woodland bordering the lake, it is fascinating to note that Aalto was not primarily driven to 'harvest views' in the way in which we would intuitively react (for example) in the UK. Clearly here other governance is at play, and that is the primal nature of dwelling. The courtyard becomes the focus of the house; a mechanism to mediate landscape; with the centrally placed hearth that is the primary signifier of human existence in this place. View is produced, of course, but in the form of 'framed views'; as if denying the apparent authority of the Western obsession with prospect.

FIGURE 3.52 Steps to the Pier Cut around Rock Outcrops.

This attitude to prospect is also resonant in the positioning of the house. Being close to the lake it affords ready access from the pier; the original means of arrival and departure of course, and thus entirely pragmatic in those terms. But to build at the base of the slope rather than at a higher level is an interesting concept given greater elevation could afford more extensive views. Yet, of course, separating the house from the lake in that manner would have been a denial of the purpose of the site; the conjunction of earth, lake, sky and mortals in a manner that Heidegger would understand and celebrate.

From the outset the Experimental House was conceived as a place for experiment. Through design making and what we might now blandly describe as post-occupancy studies, architecture could be challenged in all of its diverse manifestations. Sub-structure, structure, materials, spatial articulation, environmental issues, sustainability, utility and, of course, the *acts* of architecture were all the subject of experimentation, reflection and review.

The Muuratsalo project is, in its morphology, somewhat redolent of Utzon's Can Lis, in that it represents a series of defined spaces, distributed across a particular landscape setting. However, the dominant form of the project is the house itself and courtyard that addresses the lake. The house was constructed in 1952–1953; the smoke-sauna and guest room/studio wing were added a year later. The Aalto-designed boat *Nemo Propheta in Patria* ('no man is a prophet in his own land') was launched in 1954 and the boathouse that now contains it was constructed in 1998 following an international design competition in 1996 that was won by two Danish architecture students, Anne-Mette Krolmark and Claudia Schulz.

The 5,300m^2 site is heavily forested with birch and pine trees, with bilberry and lingonberry bushes and moss covered rock outcrops somewhat reminiscent of Fehn's Villa Busk site. The site falls steeply from southeast to northwest with a flatter western fringe upon which the house was constructed that borders the lake. The construction of the bridge link to Saynatsalo and the road that gives vehicle access to the site provides a relatively long, processional route down the slope past the outbuildings to the house. The morphology effectively closes to the north of the site with the exception of the positioning of the smoke sauna and boathouse that sit to the northeast of the house.

FIGURE 3.53 Experimental House.

The house is of an L-form configuration, the wing running southeast containing the bedrooms, the northwest wing containing the living space. The geometry is mediated at its conjunction by the kitchen. The internal hearth articulates the intersection of the two wings that provides a threshold between servant and served space. The L-form configuration is 'held' by the courtyard to the southwest, through which entry to the house is made. The courtyard is contained by high walls, pierced to allow directed view and allow entry to the west and south respectively. Central to the courtyard is the external hearth – the fire-pit that resonates of the hunter making fire in the forest clearing that Fehn wrote of. In an article in *Arkkitehti* in 1953, Aalto wrote:

> The entire building group is dominated by the fire in the center of the courtyard, with exactly the same role in providing functionality and comfort as a central campfire, with the fire, reflecting in the surrounding walls of snow, evoking a pleasing almost mystical experience.
>
> *Aalto 2013: 15*

The house was constructed only a year after Aalto's seminal trip to Morocco of 1951 and we might speculate that the courtyard typology was inspired by and represents a reinterpretation of that omnipresent Moroccan archetypal precedent.

Servant and served spaces are equally articulated within the section, the living space soars upwards southeast to northwest under the mono-pitched roof that provides a small studio gallery space hung from the roof, above the western end of the living space. The height of the western wall to the living space and courtyard provides an almost bastion-like form when viewed from the lake. Over the bed-spaces and kitchen, the roof has a reciprocal slope forming a butterfly configuration.

If the living space is the focus of dwelling, it is the courtyard that is the place of reverie, play, imagining and experiment. The courtyard walls are formed of some 50 panels that exhibited a diverse range of material response in ceramic tiles and bricks, each articulated in particular ways with particular joint systems. The floor of the courtyard too exhibits a diverse range of brick and tile; however, the colours, textures and materials of walls and floor give the impression that the two surfaces are one and the wall appears to grow out of the ground, very much in the manner of the Kingo housing project in Denmark by Utzon. Like the Kingo project, the internal spaces are orientated to the courtyard; large glazed areas form the threshold between inside and out affording views through and across the defined external space.

In the *Arkkitehti* article of 1953, Aalto set out four particular areas of experiment within the tectonic resolution of the project:

1. Experiments with a building without foundations.
2. Experiments with an irregular row of columns (non-linear colonnade).
3. Free-form brick constructions.
4. Experiments with solar heating (Aalto 2013: 15).

FIGURE 3.54 Brick Detailing.

FIGURE 3.55 Log and Stone Detail.

Taking each in turn:

- *Building without foundations.* The timber framed, timber clad guest wing sits upon baulks of timber set at 45° to the house that span between and sit upon large rock outcrops. The superstructure thus appears to float over this rugged landscape.
- *Irregular row of columns.* The positioning of columns to the woodshed was determined by the presence of the rock outcrops upon which they sit, and thus the tectonic response is effectively born of place and, in the phenomenological sense, reveals place to us.
- *Free-form brick constructions.* To the north of the site, Aalto designed three free-form brick enclosures that experimented with the idea of brick as fluid-form that were never constructed but which were later to manifest themselves in the House of Culture project (1952–1958) with the purpose-designed radiating brick, which facilitated the fluid external wall form of the auditorium.
- *Experiments with solar heating.* The experimental studio that Aalto designed to the north of the site was not to be connected to the heating of the main house and Aalto wished to experiment with principles of thermal mass and heat storage and radiation to provide a heat source, but again was not constructed.

The *objective* of experimentation is to test, and the *nature* of experimentation is some, if not all, of those tests will fail. And that was indeed the case. The floor supported by the logs spanning between the rock outcrops apparently in places subsided, with the consequence that the doors and windows of the guest wing became difficult to open and close. But that was surely the point; it was only through experimentation within their own 'territory of implication' that such outcomes would emerge.

In the tradition of the Nordic summer house typology, the Experimental House is meagre. The spaces are compact and exhibit qualities of 'just-enoughness' and are responsive to attitudes of utility and humility within this exceptional landscape setting. Yet one might also imagine excess here. The apparently often gregarious Aalto hosting his friends such as the Gullichsens, gathering around the fire as evening fell, tales told as the alcohol flowed that further fuelled the conversations.

In the Experimental House we find the archetypal and essential dwelling; subservient yet responsive to its landscape setting, the courtyard subtly mediating between landscape and dwelling, inside and out, here and there, and the courtyard fire-pit redolent of the forest clearing, around which man gathers and dwells, poetically, allowing reverie, play, imagining, and experimentation.

> There is but one rule in architecture: build naturally. Don't do anything stilted, don't do anything unnecessary. Everything that is superfluous becomes ugly with time.
>
> *Aalto in Schildt 1998: 18*

Notes

1 An indispensable condition or action.
2 Weissenhof – literally 'White Housing'.
3 A Danish architect who worked in Aalto's Office between 1948 and 1954.

References

Aalto, A. 2013. *The Experimental House*. Jyväskylä: Alvar Aalto Museum.

Bak, A., Birket-Smith, T., Hansen, G., Hansen, P. M. and Holbolth, N. (eds). 1999. *Nordjyllands Kuntsmuseum*. Copenhagen: Fonden til udgivelse as Arkitekturtidsskrift.

Gideon, S. 1969. *Space, Time and Architecture – The Growth of the New Tradition*, 5th edition. Cambridge, MA: Harvard University Press.

Pallasmaa, J. (ed.). 1998. *Alvar Aalto: The Villa Mairea*. Helsinki: Alvar Aalto Foundation and Villa Mairea Foundation.

Pallasmaa, J. 2005. *Encounters: Juhani Pallasmaa Architectural Essays*, ed. P. MacKeith. Helsinki: Rakennustieto Oy.

Schildt G. 1998. *Alvar Aalto – In His Own Words*. New York: Rizzoli.

Walters, R. F. 1913. *Sanatorium Treatment in Pulmonary Tuberculosis*. London: George Allen & Co. Online version retrieved 18 November 2016 from https://archive.org/stream/b24907881/b24907881_djvu.txt.

Weston, R. 1995. *Alvar Aalto*. London: Phaidon Press.

4

JØRN UTZON – THE THEŌROI

> To understand all the inspiration present in every one of man's countless means of expression, to work with our hands, eyes, feet, stomachs, on the basis of our movements and not of statistical norms and rules created on the principle of what is most usual – this is the way forward to an architecture that is both varied and human.
>
> *Jørn Utzon in Weston 2002: 11*

Utzon is the Theōroi. Like an ambassador of architecture, he travelled consistently to lands and cultures that were not his own with one simple objective: to understand. Like the ancient Greek ambassadors that preceded him in this task, drawing upon the etymology of the word theory discussed in Chapter 1, he observed what he found and speculated upon it. He brought back his understanding and through a process of intelligent re-interpretation, re-appropriated these archetypal precedents. Utzon travelled primarily to places of what we might term 'cultural density': more often than not ancient cultures where the origins of things remained evident. From the Mayan ruins of Mexico, the ancient hill settlements of the High Atlas Mountains of Morocco, to the ancient temples of China and Japan, each precedent discovered made a substantial contribution to his ways of being, thinking and acting.

Jørn Utzon (1918–2008) was born in Copenhagen, Denmark, on 9 April 1918 to Aage Oberg Utzon and Estrid Hauna Waleska Utzon (née Olsen); the second born of three brothers. This was a period of significant social and political change as the First World War drew to a close; for the first time women held a vote in Denmark and in 1918 the first women were elected to the Danish Parliament. In parallel in the UK women's suffrage gave rise to women's votes. In Russia, the year before Utzon's birth marked the commencement of the Russian Revolution and 1918 marked the start of the Finnish Civil War. In the USA, the Washington Declaration proclaimed the newly independent Czechoslovak Republic, formed as the Hungarian Government dissolved its special relationship with Austria, effectively ending the Austro-Hungarian Empire.

These social and political shifts were reflected within the realm of art and architecture. In the late nineteenth century we saw the emergence of modernism that was to explode in the early twentieth century and influenced all the arts including of course architecture. In Nordic architecture this movement was led by the Swedish architect Gunnar Asplund (1885–1940) and his collaborator Sigurd Lewerentz (1885–1975), who steered the transition from National Romanticism, through a period of neo-classicism onwards into the functionalism of the 1920s and 1930s and into a very particular condition of modernism, which others have termed 'humane, Nordic modernism'. This fundamental shift in cultural paradigm was reflected within philosophy, literature and fine art that, in combination with architecture, made the epoch of Utzon's birth and formative years a period of significant cultural, social and political change.

In 1918, the Utzon family moved from Copenhagen to Aalborg in Northern Jutland upon Aage Utzon's appointment as a naval engineer in the A/S P. Ph. Sturs shipyard. Aalborg has a long trading and seafaring heritage, lying on the south bank of the Limfjord that cleaves Jutland in two, providing sheltered passage between the Baltic and North seas for centuries. This rich heritage of seafaring and trade is evidenced by the Viking burial ground at Lindholm Høje, on the northern bank of the Limfjord.

Utzon's formative years in Aalborg witnessed a period of great industrial production, the town taking on the nickname of 'the town of smoking chimneys'. The cement factories and the Aalborg Shipyard were exemplars of this activity. Grainy black and white images record the huge steel hull forms created in the shipyard; the sheer scale of ambition in creating such objects of utility undoubtedly had an impact upon the young Utzon in the after-school hours he spent playing among these monoliths.

In addition to his role in the shipyard, Aage Utzon (1885–1970) was a renowned yacht designer; his most famous design was the *'Spidsgatter'*, a doubled ended yacht with fine seakeeping characteristics, the form of which pays more than a passing homage to the long-ships of the Viking tradition. The design and manufacture of these yachts and the forming of the huge and complex three dimensional form of the hulls and superstructures within the shipyard, clearly influenced the young Utzon in the appreciation of design resolution of complex shapes and the tectonic processes that brought these shapes into reality. Aage Utzon was also a keen hunter and his understanding of nature and its systems and structures were inculcated within Utzon's childhood experience, an influence that Utzon was later to use both literally and metaphorically in his work.

In 1930 Aage and Estrid Utzon attended the Stockholm Exhibition, designed by Erik Gunnar Asplund and Sigurd Lewerentz that captured perfectly the spirit of the age and was the primary exposure of functionalism (*'funkis'*) within the Nordic world. Anecdotes suggest that the Utzons were so inspired by this experience that upon returning to Aalborg they removed their heavy wooden furniture, to be

FIGURE 4.1 'Spidsgatter' Yacht Designed by Aage Utzon, housed in the Utzon Center, Aalborg, Denmark.

replaced by furnishings that represented this 'new sprit'. In addition, apparently new eating habits were introduced to the Utzon household, encouraging a healthy diet, augmented by exercise in nature (walking, hunting, swimming, cycling and sailing), and this formative connection with nature was later to profoundly influence Utzon.

His academic experience at school was somewhat unremarkable; by his own admission he far from excelled in mathematics and required further private tutoring to pass his examinations. He was apparently nicknamed by his peers '*Utz-drømmer*' (Utz-dreamer) due to his penchant for daydreaming in class: the early signs of Utzon's capacity for reverie? The teenage Utzon became enthused by contemporary art and came to know the Danish artist Poul Schøder (1894–1957) and Swedish artist Carl Kylberg (1878–1952). In particular perhaps Kylberg's masterful capturing of the qualities of light and landscape resonated with young Utzon. After being dissuaded of an artistic career by his uncle Einar Utzon-Frank, a distinguished sculptor and a Professor at the Royal Danish Academy of Arts in Copenhagen, Utzon opted for what perhaps he judged to be a more secure future in Architecture, attending the Royal Danish Academy, and he sought out Kay Fisker and Steen Eiler Rasmussen; the former reinforcing the concept of tectonic integrity, the latter providing a formative phenomenological influence.

Utzon graduated in 1942 and migrated to Stockholm, Sweden, immediately, at least in part due to the German occupation of Denmark. In the same year, Utzon married Lis Fenger. They had first met in Copenhagen and when Utzon migrated, Lis followed shortly after. Utzon completed his training working for Hakon Ahlberg

(1891–1964), a functionalist by disposition, who had published a book on Gunnar Asplund in 1943. Ahlberg was the founding president of the Swedish Architects Association (SAR), and Editor in Chief of architecture journals *Arkitekten* in 1922 and *Byggmästaren* 1922–1924 and was also President of the Swedish Academy of Fine Arts from 1954 to 1962.

Following the end of the Second World War Utzon travelled extensively within the rest of Scandinavia, Europe, Morocco, the United States and Mexico. His travels provided significant inspiration that would be later manifested in a range of projects that exhibited sophisticated trans-cultural influences. Utzon subsequently worked with Paul Hedqvist (1895–1977), who was of a modernist tendency and was professor at the Royal Academy of Arts in Stockholm between 1938 and 1948. It was here that he met the Norwegian architect Arne Korsmo (1900–1968) who was to become a close friend and significant influence. In October 1945 he joined the office of Alvar Aalto albeit for a brief period, ending in December 1945. Utzon later identified both Asplund and Aalto as being significant figures in his understanding of architecture.

Utzon set up a practice in Copenhagen 1950, completing a range of largely domestic, small-scale projects, including most influentially his own house and the Kingo housing development (1956) near Helsingør. His most significant commission, the Sydney Opera House, was won through an open international competition in 1957.

The eventual politicised debacle of the Sydney Opera House is well known. Utzon withdrew from the project in 1966. However, while working on the Sydney Opera House, but prior to moving to Australia in 1963 he designed such seminal projects as the Melli Bank, Iran (1959–1960), the Fredensborg Houses (1959–1963) and proposal for the Madrid Opera House Competition (1962 – unrealised).

While living in Sydney, he produced the first design proposal for the remarkable underground Silkeborg Museum of Art (1963 – unrealised) dedicated to the artist Asger Jorn, a first-prize-winning proposal for the Zürich Theatre competition (1964) and a proposal for his own house at Bayview, north of Sydney (1964–1965 – unrealised).

After leaving Australia in 1966, Utzon lived variously in Denmark, Hawaii and subsequently, for much of the rest of his life, on Mallorca. During this later stage of his life and without an established office, Utzon continued to produce a range of distinguished projects, including the Bagsværd Church (1968–1976), the Kuwait National Assembly (1972–1982) and his own houses, Can Lis (1971–1972) and Can Feliz (1991–1995). In 1999 Utzon accepted an invitation in collaboration with his architect son Jan, to provide design proposals and guidelines for the refurbishment and reconfiguration of the Sydney Opera House, which he continued to be involved in until his death in 2008. He was also responsible, together with his architect son Kim, for the design of the Utzon Center in his adopted hometown of Aalborg, which was opened to the public to celebrate his ninetieth birthday earlier in the same year. It is, however, his Bagsværd Church the two family villas on Mallorca, and particularly Can Lis, that together with the Sydney Opera House, represent some of the most poetic essays in phenomenological and tectonic engagement with place. His last commission was to design and oversee the production of a white grand piano for Bagsvaerd Church. A fitting finale for an architect who transcended scales, transgressed cultural boundaries and transformed modern architecture yet, throughout, remained a private and modest man.

Jørn Utzon is now internationally recognised as one of the most original, innovative and socially concerned of modern architects, perhaps the last great exponent of the humanistic Nordic tradition within modern architecture. He is the architect of what is still widely considered the most noble and humane housing built in Denmark, a simple, yet poetic modern church at Bagsværd and the most iconic and popular building of the twentieth century, his great unfinished masterpiece, the Sydney Opera House. Tadao Ando suggested:

> My spaces are born not of intellectual operations, but of the emotions rooted in the desires of many different people … my spaces transcend theory and appeal to the deepest spiritual levels. In other words, my spaces relate to the fundamental aspects of humanity.
>
> *Pare 1996: 17*

In the same way that Ando eschewed an overly theoretical approach to architecture, we find parallels in Utzon's approach. Utzon's method was not predicated upon or populated by a priori theoretical positions. He was inhabited not by intellectual ruminations and postulations, but by interrogations of the nature of human existence. These diverse formative influences provide the platform for the development of Utzon's particular paradigm which when first defined was articulated as shown in Figure 4.2.

Through further interrogation a more developed, refined and appropriate paradigmatic model has been developed (Figure 4.3).

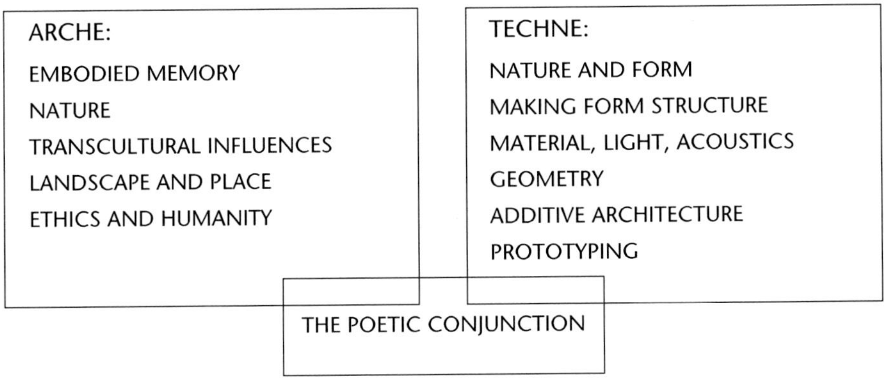

FIGURE 4.2 Utzon's Paradigm.

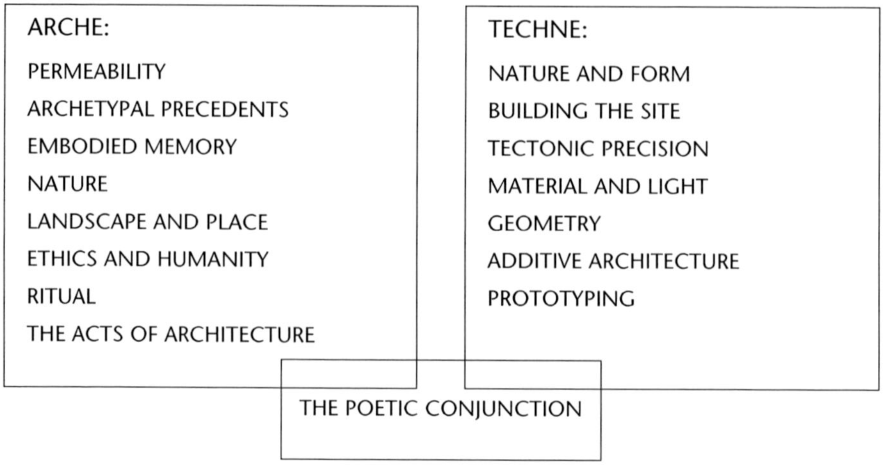

FIGURE 4.3 Utzon's Revised Paradigm.

Of Arche

Utzon was permeable – consistently open to influences that might inform his work. One such influence was the natural world: what lessons could be learned and how could these discoveries inform his work? Indeed Utzon conceived of architecture as 'nature's seed':

> The true innermost being of architecture can be compared with that of nature's seed, and something of the inevitability of nature's principle of growth ought to be a fundamental concept in architecture.
>
> *Weston 2002: 11*

This reference to nature's seed is literal and metaphorical: literal at the level of nature providing a 'model' for architecture, and metaphorical in describing an 'inter-connectedness' that nature exhibits and demonstrates within eco-systems. This notion of inter-connectedness provides, within architecture, the necessity to acknowledge and respond to particular contexts in which we work.

Utzon's work held a fascination for the forms and processes of nature, which he later shared with close colleagues Tobias Faber and Arne Korsmo, as exemplified by D'Arcy Thompson's book *On Growth and Form* (1917), which Utzon later insisted all employees owned.

Utzon was always hungry to understand natural phenomena. Richard Leplastrier, an employee of Utzon's in Sydney, once told me of a sailing trip he and Utzon made, and when sailing along the coast at Pittwater, North of Sydney, Utzon studied a bird in flight and as it dipped behind the dunes to land Utzon asked the rhetorical question, 'Why land there?'[1]

The propensity to travel is another dimension of Utzon's permeability, like Aalto, to locations of 'cultural density' where examples of the origin of things are exposed.

There is something 'of the origin' in all of Utzon's work that consistently informed his understanding of architecture. This concept of 'going back' as Fehn suggested, to rediscover that which we may have forgotten, was a seminal influence upon Utzon's oeuvre. Drawing from these experiences he developed a number of archetypal precedents that consistently informed his work.

> The platform as an architectural element [archetypal precedent] is a fascinating feature. I first fell in love with it on a study trip to Mexico in 1949, where I found many variations, both in size and the idea of, the platform, and where many of the platforms are alone without anything but the surrounding nature.
>
> *Weston 2002: 247*

The reinterpretation of the ancient Mayan temple platforms within (for example) the Sydney Opera House project have been extensively discussed but perhaps the more subtle reinterpretations of other archetypal precedents remain less explored. One such exemplar is the ancient hill villages of the Atlas Mountains of Morocco, visited by Utzon and subsequently, upon Utzon's advice, Sverre Fehn.

Here Utzon undoubtedly found 'something of the origin' – another archetypal precedent – the courtyard house. These villages presented timeless ways of building that Bernard Rudofsky[2] illuminated to the world of architecture. Arising seamlessly from the landscape, the houses are only distinguishable as places of habitation, as Fehn observed, by the throw of the shadow on the vertical walls. Utzon also discovered subtle ordering of space from the urban scale to the domestic scale that

FIGURE 4.4 Ait Benhaddou, Southern Atlas Mountains, Morocco.

FIGURE 4.5 Kingo Housing Project, Denmark.

was informed by particular climatic, social, cultural and spiritual influences that in combination provided anonymous, meagre yet poetic response to the particularity of place. The potential of the courtyard typology as an archetypal precedent was exposed to Utzon.

This courtyard archetype was most famously reinterpreted within the Kingo housing and Fredensborg housing projects and was later extended to the Nature Center project at Skane, the Utzon Center in Aalborg, and Utzon's two houses on the island of Mallorca. This precedent was reinterpreted within different cultural and climatic contexts with the same intention as the origin: to provide mediating space. Other elements of precedent such as the authority of the wall as mediator of space and lack of fenestration to the public face of the building signal the primal need for privacy and separation within the act of dwelling was reinterpreted within these new contexts by Utzon.

Yet the layering of space evident within the original precedent allowed his reinterpretations to open progressively to the world as one crossed external and internal spatial thresholds.

In the Kingo housing particularly, the houses seem to grow from the territory upon the maturation of the surrounding landscape. In part, this is due to the subtle articulation of the junction of the ground-plane of the courtyard and the external wall to the house where the same brick is used as pavior and walling and the floor of the house is not expressed as a plinth but rather a verticised extension of the ground-plane. In this detail we see the archetypal precedent of the relationship between the village and landscape at Ait Benhaddou, given expression in another context through thoughtful and precise tectonic manipulation.

Central to our collective and individual understanding of the archetypal precedents is our subliminal engagement with individual and collective embodied memory. In this realm Aalto, Utzon and Fehn have parallel paradigms. Peter Zumthor writes poetically of such things:

> There was a time when I experienced architecture without thinking about it. Sometimes I can almost feel a particular door handle in my hand, a piece of metal shaped like the back of a spoon. I used to take hold of it when I went

into my aunt's garden. That door handle still seems to me like a special sign of entry into a world of different moods and smells.

Zumthor 1998: 7

Many of these perceptions stem from our own childhood experiences yet, as is suggested in Chapter 2, we appear to have innate capacities that are perhaps hard-wired within our DNA that hold currency across cultural thresholds.

The impact of Utzon's formative experiences are clear in his work and methods. His childhood presence in the Aalborg Shipyard witnessing the construction of huge hulls of ships made the conceptualisation and realisation of large and complex forms tangible, and his father's renowned yacht designs perhaps inculcated the complexity of manipulation of three dimensional form.

His propensity for travel was similarly a well of embodied memory from which he drew; of course within the forms and elements he discovered, such as the platform, the threshold, the landscape, the wall, but also in the tectonic manipulation of these concepts. Within, for example, the Sydney Opera House project we see the stereotomic form of the plinth over-sailed by the (apparently) light forms of the shells that appear almost as woven fabric billowing in the harbour breezes.

The paradigmatic element of embodied memory extended to Utzon's fascination with the structures and forms of nature that were encouraged and inculcated by his father, which became embodied within Utzon's being and were, in diverse ways, to later inform not only his design synthesis, but also his design approach.

Fundamental to Utzon's understanding of architecture was a tangible sense of the relationship between landscape and place. As suggested in Chapter 1, Denmark is a place of big skies and low horizons; essentially a flatland, the smallest depression within the landscape is the traditional territory to make place, to hunker down in the landscape like a fox in the hedgerow.

In the Kingo housing project particularly, we see this concept of hunkering down in the landscape made explicit. Here the buildings are anchored within the soft folds of the earth, each allowing the elements of the landscape to camouflage the threshold between inside and outside dwelling and context. The genesis of this

FIGURE 4.6 Sydney Opera House – the Stereotomic Base and 'Woven' Shells.

FIGURE 4.7 Typical Summer House Landscape Setting – Near Elbetoft, Denmark.

relationship between dwelling and landscape lies in Utzon's subtle manipulation in placement of the houses, but in the case of Kingo is enhanced by the purposeful management of the common landscape by the residents that embraces the landscape rather than seeking to control the flora; providing a sharp contrast perhaps with managed attitudes in the Fredensborg housing project that exhibits a far more manicured attitude.

In contrast, with the Sydney Opera House project Utzon 'builds the landscape' of the site, using the archetypal precedent of the plateau. Here the act of Opera is literally raised to another level that is redolent of the tradition in Denmark of siting culturally or spiritually significant buildings, such as churches, on the highest land available. While there may be merely a slight lift in ground-plane, the consequence is clear: this is an important place.

FIGURE 4.8 The Kingo Housing Project.

Given the intellectual tradition in Architecture of Utzon's Nordic world encompassing the writings of such luminaries as Norberg-Schulz, Rasmussen, Aalto, Pietilä, Pallasmaa and others it is no surprise that Utzon was absorbed in the architectural dialogue upon the nature of place and the mediation of climate that the act of making place required.

Utzon's work also reflects a continuation of a Nordic tradition both within modern architecture and in society as a whole, that focuses on social well-being, equality and of ascribing value to the collective community illustrated powerfully at the Kingo project. As with Aalto and other Nordic architects, this is manifested in providing architectural solutions to the large numbers of displaced refugees following the Second World War, and his considerable interest in the provision of affordable collective housing projects, most famously the Kingo and Fredensborg courtyard housing developments north of Copenhagen.

These projects are still considered to be some of Denmark's most successful suburban housing. Not only in terms of the fine balance between the privacy of the individual and the strong sense of community that is engendered by the architecture, but also the efficiency of the planning that allows considerably higher density to be achieved than is normally the case in such a suburban context, while allowing large parts of the sites to remain undeveloped and landscaped, as shared communal space.

One of the governing elements of the brief at Kingo was that the cost of the houses should be no more than three times the average wage of the shipyard workers of Helsingør, in order that the houses were affordable to blue-collar workers. This a priori decision of course limited the floor areas of the properties, but from the outset the courtyard configuration gave the possibility to later extend the houses within the footprint that the courtyard provided.

A second opportunity afforded by the courtyard typology was to redistribute landscape outside of the footprint as common territory, managed by the community. The height and disposition of the courtyard walls allows each house to 'borrow views' from this communal realm, ensuring a sense of space and prospect within each dwelling. Given the sheer volume of commonly shared landscape it is telling to note that the density of the site (dwellings/hectare) is the same or higher than the surrounding suburbs where no such elements of shared landscape exist.

Bagsvaerd Kirke, in the northern suburbs of Copenhagen, is another exemplar of this overarching sense of humanity articulated by Utzon's architectural endeavour. This is not a church that shouts to the world, indeed its external form and materiality, reminiscent of grain silos and barns of rural Denmark, has often been a resounding disappointment to generations of students that I have taken there. Externally it speaks of modesty, subtlety and stereotomic mass, so delightfully carved internally in three dimensions with fluid, flowing forms that initially compress one upon entry and subsequently expand, to draw one's eyes upwards to the light emanating from the domain of the deities. Inside one has a sense of the dissolution of mass, the clerestory lighting washing the walls and billowing ceiling with light in an ever-changing

FIGURE 4.9 Bagsvaerd Church Exterior.

FIGURE 4.10 Bagsvaerd Interior.

kaleidoscope of soft light and shadow. Here man can subtly commune with his God through the implicit rather than explicit conduits Utzon provided.

Implicit with Utzon's permeable understanding of the complex inter-relationship between the origins of things, archetypal precedents that are drawn from those origins, embodied memory, nature, landscape and place, and ethics and humanity is a further understanding of how man through his inner being responds to such phenomena; through what we might term 'ritual'.

The process of ascension of the Opera House plateau allows divestment of the everyday, the high level light of Bagsvaerd Kirke leads our eyes upwards, the layering of space of the Kingo Houses defines spatial privacy and the hearth at Can Lis encourages gathering and allows the stories to flow. In this sense ritual is meant as the human responses engendered and facilitated by Utzon that are core elements of human experience that exist within our innermost presence as primal experience.

But at the core of Utzon's understanding are the *acts* of architecture. What it is to dwell, bathe, sleep, gather; and implicit within the recognition of these primal acts is Utzon's poetic response. To wake in Can Lis within the aedicule bed, to stare out of the cavernous opening across the sea to the horizon, is to amplify reality to a primal, visceral level; for one moment, this was the cave, I the dweller within the cave and for a second the only human in existence. However, the potentials for such amplified experience would remain only as potential if Utzon had not revealed them to us in material form through the processes of *techne* that he adopted.

Of Techne

Just as nature inspired Utzon, he reinterpreted natural forms as an effective response to tectonic challenges. Much has been made of the relationship between the palm frond and the resolution of the ribbed roof structure of the Sydney Opera House.

> Assistants recall being told that Utzon was seen waving large rhubarb-like leaves – most likely Gunnera – over a model of the podium (of the Opera House project) still uncertain how to roof his built landscape …
>
> *Weston 2002: 121*

In the original form at competition entry, the roof forms of the Opera House were conceived of as 'shells'. However, in testing such construction within the design process, the appointed engineer, Ove Arup, was clear from the outset that a thin shell roof configuration could not be constructed as originally drawn. Furthermore, Arup later reported that the shapes and scale were unprecedented and radical reconsideration was required.

> … and his friend the photographer Keld Helmer-Petersen describes the first (revised) sketch as being done in large size charcoal with a series of strongly curved natural shapes that radiate in all directions, reeds or grasses, a tuft that seems to grow, energetically unfolded on paper and kept in place by a broad horizontal line.
>
> *Weston 2002: 121*

FIGURE 4.11 Structures of Nature.

FIGURE 4.12 Reinterpreted at the Opera House as Structures of Man.

As the design process progressed it was agreed that the structural form would be conceived of as 'ribs', skeletal in nature; a system described by D'Arcy Thompson in Utzon's 'bible', *On Growth and Form* (1917). For Utzon the inspiration was also drawn from the structure and form of the giant palm leaves. The breakthrough came in regard to the form of the roofs when Utzon, experimenting with geometry, sliced the skin of an orange into triangles and those peeled elements became not only the geometry of the roof form but as Utzon knew, being a geometric form, all the elements could be prefabricated utilising Utzon's concept of 'additive architecture'.

Yet it is perhaps the plinth, the plateau as Utzon called it, of the Opera House that represents Utzon's masterstroke. The idea of ascension from the everyday to the realm of the extraordinary has been earlier discussed, but in this act of 'building the site' Utzon formed a new landscape for the project and within this 'new ground' all the 'stuff' of Opera could sit. In Can Lis equally Utzon 'builds the site' and in this case, 'builds from the site'; the project resonant of hill villages of the island.

Central to Utzon's paradigm is a complex engagement in the relationship between structure, construction, meaning and form: a tectonic approach. Kenneth Frampton's writings on Utzon, first in relation to a critical regionalism in architecture, and later, more notably, in his dedication of a chapter on Utzon in his seminal publication *Studies in Tectonic Culture: The Poetics of Construction in Nineteenth and Twentieth Century Architecture* (2001), reinforces Utzon's significance as an exemplar of a tectonic approach within modern architecture delivered with great precision.

Bagsvaerd Church is an exemplar of such an approach. The structural system could hardly be simpler: reinforced precast concrete frames set out on a 2.2-metre grid, the frames clad externally in precast concrete planks with a ceramic finish to the external face. It is inside this rather simple and restrained form and structure that the narrative on man's relationship to the deities unfolds. Utzon conceived of the major interior space of the church as a promenade of humanity under the clouds that house the deities, apparently while he was sitting on a Hawaiian beach, watching cumulus clouds form on the horizon, translated as the now famous sketch where the promenade of humanity is lit by shards of sunlight emanating between the clouds.

In Bagsvaerd Church, the section is everything; the apparently free-form concrete shell vaults of the interior were informed by Utzon's interest in Arabic calligraphy and, again, Utzon used the geometric form of the circle to articulate the curvature of each vaulted form. They were constructed of *in situ* sprayed concrete reinforced with mesh, on plywood shuttering and finished internally in lime mixed with white cement, providing a very particular quality of luminosity when the soft light from above falls upon the surface.

Extending Utzon's engagement with a tectonic precision is his sense of materiality in the context of 'utilised light' as articulated by Louis Kahn: 'You can say the light, the giver of all presences, is the maker of material, and the material was made to cast a shadow, and the shadow belongs to the light' (in Latour 1991: 235). This response to light was always 'place-specific'. His response to 'the fifth elevation' of the Sydney Opera House was to use reflective ceramic surfaces to reflect direct light

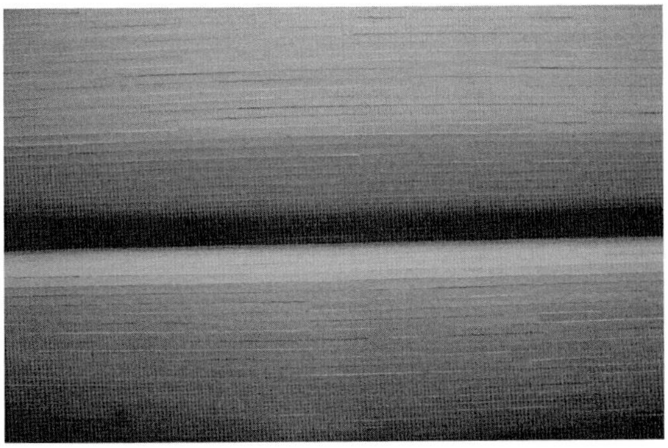

FIGURE 4.13 Light Falling on Vaulted Surfaces, Bagsvaerd Kirke, Denmark.

FIGURE 4.14 The Ceramic Shells of the Opera House.

providing shimmering roof forms, drawing from his experience of such surfaces in the Middle East and North Africa.

His design response in Bagsvaerd Church was, in contrast, to draw in the more subtle indirect glancing light of the North that encourages human dialogue with the deities. But perhaps the most powerful exemplar of Utzon's attitude towards light and material is within his own family home, Can Lis on the island of Mallorca. Here, within the living space, mid-afternoon (certainly in April when I was there) a slim shaft of sunlight slices through the shadow of the interior, animating the surface of the rough-hewn stone below this slot opening. Momentarily, the texture and colour of the wall are exposed until as the light shaft disappears, the space falls into shadow once more and we are left with only memory.

In geometry, Utzon found tectonic solutions. For him, geometry was not an end in itself, but rather the means by which effective and efficient tectonic solutions could be achieved. The complexity of the shell roof forms of the Sydney Opera House were brought to magnificent resolution through the application of geometry. One should amplify that this work was carried out by hand, ahead of any computer aided design programmes, and apparently when Raphael Moneo, an employee of Utzon's on the Opera House project, arrived at the opening of the Utzon Exhibition held at the Louisiana Museum of Art in Denmark and was confronted by a huge facsimile of one of the incredible hand-drawn geometric section drawings he famously muttered 'I made hundreds of those'.

While most commentary available on Utzon's relationship to geometry is related to the Opera House project where it is at its most explicit, it is a consistent element of his paradigm, given expression in the vaulted ceiling forms of Bagsvaerd Kirke, and is evident within his earliest work such as the unbuilt project for the Aalborg Convention Center of 1945, designed in collaboration with Tobias Faber, through to his later work such as the Nature Center in Skagen, Northern Jutland, Denmark, designed in collaboration with his sons, Kim and Jan Utzon (1998). Here the geometry of just a single pavilion is shifted 45° off-grid to accentuate its hierarchy, as both the place of socialisation and respite and as the only two-storey element, affording a view out into the surrounding landscape.

Engagement with geometry also facilitated an opportunity for Utzon to engage with the utility of additive architecture. Utzon's organic understanding of design led him to what he referred to as additive architecture; a concept, based in-part upon his understanding of the ancient Chinese building manuals, whereby a one-family house and also complex larger scale architecture could be created using a limited number of pre-fabricated components. Whether we consider the repetition of the shell structures in Sydney or the typological development of the Kingo or Fredensborg projects, we see addition and repetition as a core characteristic of Utzon's work.

> I happened to say something that Jørn asked me to repeat. He then got up and with his 6B pencil wrote the words ADDITIVE ARCHITECTURE on the wall, and said we had broken through the sound barrier.
>
> *Prip-Buus 2009: 8*

At the scale of urban and suburban morphology, we see the additive principles employed in a diverse range and scales of projects such as the unbuilt Herning Export College (1969), the Jeddah Stadium project (1969) and the second Museum

FIGURE 4.15 Clerestory Light Slot, Can Lis.

of Art proposal (1969–1971). Perhaps the best example of this approach to design is in Utzon's Espansiva Housing system of 1969. Designed as a prototype low cost mass housing solution, it utilised modular components that provided for a diverse range of spatial variation and organisation.

Underpinning and supporting Utzon's response to the 'bringing forth' or 'revealing' of architectural intent was his process of design development through prototyping. The Espansiva project is an excellent example of this element of Utzon's paradigm; being constructed up to and including a full-size prototype, just as he did with the Opera House roof panels to test the ceramic tiling layouts.

More usually seen in processes of industrial production in motor manufacture, product design and engineering, prototyping allowed Utzon to finesse complex three-dimensional design proposals, producing elegant solutions that could be constructed with efficiency. The concept of prototyping goes beyond merely making a model that in some way represents the 'thing'. For Utzon the prototype was the means of testing, evaluating and developing the thing through an iterative process rather than merely being a means of representation.

Of Poetic Conjunctions

Underpinning Utzon's work is a poetic, metaphysical dimension that simultaneously transcends the plurality of this paradigmatic investigation yet paradoxically fuses the elements together. To look up in Bagsvaerd Church as the soft light moves fluidly across the sculpted ceiling is to commune with the deities. To walk down the internal stairways of the Opera House is to be alongside the tumbling mountain streams of Utzon's Nordic world. To sit in Utzon's living room in Can Lis looking out through the apparently frameless, deep sandstone window bays to the sea and sky beyond is to return to the cave and a sense of the core of human existence.

Inculcated within such an approach is that Utzon never lost sight of the experience of the individual, which is always central to his architecture. Whether in the sheltered enclosures of his courtyard housing or the sense of sacral procession up the podium steps of the Sydney Opera House to be presented with a grand panoramic overview of the harbour, before entering the halls of the Opera House, sublimely prepared to profoundly appreciate the artistic endeavour taking place within.

Such poetic qualities consistently resonate in the Nordic world. In art, music, literature, poetry and film, we find a melancholic and reflective attachment to the metaphysical realm and it should be no surprise that Utzon too inhabited this realm.

While Utzon's output may be considered by some commentators as being relatively limited in comparison to other architects of his generation, it was, however, remarkably varied in terms of scale, function and context. But there is nevertheless a clarity, consistency and continual reworking of essential ideas throughout all of his work. It is this possibility to be able to more clearly identify, illustrate and discuss certain significant themes in architecture and design, with reference to Utzon, that gives relevance to the Utzon Paradigm.

What follows is a narrative that seeks to explain the poetic and substantive qualities of one of Utzon's projects – his own home, Can Lis, on the Balearic Island of Mallorca. It is not intended as a work of analysis so much as a recording of a process of how, across space and time, this beautiful house revealed itself to me and my friend and colleague, an erstwhile PhD candidate, Line Nørskov-Eriksen, who collaborated in the writing of the piece.[3]

Existential Conversations in a Cave 2: Reconciliation of Oppositions (Theory as Architecture – Architecture as Theory)

Of Theory

Dwelling within this magnum opus of the humane modernist tradition of architecture that is Jørn Utzon's Can Lis, we are inspired to ruminate upon a defining existential question: 'Why can we not just drop things anymore?'

> A long time ago … people used simply to drop things from time to time. But nowadays we have physicists to inform us of the laws of gravity by which objects fall; philosophers to doubt whether there are really any discreet objects to be dropped at all; sociologists to explain how all this dropping is really the consequence of urban pressures; psychologists to suggest that we are all trying to drop our parents; poets who write about how all this dropping is symbolic of death; and critics to argue that it is a sign of the poet's castration anxiety. Now dropping can never be the same again. We can never return to the happy garden where we simply walked around dropping things all day without a care in the world. What has happened, rather, is that practice has now been forced to take itself as its own object of enquiry. Theory is just human activity bending back upon itself, constrained in a new kind of self-reflexivity. And in absorbing this self-reflexivity, the activity itself will be transformed.
>
> *Eagleton and Payne 1991*

Speculating upon Eagleton and Payne's observation of contemporary theoretical endeavour as rather pointless 'bending back', our conversation within Can Lis is born of a shared contention that architecture struggles with our contemporary understanding of 'this thing called theory'.

This struggle is not one of a singular origin, but rather represents a complex set of conditions. One dimension of this complexity may be that since the period of the Enlightenment, our understanding of theory has been predicated upon Cartesian frames of doubt, proof and scientific method. This has as a consequence, forced architecture to question its relationship with the arts due to the inherent technical challenges that lie within our discipline. A second dimension may be that theoretical praxis in architecture has been subjected to the manifestos of the modern movement that shared the Enlightenment's rather ambivalent view towards history

FIGURE 4.16 Can Lis Viewed from the Sea.

in order to liberate 'betterment' from past conventions. This tendency was revealed through a heroic belief in the new era, entrusting architecture with the capacity to surpass the creations of all previous epochs that as a consequence, subjugated and compressed the status of the history and, thus, the 'origin of things'.

As we dwell in Can Lis that so poetically articulates the origins of human existence in its archaic qualities, we develop the view that the Cartesian paradigm and the modernist project have led to binary, oppositional distinctions between intellect and emotion, knowing and unknowing, new and old, modern and ancient, innovation and origin, theory and practice which have been abstractly constructed in an effort to establish theoretical credibility within contemporary architectural discourse.

Inspired by the archaic spaces of Can Lis, we speculate: What if we were to return to the origin of things themselves, and more specifically the origin of the word 'theory' (see Chapter 1)? What possibilities would then arise from the relationship between theory and architecture? Is there something here that perhaps is not lost, but may have been forgotten?

Of Archaeology

By *archaeology* of course we mean the 'revealing of something'; in this case the essence of the place that is Can Lis. We contend that the methodology of archaeology draws attention to not only the origin of architecture, its prehistory, but also exposes the archaeological process. This process of revelation by searching below the surface is of paramount importance.

The archaeologist cannot discover or reveal from the office. He or she has to be at the end of the spade, the trowel or the brush. Fundamental to archaeological praxis in architecture is this 'being in the presence of' that invites an experiential and visceral understanding. Back in our offices before arrival here, we had studied Utzon and Can Lis at a distance. Those studies had suggested where we might dig.

Archaeology holds another potential dimension in the understanding of place. By nature, archaeological praxis is formative rather than summative, speculative rather than absolute. Archaeology can only uncover what it is that remains, and then speculate upon the authorship, values and zeitgeist of the antiquities. That speculation is of course underpinned by comparative knowledge, but in essence it allows space for the 'as yet undiscovered' and as such defies absolute conclusion.

Once in Can Lis, we uncovered layers of meaning and visceral experiences that we never anticipated from the office. We were able to uncover some essences, hopefully without contaminating the place. We have striven in the context of Prip-Buus's words to 'look beyond the girls on the beach' and through dogged and determined acts of archaeology reveal the anatomy of both idea and place.

This methodology has suggested to us that the problem with 'this *thing* called theory' is not the *thing* itself, but rather the way in which we have collectively allowed the origin of the word theory to be silenced; theory as vehicle for personal, immersive experience. Furthermore, we contend this liberates theoretical endeavour developed through the concept of 'archaeology' that can inspire and encourage an immersive study of architecture.

We? We are apparently teacher and student. The teacher has always taught what he wants to learn; the student hungry to understand the mysteries. Yet as time has progressed, the student has become the teacher, the teacher has become the student, and teaching for both has become learning. In order to further understand, they retreated to the existential cave of Can Lis.

For years we have studied Utzon's oeuvre. The teacher inspired through his work upon the Utzon paradigm, the student inspired by the transcultural dimensions of Utzon's oeuvre. We have written variously about Utzon's diverse range of work, speculated upon his influences and have striven to understand his methodologies. It is this quest to understand that brought us to Can Lis, in the spirit of expectation that by the mere act of being there, we may more deeply understand that place, and of course the complexity that lies behind its physicality.

Can Lis was designed by Jørn Utzon as a family home on the island of Mallorca. After his self-exile from Australia, Utzon found on Mallorca a climate and landscape that reminded him of New South Wales, and during a visit with friends who had already adopted the area Migjorn as their home, Utzon's wife Lis asked a group of farmers whom they met if there was any land for sale in the area. Apparently, one of the farmers knew of three places – one beautiful, one a paradise and the third incredible; and accordingly, they bought the 'paradise' immediately, the site upon which Can Lis was built in 1972.

An import part of the Can Lis story is that Utzon would eventually build another house further inland. Since childhood Utzon had lived close to the sea, but the harsh reflected light of this place would eventually be too much for his ageing eyes. The cold winter months on the cliff edge grew longer; an explosion of tourism ensured that eager students of architecture would arrive unannounced by land and water, and would exclaim: *here is the adopted home of the architect who built the Sydney Opera House*, disturbing the silence and privacy which undoubtedly was important to a man who was no self-publicist and often portrayed himself naked in his sketches.

The house nestles within the dramatic landscape of the southern cliff of the island, with Africa over the horizon. This is an essay of poetic place making that seems to grow effortlessly out of the particular landscape, yet it exposes core elements of what it is to dwell poetically, joyfully and with dignity. It is place that encourages and facilitates the *acts* of human habitation yet fuses modernity with the epoch we now record as pre-history, that is embodied deep in each of our collective memories.

It is the cave. The existential cave. William Curtis observed when interrogating the works of Alvar Aalto that the cave condition is a 'cosmological seismographic' (Curtis 1982) – a designed collective memory laid bare by the intuitive hand of the architect and, we sense, an internal existential conversation in architecture. In the depths of the cave, we talk, ruminate, uncover, discover, speculate and make fire; testing and honing the idea of archaeology as a paradigm for authentic intellectual praxis in architecture.

Of the Origin

Perhaps poignantly within the context of our archaeological methodology, there is something 'of the origin' that is coincidental with his 'peregrinate praxis' in all of Utzon's work, that suggests the potential value of returning to the 'things themselves'. As a dedicated pragmatist in the midst of an exploding modernist revolution in the 1960s, Utzon was unique in his distrust in an overly academic and theoretical approach to architecture. Rather, he maintained a simple principle for his own ethical and creative formation; wishing to further enhance his understanding of architecture beyond what could be drawn from the academic realm, he maintained that architecture had to be experienced. Thus, in response to this position, our starting point naturally had to be rehearsing the ability to experience our surroundings. This 'experientialist ethos' was first expressed within a rare essay, 'The Innermost Being of Architecture' (1949), where Utzon speculated upon uncovering the 'seed' as a metaphor for the origins of architectural endeavour:

> The true innermost being of architecture can be compared to nature's seed, and something as inevitable as nature's principle of growth ought to be a fundamental principle in architecture.
>
> *Jørn Utzon in Weston 2002: 10*

Utzon's idea of the seed is analogous to the concept of *arche*, in that it speaks of ontologies and origins of architecture. Utzon's idea of 'nature's principle of growth', is analogous to *techne* in that it reveals and brings forth architecture dependent upon

FIGURE 4.17 Can Lis – the Existential Cave.

the specific conditions encountered; perhaps climate, prospect, aspect, orientation that also captures the nuances and complexities of a metaphysical understanding of place.

The genius of architecture is in revealing the seed and nature's growth through matter; the tectonic intention in the manipulation of matter, responsive to the analogy of nature's growth. Utzon proposes we design from the inside, the 'seed', outwards into the world of existence.

Utzon consistently sought the seed, the origin. We cannot believe that it was accidental that he journeyed to places that exhibited a density of the condition of origin. In Mexico he uncovered the idea of 'plateau' within the ruined Mayan temples, in China and Japan he found the idea of the floating roof, in Morocco the courtyard, the blind wall to the street, and in all these places of density he uncovered the articulation of social, cultural and spiritual mores, given expression through Architecture.

These glimpses of the origin were to be consistently translated within his being, thinking and oeuvre. The plateau and floating roof, reinterpreted perhaps most notably in the Sydney Opera House, the blind wall and courtyard (and layering of space) in the Kingo and Fredensborg projects, the plateau and courtyard in the Utzon Center in Aalborg, Denmark, and the idea of courtyard resonated again in the Nature Center in Skagen, Denmark.

Utzon led us to this idea of archaeology and it is therefore appropriate that we should utilise this methodology in understanding what is the most intimate and difficult act for any architect: the design of his own house. Can Lis, our existential cave.

Of Experience

Of Harbour

> Roger, this is a beautiful little harbour you have made here.
>
> *Richard Leplastrier, in conversation with the author*

Since the thirteenth century when the Catalan peoples settled on Mallorca, the island has been a nexus of trade in foods, craft, valuable commodities, and of course ideas, between Africa and Europe. It is thus of little surprise that an architect, with his love of North African culture, would make the Mediterranean, the cradle of Western and Central civilisations, his last home.

As a last attempt to understand not merely this southeastern corner of Mallorca, but also this particular cliff edge, the student is again compelled to dig below the surface and picks her way down the rock face.

The cliff is a 30-metre sheer drop that forms a right angle with the sea, until the wall reaches the surface of the water, where the waves century after century have been washing away the bottom of the cliff lifting it from the surface of the sea. Occasionally the cliff provides plateaus where the student can stand back and let her eyes wander across the Mediterranean before she journeys further down towards the ocean. Just a few paces east of Can Lis, the cliff lifts the sandstone free of the water like a woman lifting her skirts. Here you discover that nature has bequeathed a beautiful cave with the diameter of at least 40 metres and a mouth the height of a three-storey building.

Inside, the sun reflected from the water is dancing on the ceiling, and the sounds of the surf fill the space so dramatically that you feel it in your chest. Curiously, like the crescent window that greets you upon entrance to Can Lis, the cave takes the shape of a perfect half-moon; a mouth, an arc, a crescent, an embrace, a harbour.

Utzon never described this primal space below Can Lis in words, but he often communicated an almost spiritual fascination with natural caves, in parallel with the consistent references to sailing and sailing boats, so deeply ingrained within his Nordic psyche.

FIGURE 4.18 The Cave Below Can Lis.

Source: Line Norskov-Eriksen

The student and teacher speculate on the importance of the relationship between this cave and Can Lis, searching again in language for the origin of the word harbour that is rooted in the old English word *herebeorg* (meaning shelter, refuge) or French *auberge* (meaning inn or place of rest and repair). The etymology suggests that perhaps the seed of Can Lis is an archetypal harbour village; a place to drop your anchor, from where dreams set sail, and where foreign influences from across the sea are given shelter. Alberti suggested to us that a house is a miniature city in the layering of space, the disposition of spatial hierarchies and its purpose in providing shelter and health.[4]

Of Gate

The front door to Can Lis is received by a vestibule of interstitial space that mediates between the two geometries; that of the static, classical and ordered *agora*, and that of the almost mischievous dancing disposition of *chora* and *domus*. From this vestibule, a glancing view is presented through the carved crescent moon, past the pines to the horizon beyond.

Here is the point of distribution; west to the formalism of the *agora*, east towards the condition of *domestica*. The gatekeeper becomes the conductor in the orchestration of space and acts. It should be thus in a home.

Of Streets and Stairs

The dancing route to the east is populated with controlled external courts through which your passage crosses or, perhaps, you linger for a while. The two northern

FIGURE 4.19 The Gate.

FIGURE 4.20 The Dancing Route.

FIGURE 4.21 The Ordered Route to the West.

courtyards provide cool respite from the hot Mallorcan sun, yet behind the wall to the north, you are aware of the existence of humanity as folk pass down the street beyond.

The route to the west is more ordered, controlled; classical in character. From the gatehouse you are captured within the arcade that terminates visually to the west, in the closing wall of the temple. Here another layer of arcade is exposed, the inner arcade of the dining space to the north, that mirrors the external space.

These streets and squares reinforce the subtle differences in character as we move through space, reminiscent of the increasing layers of privacy one experiences, moving through the dense morphology of a city such as Marrakech where the alleys reduce in scale, compressing the traveller until eventually one perceives that one has arrived at a point where the threshold of privacy has been accidentally crossed. This is the realm of *domus*.

Of Domus

The teacher awoke the first day at dawn. His head rested on the pillow as his gaze was drawn to the thin slot of glass that stole his sight, past the pines, over the cliff edges, across the sea to the horizon and beyond into the sky; the territory of the deities. He remained still and slowly, as the sun rose, and the earth spun on its axis, the first slither of sunlight kissed the sandstone wall, the frame of his world, and the wall became animated. As the world turned further and the sun arose further, that

FIGURE 4.22 Desk in the Bedspace.

animation slowly penetrated his being and he orientated his existence in space and time.

The bed is on a low dais, within a compressed aedicule, the space beyond half as tall again. The oriel projecting spaces form antechambers to the room that comprise four distinct spaces, bed, slot oriel, oriel of gathering and prospect and the space between, simply furnished with desk and bamboo chair. This interstitial space led him into the small external courtyard that mediates between bedrooms.

The room is the monastic cell, the hermitage, a place of contemplation, speculation, meditation, and of course sleep. In other circumstances it could be a place of union, conjunction, passion and stillness. Whatever the occupants ordain, the silence of the space will resonate, as will the prospect of the horizon. The cross-section opens from back (bed aedicule – compressed) through the mediating volume (expanded volume), to the compression of the oriel spaces to the south. In this primal archetype of cave the teacher had never felt more like he was, at last, dwelling – poetically – within all of this density.

In Can Lis there are two distinct elements of the condition of *domus*. One for the adults held in the dancing morphological disposition. The second, the *domus* of the children, re-aligned with the *agora* and temple to provide a static and balanced termination of the composition.

Of Chora

Here is the place of becoming. Double storey-height with a modest footprint of seven by six paces. The wrapping wall to the north, east and west dissolves into five oriel projections to the south, of varying volumes that each draw in the prospect of sea, horizon and sky by day. If the three pairs of doors to the north are opened, the volume becomes transparent at eye-level; the small courtyard to the north, celebrated for its cool disposition, becomes the place of audience of the spectacle to the south.

The clerestory light slot (Figure 4.15) high in the southwest corner lures in the mid-afternoon sun as a piercing shaft of light that kisses the floor and wall, momentarily exposing the density and tactility of the stone. The light disappears as quickly as it arrived, a reminder, if one were needed, of our human impermanence and fragility, within the greater cosmic order.

As day gives way to night, the prospect evaporates and the space becomes internalised. The student ritually lights the fire each evening, and she and the teacher are transported to the Finnish woodland clearing Sverre Fehn described; where the throw of light from the fire defined the primal room. Beyond this light lie the spirits of the wood, some evil, some good and many simply benign. Fire lit, words are exchanged, speculations made, questions asked, propositions and counter propositions made. Observations take place. This is a crucible of the revealing of the archaic construct of theory. Much is emerging. This is the space of gathering, of becoming. We imagine countless conversations, families and friends converge, ideas are discussed, laughter and perhaps tears too. We can also imagine individual acts: perhaps sitting alone in the bamboo chair within an oriel, staring out to sea in silent contemplation.

The student, as 'keeper of the keys', opens the space each morning and upon entering is treated to the unique incense of the wood smoke from last night's fire that has permeated the porous sandstone. This is the soft scent of memory, of words, silences, and nocturnal speculations, all gently fuelled by the good grace of Bacchus.

Of Resolution

Moving west from the *chora* we arrive back at the gatehouse that is the point of resolution of the two geometries of counterpoint. This resolution is articulated by absence, the walls of the geometrical conjunctions do not touch, they manifest in spatial and temporal slots, populated with the tension of two hands about to conjoin as one.

Of Agora

To the west of the gatehouse lies the *agora*, complete with three arcaded sides, one directed west towards the temple, and two orientated in southerly aspect that terminate in stone frames that form 'windows to the world'. To the north are the pantry, kitchen and dining space, yet the static heavy stone table and bench in the eastern arcades makes the dining space virtually redundant in all but the most inclement weather. It was within this space that we worked, with open prospect south, again referencing the enormity of the horizon.

FIGURE 4.23 The Gatehouse.

FIGURE 4.24 The Place to Be.

The arcades are roofed within the classical tradition yet the central space is uncovered by roof, affording an impression of European Renaissance urban spaces, or perhaps the Jamal el Fna in Morocco, or the order and finesse of urban space in Regency London. Within this space, sub-spaces emerge; the 'great spot' at the southern end of the western arcade affording protection, prospect, and when seated in one of the two bamboo chairs located there, eye level connection with the horizon that provides a consistent narrative to this place.

In section the floor of the arcades of southerly aspect and central space fall-away two steps towards the cliff edge affording an amphitheatre of spaces overlooking spaces. The southerly edge of the space is kerbed providing spatial definition, yet this modest up-stand never interrupts the prospect.

Here, a sense of the origin resonates powerfully, the arcades suggestive of monastic retreat, ritual and spirituality, the central space of communing, the internal and external spaces of communing conviviality. Many of the precious acts of human existence have been played out upon this stage.

Of Temple

The final hanging Wagnerian chord of this subtle spatial composition is the temple. Set west of the *agora* in retroussé disposition, carefully aligned to the east/west arcade and children's *domus*, entrance is afforded through an offset, unlintelled opening, reached across a thin slot of an interstitial space. Upon entry we are presented with

FIGURE 4.25 The Temple.

the table of the half-moon that addresses the sky, and perhaps onwards to the deities beyond.

This is a place of both literal and metaphorical sacrifice resonant of the places of human sacrifice of the Maya, yet simultaneously redolent of the Mallorcan tradition of *medio dia*, meaning midday, from '*meridional*' with its roots in the Latin word '*meridies*' (meaning south or midday); a south-facing courtyard intended for food preparation in the open air, yet sheltered from the sun. This idea of the temple as a *medio dia* is given further place-conscious resonance, as one learns that the southeastern corner of the island where Can Lis is located, is known among that locals as *Migjorn* (meaning 'midday', as well as 'junction east and west'). This region is also the most fertile area of the island, sheltered from the north by the mountains and confined by sea to the south. Curious to understand this new condition, revealed through archaeology, the student and the teacher again return to the table, which reveals itself now as both a half-moon and a compass, which does not point south as is the tradition of the *medio dia*, but is orientated precisely 160° to the 'southeast' in alignment with the landscape upon which it sits.

To the south and west of the temple are two Kahnian half-moon carvings within the wall mass, of differing proportions: the larger, that to the south with no lintel, admitting the sea and horizon appearing as a wine glass holding the ocean; and that to the west, with lintel, admitting the forest beyond.

The walls of the temple are a stone-course lower than the *agora*, and the space is devoid of roof. One has a sense upon observation, and consideration, this is a space of the spirit, purposely designed as a ruin; it appears that the softest sandstone blocks are placed here, which when subjected to exposure to weather upon both faces, heightens the sense of designed decay.

Nature is invading this space and that will only be accentuated over time. Outside of the temple to the south are scattered blocks of sandstone that augment the sense of the ruin, spatial decomposition that illuminates the temporal nature of architecture.

Of Revealing

> The ultimate meaning of any building is beyond architecture; it directs our consciousness back to the world and our own sense of self and being. Significant architecture makes us experience ourselves as complete embodied spiritual beings.
>
> *Pallasmaa 2005: 11*

If our construct of the potential of 'archaeology' in uncovering essences is to be considered credible, it must hold the capacity to reveal. We both came here with preconceptions, predispositions and expectations. Our a priori academic studies had exposed to us both a sense of the primordial cave, a place of retreat, prospect and reason. Yet our experience here has illuminated that this is one of a number of subtle and complex multi-layer experiential conditions Utzon has provided. Being within our existential cave has facilitated reflection, immersion, contemplation and, of course, speculation. The intensity of our experience has revealed much. Our a priori readings of place were, upon honest reflection, somewhat flawed and certainly incomplete. The abstract impressions of this place garnered through photographic images, drawings, and critical writing, engendered certain preconceptions that we brought with us and once *in situ*, we struggled to overturn.

Through an intense process of persistent reflection, immersion, contemplation and, of course, speculation, we have been led by Utzon towards new conclusions: this is a place that is house and harbour village, this is a place inhabited by incredibly subtle geometric alignments, this is a place of tectonic ambitions where wall, column, lintel and roof are not only given expression, but bring revelation of Utzon's 'seed'. It is of seed and nature's principle of growth, an essay in the mysteries and tangibility of the origins and the everyday, and reveals, day after day, yet another layer of the potential that architecture holds to narrate and dignify our existence.

It is no accident that we have described Can Lis as a series of urban artefacts. At the gatehouse we arrive and are distributed according to various ordinations of formality, intimacy, purpose and familiarity. To the west lie the public artefacts of *agora* and temple. To the east, *chora* and *domus*. While these caves are resonant within the realm of domesticity, the *agora* and temple are public space of gathering. Can Lis is in Alberti's construct both house and city; in this case as harbour village rather than city.

Other layers have emerged. Utzon's idea of 'seed' is given expression through the articulation of a distinct palette of tectonic elements: the door, the window, the

FIGURE 4.26 Essences.

opening, the wall (and absence of wall), the column, the lintel, the roof. These elements are variously but always precisely disposed, providing a coherent tectonic language that speaks simultaneously of the archaic and of modernity. The choice of material is equally deliberate and precise. The soft sandstone is muted in shadow and animated in light. The mass and density of the material root it to site yet simultaneously allowed Utzon to build his metaphors with substance and meaning.

We discovered subtly and nuance in Utzon's response to landscape. Utzon's humility in pivoting the plan around existing mature trees, and our sense that the section of the house is *of* the cliff rather than *on* the cliff. The intention to design spaces that hunker down in the tradition of Danish vernacular, behind the wind wizened pines that cling tenaciously to the cliff top, affording both wind protection and summer shade. The humility to let nature in rather than strive to resist and control it. These subtleties extend to climatic response, ensuring spaces are orientated appropriately to purpose, that inhabitants may shift location dependent upon climatic conditions and time of day and season, by designing spaces that exhibit diverse climatic conditions. Utilising nature's processes of natural ventilation in cooling all spaces, enhanced by natural shading, brings simultaneously cool interiors and contact with the landscape beyond.

Can Lis also articulates the cultural, social and architectural spirit of Utzon's zeitgeist. He invites us to think profoundly upon excessive consumption and what is 'enough'. He invites us to think deeply upon the nature and conditions of dwelling. He inhabits the modernist predilection for precision in morphological alignments and tectonic detail. And within this place is a clear ambition to suggest that there are more dignified, less depleting and more poetic paradigms of dwelling that recognise vernacular ways, and suggests a new order that may helpfully carry us into the future.

However, one is left with a predominant sense that Utzon was directed by the *acts* of architecture. He has made here, places to gather, places of solitude, places of conviviality, places of contemplation, and places to stand, sit, view, walk, talk, places to be silent and places to be naked. This has been our fundamental revelation. In this age of immediacy and the apparent authority of the visual image, this focus upon the *acts* rather than the *objects* of architecture is inspiring, refreshing and moving.

Can Lis is Utzon's seed and nature's principle of growth; this place is an essay in the mysteries of the origins and everyday existence, and reveals, day after day, yet another layer of the potential that architecture holds to narrate and dignify our being-in-the-world.

To be clear, this is not a point of finality in our archaeology of Can Lis, or indeed Utzon. This is the work of a lifetime and beyond, but we sense that if our early hypothesis set out in this writing is credible, our experience of, and immersion within, the actual physicality of Can Lis will have in some way shifted and enhanced our understanding of the particularity of this place. It has.

Such an admission supports the initial hypothesis that the archaeological *experience* of architecture may better inform our understanding of what it is to make place poetically.

Of Epilogue

As our existential conversations draw to a close in Can Lis, this writing too draws to a close. Soon it will be time for the gatekeeper to walk along the streets and across squares to lock up this harbour village for the last time.

If anything, the time spent in Can Lis has reminded us (if we needed reminding) that 'this thing called theory' is not a quantitative condition but rather is a qualitative phenomenon, and that theoretical praxis can return to the 'happy garden' of 'simply dropping things', in the words of Eagleton and Payne earlier in this chapter.

We close with the words of Reuben Wheeler:

> The aim of life and the business of education should be the development of the ability to interpret experience to the end of perceiving reality. And this reality is something, which cannot be measured, analysed, reduced to constituent parts or embalmed in a set of rules. It is something which is perceived through religion, through science or through the act of profoundly living.
>
> *Wheeler 1968: 3–4*

And if this thing called theory is able once again to return to its origin of meaning, we may be encouraged to contemplate or speculate upon engaging with archaeological processes that may reveal the essence of the things themselves.

That is a beautiful idea.

Notes

1 Richard Leplastrier (1939–), RAIA gold medallist and RIBA International Fellow. All quotes from Leplastrier in this chapter are from contemporaneous notes taken in conversation with the author in April 2012.

2 Bernard Rudofsky, an architect who was responsible for an exhibition entitled 'Architecture without Architects' held at MOMA New York (1964–1965) and wrote the book of the same title published in 1964 to accompany the exhibition.

3 The text that follows was written in collaboration with Nørskov-Eriksen while her guest in a period of residency in Utzon's Can Lis house in April 2016. The house became the lens through which, in the spirit of Utzon, we discussed the role of theory in architecture and speculated upon the poetry and meaning of this special place.

4 'I come now to private buildings. We earlier described the house as a miniature city. With the construction of a house, therefore, almost everything relevant to the establishment of a city must be taken into account: it should be extremely healthy, it should offer every facility and ever convenience to contribute to a peaceful, tranquil, and refined life' (Alberti 1987).

References

Alberti, L. B. 1987. *The Ten Books of Architecture: The 1755 Leoni Edition*. Mineola, NY: Dover.

Curtis. W. J. 1982. *The Problem of Regional Identity in Modern Architecture Since 1900*. Oxford: Phaidon.

Eagleton, T. and Payne. M. 1991. *The Significance of Theory*. Chichester: John Wiley & Sons.

Frampton, K. 2001. *Studies in Tectonic Culture: The Poetics of Construction in Nineteenth and Twentieth Century Architecture*. Cambridge, MA: MIT Press.
Latour, A. (ed.). 1991. *Louis Kahn – Writings, Lectures, Interviews*. New York: Rizzoli.
Pallasmaa, J. 2005. *The Eyes of the Skin: Architecture and the Senses*. Chichester: John Wiley & Sons.
Pare, R. 1996. *The Colours of Light*. London: Phaidon Press.
Prip-Buus, M. 2009. *Jørn Utzon Logbook, Vol 5: Additive Architecture*. Hellerup: Blondal.
Thompson, D. W. 1917. *On Growth and Form*. Cambridge: Cambridge University Press.
Weston, R. 2002. *Utzon*. Hellerup: Blondal.
Wheeler, R. 1968. *Man, Nature and Art*. Oxford: Pergamon Press.
Zumthor, P. 1998. *Thinking About Architecture*. Basel: Birkhäuser.

5

SVERRE FEHN – THE STORYTELLER

> For Fehn, light, dark, fire and water have always been the physical dualities out of which the presence of place has been constituted and from this comes the political sense of 'civitas' that is brought into being with the feudal hearth, the public well, the Stoa, the Market Hall, the Butter-cross, the Cathedral and the Moot Hall. Fehn finds the domestic equivalent for such institutions in the hearth laid into the depths of the house and in the time honoured ritual of the family bath. The crackle of the fire, the gurgle of water, the hiss and surface sensation of steam; for Fehn all these sensations characterise the fullness of the traditional home.
>
> *Fjeld 1983: 15*

Fehn was the storyteller. There was narrative in all that he did and those stories were not a conceit. Their purpose was to reacquaint us with all that we have forgotten, and in that process, ground us in our own existence in the particularity of place. At the core of the narrative sits landscape.

Fehn was born in the small provincial mining town of Kongsberg, eastern Norway, in 1924. He completed his studies in Architecture at what is now known as the Oslo School of Architecture and Design in 1949, joined the Progressive Architects Group Oslo, Norway (PAGON) in 1950, and made his seminal trip to Morocco in 1952–1953. He married Ingrid Løberg Petersen in 1952 and their son Guy was born in 1960. Upon the receipt of a state scholarship, Fehn worked in the office of Jean Prouvé in Paris from 1953 to 1954 and during this time was a frequent visitor to the office of Le Corbusier.

Upon his return to Oslo, Fehn opened his practice and remained active until his death in February 2009. Fehn became professor at the Oslo School of Architecture and Design in 1971 until 1985 and also taught at MIT, Cooper Union New York and the Architectural Association in London. He was awarded the Académie

Française d'Architecture Gold Medal in 1993, and the Heinrich Tessenow Gold Medal and the Pritzker Prize for Architecture in 1997.

> The isolation of the North translated the world far beyond the horizon into dreams and fairy tales. The farther North one travelled, the more natural barriers formed through the harsh climate, and this influenced society.
>
> *Fjeld 2009: 11*

Of the three nation-states that were home to our protagonists, it is the climate and landscape of Norway that presents the greatest challenges for humans to dwell within. Norway is 385,000km^2 in area and one-third of that territory lies within the Arctic Circle, where temperatures have been recorded as low as –50°C. Extending from 13° to 71° latitude in the north, the craggy coastline is rugged with some 50,000 islands lying off the mainland. Norway is dominated by the Swedish mountain range having an average elevation of 460 metres, 32 per cent of the landmass lies above the tree line and there are significant variations in climate between north and south.

Such conditions shape people and by implication shape society. This is not a place of gregarious communing in sunlit village squares of the south. This is more a place of retreat from the harsh conditions. Retreat into a place of innerness; here the efficacy of the dwelling, as mediator of climate, is of huge importance both physically and emotionally. This is the Danish sense of '*hygge*' to the power of ten. This is also a place of mythology.

Landscape and climate were central to an embodied sense of the presence of a mythical 'otherness'; a force greater that man. Mountains soaring above fjords, the dark dense woodland and shimmering lakes combined with naturally occurring events such as the aurora borealis that must have inspired a sense of wonder and suggested to the ancients a metaphysical dimension to human existence.

This Norse mythology that is implicit within Fehn's understanding of place is rooted within the pre-Christian pagan world. Belief systems evolved that were influenced by the specific climatic and landscape conditions of this place. The pagans believed in deities such as Odin, Thor, Freya and Loki, each of whom held roles within the spiritual structure and were each ascribed certain powers. Giants and trolls further populated this spiritual realm. The Vikings believed that their destiny was in the hands of deities and spirits with the ultimate goal being transcendence to Valhalla. After conversion to Christianity, many of these beliefs remained and were fused within the new spiritual tradition; for example, finials and internal decoration of ancient sites of Christian worship such as Borgund Stave Kirke (Borgund Stave Church), that presents artefacts and imagery such as gargoyles (defence against evil spirits) and carvings of the one-eyed Odin. This embodiment of pagan spirituality with the new tradition provided a very particular version of Christianity firmly rooted in place.

These traditions were not contained to what we now understand to be Norway. Parallel narratives arose in Finland, in the form of the Kalevala. Similar structures of

FIGURE 5.1 Norwegian Landscape.

FIGURE 5.2 Borgund Stave Kirke, Norway.

FIGURE 5.3 Villa Sparre.

deities emerged again, ascribed specific powers. Inculcated within this tradition was the role of the shaman, who had the ability to communicate with the underworld. Nature and ordinary life were populated by magic and sorcery and in the more remote areas of Finland such spiritual traditions were maintained until the nineteenth century.

Again, the spirits within the epic genre were rooted to place. The bear, the rock, fire, frost, snow, snake and water provided the elemental structure and characterisation. Given the sheer longevity of this tradition these mythologies are clearly embedded within the Nordic psyche and resonate today.

A parallel yet distinct tradition exists in Denmark, perhaps exemplified by the writings of Hans Christian Andersen (1805–1875). He is most famous for his children's stories although he was a prolific author across several genres. His fairy tales, many reinterpretations of tales he heard as a child, were imbued with a strong sense of morality that encompassed the danger of ego ('The Emperor's New Clothes'), systematic abuse and bullying ('The Ugly Duckling') and of course love and sacrifice ('The Little Mermaid'). These threads of morality are woven through the texts in a manner reminiscent of Aesop's Fables or the storytelling traditions of Morocco. This dimension of morality is reflective of the Nordic sense of *civitas* and represents particular social and cultural mores that resonate to this day.

The elements that provide the complex narrative that comprise Fehn's particular paradigm may be encapsulated as shown in Figure 5.4.

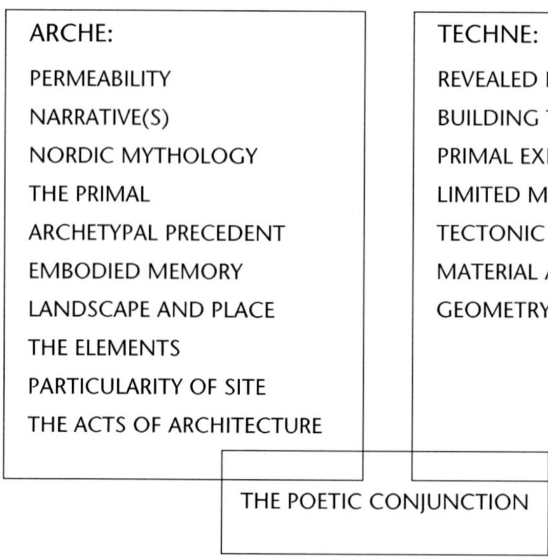

FIGURE 5.4 Fehn's Paradigm.

Of Arche

Fehn's permeability resides in his ability to absorb and embody a sense of landscape and mythology that is particular to Norway, and through built narrative reveal these conditions to us.

Perhaps nowhere is the importance of narrative, its exposure of the metaphysical dimensions of existence, and rootedness to place, better exposed that in Christian Norberg-Schultz's introductory chapter to the book *The Concept of Dwelling: On the Way to Figurative Architecture* (Norberg-Schulz 1985).

Norberg-Schulz retells the short story 'The Last Man Home' by the Norwegian writer Tarjei Vesaas and exposes the complex inter-relationships between place, the poetic dimension of human existence and what it is 'to be' in these circumstances. The central character of the tale is a young man called Knut, out in the forest to cut timber. He stayed longer than his peers and, once alone, he began to witness how the forest 'prepares itself for the night' (Norberg-Schulz 1985: 3). As the forest disclosed itself, it whispered 'Here you are at home, Knut' (Norberg-Schulz 1985: 9). Here, the use of the word 'home' is of real significance as it exposes the embodiment of landscape as place and locates us within that which Norberg-Schulz suggests is an 'objective truth which is accessible to everyone, but only if the mind is open' (Norberg-Schulz 1985: 9).

The title of the story tells, however, of another dimension of the word 'home': *domus*, the place of dwelling that mediates the climate. In this context, Vesaas exposes the fundamental human need for a fixed spot in which to dwell. For Knut, this other 'home' is a firm anchor in the harbour that is the forest. Given this literal and metaphorical context, it is no accident that Sverre Fehn was imbued with such narratives.

> Fire and water have always been the focus for the places people gather. These elements are opposed in character and are by their very nature social.
>
> *Fjeld 1983: 50*

As storyteller, Fehn exposes these primal narratives to us. At a literal level these narratives are laid bare within his extensive writing. He writes of place; for example, his journey(s) to Morocco that provide a tangible sense of atmosphere. He writes of Venice in a manner that would appeal to John Ruskin, describing it on one hand as the city of the thief and the salesman, yet simultaneously suggesting that 'Venice discovered light and colour'. He also conceptualises and speculates within his writing of core architectonic elements such as silence, light and shadow, of colour, of texture, tectonics and material.

His narratives are also explored within his speculative sketches; consistently identifying the sea, the ship, the horizon, the hearth, the forest and the minuscule scale of humans on the surface of the earth as being embedded within his psyche. Some of these sketches have a mythological quality, of characters flying in space on carpets, and others take on cosmic scales of consideration such as 'Sketch of Villa

Rotunda' (1984–1985) and 'The Discovery of an Object' (1992). Other sketches explore embodied memory such as 'A Child's First Meeting with its Column' (1993). Regardless of the means by which Fehn articulated his narratives, they are not only embedded within his work but also clearly inform it.

Villa Sparre floats across the momentous rock outcrop, the floor-line etching a new built horizon in the sky when viewed from the road below. The Skådalen School for Deaf Children is in its morphology resonant of the hill villages of the Mediterranean; as the buildings appear to tumble down the hill to be met by the playground; perhaps redolent simultaneously of the village square and of Plato's *chora* (discussed in Chapter 2); the woven mat on which we might dance.

The Oslo Architecture Centre is a narrative of the landscape; of shards and fractured ice reborn as glazing, the mass of the mountain reborn as concrete. The Glacier Museum is even more explicit in the same narrative of landscape in synthesising the dynamic form of the glaciers it celebrates. The geometry of the external stairs lifts the eye from the everyday of the ground plane up into the mountains beyond, and then above to the sky; Heidegger's realm of the deities.

Inculcated within these narratives is a sense of connection to agencies of greater significance than man. When writing of the origin of the room, Fehn takes us to the forest and writes of the hunter lighting a fire in a clearing and as day gives way to night, the throw of the light from that fire defines the first room. I speculate that this conceptualisation is embodied within all of us in the sense of holding a real

FIGURE 5.5 The Glacier Museum.

FIGURE 5.6 Skagestad House Stair.

sense of the comfort and security that the fire and its light provide. Yet, within the Nordic world I suggest that this sense is amplified in the embedded wisdom that suggests that outside of the throw of the light lay the spirits of the forest, some good, some evil and some, of course, benign. I suggest that this is far from being a romantic or fanciful notion, but rather deeply set within the Nordic psyche and given the sheer scale of landscape in Norway, is perhaps magnified further.

Fehn was inculcated with the primal. It became a way of seeing. The primal was for Fehn a way of revealing the origin and responding to and reinterpreting that revelation. The site of Villa Busk, for example, is populated as it is by dense vegetation and forest, but Fehn saw beyond those appearances to the topography and geology that represent the origins of that place, and that way of seeing allowed the house to gather the landscape; just as Heidegger's bridge gathers the banks.

Many of Fehn's narratives describe the primal; that of the origin. Like Aalto and Utzon, Fehn sought out the origins of things. He too travelled to places of 'cultural density' where such origins may still be apparent, and again like Utzon, brought such discoveries home. This represents another dimension of Fehn's permeability: the ability to travel, observe and speculate upon that revealed and subsequently, in the manner of Utzon, reinterpret. It is clear from his own writing that his first trip to Morocco in 1951, on the advice of Jørn Utzon, had a seminal impact upon Fehn and he returned with his students in 1987. As he subsequently wrote, 'I went to Morocco not to discover new things but to recollect what has been forgotten' (Fjeld 2009: 42).

In Morocco both Utzon and Fehn discovered archetypal precedents that would consistently inform their respective oeuvres. In locations such as Ait Benhaddou in the High Atlas Mountains, Fehn witnessed that the landscape was being gathered and revealed to us by the vertical walls of the village, casting particular geometries of shadow that only verticality provides. He wrote of the idea of the indeterminable space of the desert as he wrote, 'a space without dimension' (Fjeld 2009: 42). Perhaps most importantly, he reflected upon the timeless quality of architecture that he discovered and suggested that the builder's signature was anonymous 'because it is nature itself' (Fjeld 2009: 42).

FIGURE 5.7 Stair in the Bødker House.

Such a sense resides perhaps in our individual and collective embodied memory that Fehn consistently invites us to draw upon in each of his projects. In the Skådalen School, we are invited to adopt the scale of a small child in bending sufficiently to see out of the windows to the ramp that he positioned at the eye height of a child. In the Skagestad House (1962–1964), we are invited to adopt a Narnia-like persona as we climb the stairs; stairs conceived of as furniture.

Yet in the Carl Bødker House, the stairs are treated as a monolith, the floor apparently being raised to 40° like a pass in the High Atlas Mountains. The purposeful use of the same material for stair and wall through its apparently seamless

FIGURE 5.8 Hedmark Museum.

conjunction suggests that each are of each other in the manner in which landscape and walls conjoin in the High Atlas hill village of Ait Benhaddou, in Morocco.

> Architecture is bound to situation. Unlike music, painting, sculpture, film and literature, a construction (non-mobile) is intertwined with the experience of place. The site of a building is more than a mere ingredient in its conception. It is the physical and metaphysical foundation.
>
> *Holl 2007: 9*

These words from Steven Holl represent a coalescence of attitudes towards place, held by both Holl and Fehn; the concept that place is born of landscape, gathers landscape and encourages landscape to reveal itself to us through the lens of place. As Holl suggests, in this manner we consider 'site' in all of its dimensions: the physical *and* the metaphysical.

The Glacier Museum mediates between the lake and the glacier; its form while an abstract representation of the glacier, through orientation and disposition of architectural elements such as roof and stair, leads the eye to the landscape it abstractly represents.

At the Hedmark Museum, Fehn reveals the landscape of the original building through precise and differentiated insertion; this is not an act of mimesis; rather a purposeful narrative of placing of contemporary objects within the historic shell, in the manner of Carlo Scarpa at Castelvecchio in Verona, or the Querini Stampalia in Venice.

FIGURE 5.9 Bødker House Fire.

FIGURE 5.10 Bødker House Snug.

The four elements of earth, fire, water and air are integral facets in Fehn's paradigm and, I would propose, the Nordic psyche. The hearth is an essential element of Fehn's paradigm, used consistently as an organising element in space but simultaneously acknowledging the deep-seated sense of security that it provides and becomes the focus of gathering. In Villa Sparre, the fire delineates space, in the Bødker House there are two: one serving the cosy snug at ground floor level that has the arch of the stair at its head, the second directly above that delineates the living space.

Water is treated with equal respect to fire. If we take the example of bathing spaces, for Fehn this act is clearly associated with primal processes that take on a quality of ritual and performance. Nowhere is this more evident than at Villa Busk, where the bath terminates the plan and opens to the landscape like a primal forest pool. Earth is celebrated by stereotomic acts of carving mass and air celebrated in the weaving of lightness of roofs and screen walls.

A central element of Fehn's architecture is particular response to the particular place. In this sense site is for Fehn an element of chora (Chapter 2) that signals the possibility of becoming, revealing that place to itself and to us. In the Hedmark Museum project, the site is the existing stone barn and Fehn's intervention is conceived of an insertion that reveals the stone-ness of the stone and the barn-ness of the barn.

Yet all these elements of Fehn's Arche are supported and enhanced by Fehn's deep understanding of the *acts* of architecture. For Fehn, architecture is clearly born of human acts, to retreat, to gather, to bathe, to cook and to sleep, and an equally deeply held sense of the fundamental nature of what it is to dwell in refuge, prospect and reason. It is these acts, the verbs of architecture, that inform the development of the *objects* of architecture, the nouns.

The snug of the Bødker House is an exemplar of such an understanding. To reach it you descend from the light-filled floor above into stereotomic mass, where natural light is diminished. Here are placed three chairs and a low table aligned with the hearth, and the stair wraps the space like a scarf. Here is a place of intimacy, retreat and refuge. A place where we can simply 'be'; seemingly within the bowels of the earth itself.

FIGURE 5.11 Skagestad House.

Yet, the platform of Fehn's Arche lies in his sense of craftsmanship. As Heidegger suggested to us (Chapter 2), there is a *need*, we *build* and within that act of building there is *poetry*, because man is at heart poetic. Fehn is an exemplar in this respect, connecting the head to the hand, the idea to the manifestation of the idea, at all scales of architectural endeavour.

His craftsmanship spans scales. At one level it is the parti diagram. At another level it is the intuitive sense of the acts of architecture. It is the window that separates ventilation from view, or the light fitting or the door handle. This ability to cross scale is redolent of similar abilities we identify of course in Aalto.

Of Techne

> The use of a given material should never happen by choice or calculation, but only through intuition and desire.
>
> *Fjeld 1983: 46*

Here we are directed by Fehn to draw from our intuition in order to make or reveal place. For Fehn that intuition is directly connected to his narrative, and that narrative is itself embodied within broader narratives of landscape, mythology, embodied memory, archetypal precedent, the four elements and the acts of architecture.

For Fehn, to build is to reveal the narrative, through layers of tectonic endeavour that provide the tangible built form in structure, construction and material. Each narrative is particular to the conditions of place: in the Bødker Houses we see a largely stereotomic approach, carving voids from mass. At Villa Busk we detect a dichotomy of carving mass and weaving light fabrics to drape over, forming roofs and framed glazed walls. These are the revealed narratives.

Yet part of the narrative is the narrative of place, the way in which Fehn draws from the particularity of place, effectively 'building the site'.

At Skagestad House (1962–1964) as one climbs the steep steps up to the front door, one has a sense of departure from the everyday and as one ascends, crossing a threshold and entering the intimate world of *domus* beyond. The escarpment provided by the site allows entry into the bowels of the house and upon ascending the stairs to the floor above and moving into the lounge with our back towards the hearth our eyes are drawn to the glazed wall of the cave mouth that transports of view to the spectacular landscape beyond. Fehn 'builds the site' utilising these primal archetypes.

Building the site was clearly a constant preoccupation for Fehn. The Glacier Museum is an abstracted representation of the powerful landscape that it celebrates. In the Hedmark Museum, the purposeful articulation of the inserted route reveals the qualities and form of the existing building. These techniques resonate in the work of Jørn Utzon, evidenced through the morphological disposition of the elements of Can Lis and the primary tactic of defining the plateau for the Sydney Opera House project.

Of course primal expressions dive deep into our individual and collective memories and resonate of Fehn's narratives of landscape, mythology, embodied memory, archetypal precedent, the four elements and the acts of architecture discussed earlier in this chapter, that in the terms of Maurice Merleau-Ponty are the 'things themselves'.

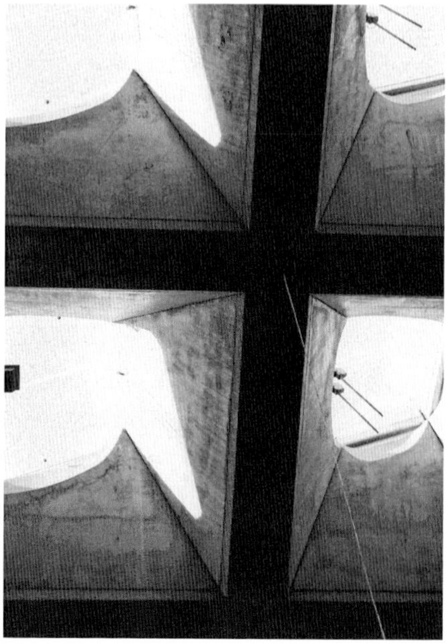

FIGURE 5.12 Publisher's House, Oslo.

These primal expressions in all of Fehn's projects are revealed through his attitudes of craftsmanship and tectonic precision. The articulation of joints mattered to Fehn, as did how the building meets the ground, the nature of threshold, the appropriate nature of material used and of course tectonic expression in exposing structural elements as a key ingredient of the developed narrative. He wrote:

> Construction is with me from the very beginning, but it takes time for the project to find its structure. The story I am seeking must be edited, and how much of the story shall the structure decide?
>
> *Fjeld 1983: 182*

Fehn's tectonic narrative is always revealed with less. He, like Aalto and Utzon, used a very limited material palette and one has a sense that such a tactic was deliberate. If we return to Gottfreid Semper's writing on the essential nature of architecture we identify both the stereotomic and the woven in Fehn's projects each given presence through few materials. The stereotomic elements are given expression through stone, brick and concrete, which appear as carved platonic solids. The woven is the narrative of timber and glass, the warp and weft of the weave. In this Fehn reveals tectonic precision, every junction and joint is carefully considered and articulated in order to reveal the desired primal expression.

Yet one has a sense that within this tectonic precision rests the type of craftsmanship that Richard Sennett (2008) writes of, qualities of execution of any act that demands we do a job well, for its own sake. Such craftsmanship and materials are revealed in light. There is an almost Kahnian sense of the admittance or exclusion

FIGURE 5.13 Villa Busk.

of light within Fehn's projects. The huge roof-lights of the Publisher's House project in Oslo allow us to locate ourselves in space and time within this cavernous space, and in contrast, the clerestory lights of the roof of the Bødker House I apparently allows the roof to float free of the wall. Similarly the clerestory lights on the south wall of Villa Busk invite the winter sun to enter but exclude summer sun, yet simultaneously appear to detach the wall and roof allowing the stereotomic and woven elements to be revealed.

Organising this symphony of devices in rigorous geometry and spatial articulation of the plan is redolent of architects such as Glenn Murcutt and before him, Mies van der Rohe. The Hedmark Museum project is defined by its ramps and walkways that ascend to the exhibition (internally) and descend from the exhibition (externally) designed as a promenade through space. But it is perhaps the plan of the A. Bødker House (1961–1965) that is the clearest example of Fehn's use of geometry; the red brick walls are orientated at 45° to the façade, creating a gallery space for the exhibition of his client's art collection.

While each of the paradigmatic elements described above articulate Fehn's design tactics each standing alone to not explain the poetic and metaphysical qualities of his work. Each of the elements contributes to these qualities but as is the case with Aalto's and Utzon's oeuvres there are almost inexpressible qualities to the projects, which I term the poetic conjunction.

Of Poetic Conjunctions

Existential Conversations in a Cave 3: The Fundamental Nature of Dwelling

The Degenerate Noun and the Generative Verb Seen through Anthony's Eyes

This chapter posits the potential of the *acts* of architecture (the verbs) informing the *objects* of architecture, the nouns. Architects ponder endlessly upon the essence of what it is to dwell poetically. We speculate, and we theorise in order to arrive at that great 'truth', yet as I discovered recently, that essence resides within each of us if only we were open to it. Perhaps with the passage of time we increasingly distance ourselves from such embodied wisdom.

> The roots of our understanding of architecture lie in our childhood, in our youth; they lie in our biography.
>
> *Zumthor 2006: 65*

Anthony is my wife's four-year-old nephew. He and his two sisters came to stay for a weekend and after two full days of laughter and adventures he sat on the sofa and quietly asked me, 'Uncle Roger, can we build a den?' My reaction? Well of course we could. As an architect and now teacher of architecture my 'den-ness' knew no bounds. However, as I soon learnt, Anthony, not me, was in control.

He began by surrounding himself on the sofa with cushions, building them higher until he had disappeared within. He had made *refuge* but it was unsatisfactory because he had lost all relation with that which surrounded him and I guessed that was in some way threatening. How could he defend himself from his sisters, if he was unaware of their approach? Almost immediately the cushions were abandoned, scattered across the floor in frustration.

'What else can we use, Uncle Roger?' he demanded. I suggested bath towels; we could hang them between sofa-back and dining table providing a roof. We did just that, and Anthony gathered his cushions and took them in under his roof … giggling. Some cushions were seats, others became walls but he had, in the simplest possible way, defined dwelling as both *refuge* and *prospect.* Yet something was missing …

'Uncle Roger, will you be a lion?' Happy to oblige, on all fours I prowled around roaring, which had the effect of making Anthony's giggles uncontrollable. His 'dwelling' was complete; *refuge, prospect* and what I term *reason*; the lion was Anthony's reason why refuge and prospect were required.

Anthony was driven by the verb. The actuality and materiality of the object were secondary to his pursuit of the *act* dwelling. He made place from available material and space. What was clear to me was his innate desire to retreat, make place and in the sense that Heidegger would understand; *to be.*

> Poetry is what first brings man onto the earth, making him belong to it, and thus bringing him into dwelling.
>
> *Heidegger 1971: 218*

Anthony dwelt poetically. Certainly his pragmatic needs were met. He had *refuge* and of course *prospect* and, albeit as an afterthought, *reason.* Here was a young man in control, holding a real sense of *being,* in the Heideggerian sense of that term. He had some control, territory and refuge, paradoxically in the most benign and invented context. He had through his act inhabited the verb and formed the noun.

With a real sense of humility I realise that Anthony taught me much that day. I had pontificated for years regarding the essence of architecture, intuitively having a sense of the importance of 'the origins of things', yet not knowing how to articulate that intuition. In that afternoon, a four-year-old boy had exposed to me the essence of my subject. He had exposed the verb of the act of dwelling; the noun of course followed; the object within which to dwell, but for Anthony, the verb came first.

It was not that the noun was unimportant, but that it was the verb that drove the making of the noun. It became clear that the essence was delivered by the a priori value of the verb informing the development of the noun. For Anthony, the issue was not the actuality of the material nature of the noun, but how, when focused upon the verb, the noun fell into place. It became clear to me that the issue was not verb v. noun, but how they might conjoin … poetically. I have no sense that Anthony had been taught to build a den. It was an apparently intuitive act that we can all relate to; the primal need for place that offers us retreat and prospect, given sufficient reason.

> The dwelling is the theatre of our lives, where major dramas of birth and death, of procreation and recreation are played out, and, in which the succession of scenes of daily living are enacted, and re-enacted in the process of dwelling.
>
> *Oliver 2007: 17–18*

The noun objectivises architecture, and through the seductive images, anchors that objectivisation. As Pallasmaa suggests, the image provides a perceptual immediacy; but in semiotic terms, that immediacy is all too often an empty sign. Our contemporary world is increasingly dominated by the power of the image and nowhere is that clearer than in architecture. Magazines, websites and TV set the image in front of us, providing a seeming immediacy of understanding. Yet both literally and metaphorically, all those images are filtered through many lenses, each lens having a particular intent.

The sheer volume of such visual exposure ascribes an apparent absolute authority to the image, to the extent where our desire to understand what informs what we see, evaporates. This encourages a level of superficial understanding that resides only within the image of the object and encourages ever more, again literally and metaphorically, retouching; in search of a perceived perfection. This trend is of course a self-perpetuating mythology but, in turn, encourages a shift towards the superlative domain of architecture: biggest, tallest, longest …

> Yet how are we to achieve this wholeness in architecture at a time when the divine, which once gave us meaning, and even reality itself seem to be dissolving in the endless flux of transitory signs and images.
>
> *Zumthor 2006: 32*

In contrast, part of the value of the verb is that it is indeterminate. It does not presume outcome in terms of object, merely acknowledges the desire to develop an object. It focuses upon process, act and being. The verb is, by definition, devoid of pre-determined architectural solutions, and invites speculation upon possibility, rather than prescribing outcomes. The verb demands a response to the human condition and that in turn informs the development of the noun. With the verb we are forced to interrogate all that which sits in front of the noun, and is implicitly responsive to the diverse range of human needs, aspirations and potentials. To encourage the verb we need to develop points of resistance to the apparently absolute authority of the noun.

These points of resistance are provided through paradigmatic study of those who have in terms of theoretical positioning and/or the process of the synthesised design, clearly engaged with the potential of the verb. Immediately one would reference the Nordic spirit of Aalto, Utzon and Fehn, in understanding such concepts and praxis. Outside of this geographical realm, designers such as Louis Kahn, Carlo Scarpa, Richard Leplastrier and Peter Zumthor and others describe through their praxis and writings clear speculation regarding the core of existence. Additionally the phenomenological agendas of Juhani Pallasmaa, Stephen Holl and others represent a particular strand of engagement with the act of being. The philosophical strand (at least in modern history) reaches back to Heidegger with additional sediment and dimension supplied by Merleau-Ponty, Husserl and Sartre, and is discussed in Chapter 2.

However, within the creative realm of architecture the verb/noun relationship should not be considered as linear but rather providing two points between which the creative act may oscillate. What is clear in the theoretical position and praxis of those defined as exemplars (above) is that this process of oscillation between the verb and noun results in sublime design solutions that resolve the 'design problem' at metaphysical and physical levels of existence.

As Anthony showed me, the inner construction of the act of dwelling holds an embodied resonance that connects us all at some primal level of our common, and perhaps universal, existence. Yet, as individuals our particular interpretations will be unique, predicated upon our particular experiences; what Peter Zumthor describes as 'our biography'.

The potency of the verb encourages dialogue with act, being, and what, in place of a better term, we might call 'the poetic', albeit eventually expressed as a noun.

> Postmodern life could be described as a state in which everything beyond our own personal biography seems vague, blurred and somehow unreal. The world is full of signs and information that stand for things that no one fully understands because they, too, turn out to be mere signs for other things. Yet the real thing remains hidden.
>
> *Zumthor 2006: 32*

Villa Busk reveals to us meaning by exposing the origins of what it is to dwell in a visceral manner and that is Fehn's intention. Within my experience Villa Busk resonates with the primal acts of dwelling expressed poetically.

> 23rd January.1973. A long time has passed ... But the problems are more or less the same. What matters is to give form to what is already within us. To find an expression for the harmonious union of impulsive and intentional behaviour. In our formless existence-without fixed rituals of any sort there is little reason to have confidence in impulsive actions. Meditation on the various problems is necessary in order to solve them in a morally justified way.
>
> *From Fehn's sketchbook, reproduced in Helsing Almaas 2009*

FIGURE 5.14 The Villa Busk Tower from the West.

These words help hugely in uncovering Fehn's intention. There are key words that we might usefully focus upon:

- 'problems';
- 'rituals';
- 'meditation';
- 'morally justified'.

We will examine each of these in turn.

'Problems': Here Fehn acknowledges the loss of existential meaning and alludes later to the paucity of ritual within contemporary life. In acknowledging such loss he invites our transportation to earlier times when such rituals were implicit within human existence. This is not a plea to return to 'the good old days' but rather a suggestion that we might return to the origin of things to rediscover that which we have subsequently lost. Here Fehn takes us back to the forest, the stream, the fire and the landscape and invites rediscovery of our innerness and our being-in-the-world.

> [Fehn] has often commentated upon the effect of the slow loss of the understanding of the fire/water/earth relationship within a house: the changing conceptual awareness of places of rest and nourishment is moving the house away from a basic understanding of home to that of a temporary rest stop.
>
> *Fjeld 2009: 70*

We live within a compressed space–time continuum where communication flows instantly; we can physically travel from one side of the globe to the other within 24 hours and our conceptualisation of our existence is increasingly boundless. The authority of the nation-state is eroded, and in parallel our individual and collective sense of identity evaporates.

Fehn suggests a counterpoint and returning to Terje Welle-Busk's invitation to Fehn upon commission – in Villa Busk he makes a place 'to be.' He does this through narratives; the story of the hearth, the forest, the rock, and the bath utilising primal archetypes that our collective and embodied collective memory recognises and delights in.

'Rituals': Today we flick a switch and there is light. We turn a tap and there is water. We turn a knob or press a switch and we can cook. Where is the ritual in the microwave ready-meal? Fehn suggests to us that somehow we became poorer when the fire left the kitchen, when light became available through a finger-flick and water flowed conveniently, according to our will.

> Fehn argues that in the day-to-day rituals embedded in these two elements (fire and water) lies an aspect of time, in particular an aspect of waiting, and that this time aspect is a resistance force; it sets limits. Today a house is equipped to perform everything at all times with little or no effort. Basic no longer exists.
>
> *Fjeld 2009: 70*

'Meditation': Earlier in this book I explored the nature of theory in the context of architecture, and suggested there is a value of returning to the etymology of the word in discovering in its original term theory meant 'observation and speculation-upon'. Within the context of Fehn's use of the word *meditation* I see an interesting coalescence in that acts of meditation, observation and speculation-upon are acts that require time and by their very nature are counterpoint to much of our contemporary world. Perhaps there is something important in such words and their consequence for the architect.

'Morally justified': This is a term we hear rarely these days – rarely certainly in schools of architecture. Yet the position is resonant of the unique quality that characterises Nordic humane modern architecture; a sense of collective responsibility and ambition for collective, as opposed to individual, betterment. A sense that architecture has at its core social responsibility and the potential to enhance circumstances through appropriate practice.

In these few words Fehn captures both a spirit and a challenge. The spirit that is inculcated within this particular genre of architecture yet simultaneously defines the challenges faced. These challenges were surmounted by a four-year old boy, with some cushions, and a bath towel. An object lesson perhaps?

In his pioneering book *Architecture without Architects*, published in 1964, a companion text to his Museum of Modern Art Exhibition of 1964–1965, Bernard

Rudofsky provides a counterpoint to the modernist tendencies of his zeitgeist in the exploration of what he termed 'non-pedigree architecture'. In the preface Rudofsky suggests that the tradition of architectural history as taught in the Western world is selective and exclusive and captures only a very small proportion of the world's cultures. He explores the 'vernacular, anonymous, spontaneous, indigenous, rural' (Rudofsky 1964: preface 1).

He goes on to suggest:

> There is much to learn about architecture before it became an expert's art. The untutored builders in space and time – the protagonists of this show – demonstrate an admirable talent for fitting their buildings to their surroundings. Instead of trying to 'conquer' nature as we do, they welcome the vagaries of climate and the challenge of topography.
>
> *Rudofsky 1964: preface 2*

It is these primitive forms of architecture that Fehn sought when travelling to Morocco in rediscovering that which had been lost. In this context the term primitive is used in the original meaning rather than in its contemporary pejorative meaning:

> Primitive (adj.): Late 14c., 'of an original cause; a thing from which something is derived; not secondary', from Old French *primitif* 'very first or original' (14c.) and directly from the Latin *primitivus* 'first or earliest of its kind'.
>
> *Online Etymology Dictionary undated*

And so to Villa Busk. The house is located in Bamble in the Telemark region of Norway, some 200 kilometres west of Oslo. The area is characterised by rocky pine-covered headlands and inlets populated by a sparse distribution of 'seahouses'; summer homes, many of which have been handed down through generations. It was here that I met Terje and Astrid Welle-Busk. They commissioned Fehn after the land was gifted to Astrid and Terje as a wedding present by Astrid's parents who were local farmers.

The site is high on a rocky escarpment characterised by huge boulders that emerge from the surface of the earth, and the promontory away to the southwest turns to meadow and forest cleaved by a stream in the base of the valley that flows into the coastal inlet that is overlooked from the western end of the house.

Recounting the process of commissioning Fehn, Terje shared that upon being gifted the land they knew nothing of architecture. They bought books and journals to acquaint themselves with current trends in design but that brought them no further to choosing an architect. On a whim, Terje telephoned the National Association of Norwegian Architects (NAL) for advice and was told that they understood Sverre Fehn was looking for work. Terje telephoned Fehn and explained their situation, perhaps significantly telling Fehn not that they wanted a house designed, but rather they wanted a 'place for us to be'.

FIGURE 5.15 Villa Busk Wall.

Terje Welle-Busk told me of his first meeting on site with Fehn: standing on the westernmost boulder overlooking the fjord he told his assistant Heinrich to walk due east and he marched off into the undergrowth. When he emerged high upon the next significant bolder, Fehn shouted for him to halt. Turning to the Welle-Busks, Fehn stretched out his arms pointing towards his assistant and said: 'Here is your house'. And so it was.

> The Busk House was a fairy tale project. I clapped together a summer and a winter house in one project. The site had a beautiful view and a fantastic rock formation clinging to the sea. Here as in Palladio's Villas, summer breezes can ruffle silk shirts. What can sustain one when once again production is moved out into nature? Nature, the hillside is untouched. You can run around in this nature and scream, 'Here is beautiful'. And the daughters will have their own fairy tale: their home in the Tower.
>
> *Fjeld 2009: 217*

Villa Busk comprises three distinct elements each of which are generated from the particular landscape qualities of the site and of course orientation. Running east–west is main the body of the house, with a spine of circulation to the north that terminates in the living space to the west and gives way to the landscape to the east. To the south is the tower designed to provided distinct sleeping accommodation for the children with an independent spiral stair to the northeast corner that connects the bedrooms vertically and facilitates private access and egress to the tower; providing a sense of independence for the young inhabitants. These two elements are connected by a glazed linking element that floats high over the landscape mediating between tower and house that balances the independence of the spiral stairs with a sense of security in the umbilical bridge.

FIGURE 5.16 Villa Busk Tower.

The narrative of Villa Busk is complex. Of course it is about the particularity of place, but it is also about how Fehn mediates between landscape and man. The wrapping wall to the south of the main house signifies the containment of the *acts* of the house; gathering, cooking, dining, sleeping and abluting are distributed within this organisational element that evaporates at each end and builds relationship back to the landscape. The wall also terminates in the two fundaments of Fehn's architectural narrative: the hearth and the bath.

The density and materiality of this wall produces a profound sense of containment punctuated only by relatively small window openings that themselves separate the functions of view and ventilation. The circulation route to the north has a largely glazed façade and is populated with storage areas the project out from the spine that is defined by a steady rhythm of timber columns that support the distinctly articulated roof. The dense wall to the south provides a 'horizon' in the landscape over which the roofs float, propped by a clearly articulated structural system. In combination these elements expose Fehn's paradigm.

Villa Busk when viewed from the south appears to grow out of the rock of the landscape, the concrete wall soaring as the site falls away. The tower, separately articulated, is the place for young dreams and adventures, albeit connected by the umbilical glazed link that bridges to parents and safety. The tower is also in a semiotic sense a signifier of habitation within the landscape resonating of the

FIGURE 5.17 Villa Busk Entry Path.

lighthouse or church tower when seen from the sea; a marker of safety and human existence.

In Villa Busk there is nothing that is superfluous. The house presents us with a narrative of the essence of what it is to dwell, as Heidegger suggested, poetically. It is the cave and the rock-pool, the fire in the forest clearing, the monastic cloister and ambulatory, and the subterranean territory of Orpheus; the recording studio that sits deep within the landscape.

That narrative begins at the entrance pathway; the entry route, aligned precisely with the hearth angled obliquely to the house. It is here that the narrative of landscape commences. The orientation of the path towards the hearth provides a route of entry that is askew to the alignment of the house. The pathway appears to float across the landscape and as one walks towards the house and is captured by the canopy overhead we are confronted by the substantial rock outcrop that demands that our route must deflect in deference to the mass of the landscape. We are thus met by the northern façade and the door.

But to understand Fehn's depth of ambition we need to attune to embodied memory; memory that resides deep within each of us, allowing us to make sense of our presence in the world. Fehn consistently encourages us to (re?)connect with our own essence in the phenomenological understanding of place at liminal and sub-liminal levels.

This concept of collective embodied memory is a core component of Fehn's work that in Villa Busk is given expression in the sophisticated and carefully articulated placement of the hearth and the bath, the tower, acting as signifier of

FIGURE 5.18 The 'Bridges': Villa Busk.

FIGURE 5.19 The Stair from the 'Cave', Villa Busk.

human habitation in the landscape, the wrapping wall forming the cave and the open aspect to the north providing prospect and connection to the landscape beyond. A further tensile dimension is provided in linear form between the two outcrops of rock that define the extent of the house that effectively allow the house to bridge the landscape; another primal act of human habitation within the landscape. The bridge gathers the landscape.

> The bridge gathers to itself in its own way earth and sky, divinities and mortals.
>
> *Heidegger 1971: 153*

The concept 'bridge' with Villa Busk is both literal and metaphorical: literal in connecting the tower to the main body of the house, metaphorical in bridging between landscape elements. In this metaphorical sense, the house gathers the landscape in the manner that Heidegger suggests that the literal bridge gathers the banks. The two opposing rock outcrops to the east and west are mediated by the house and define the extent of habitation yet the porosity of the walls to the north, east and west provides the most ephemeral threshold between inside and outside; and the pine forest is invited inside by the eye.

Furthermore, when viewed from the valley to the south, the house provides a 'built horizon' for the site; the top of the wall presents a strong horizontal benchmark, another bridge, while the undulating landscape at the base in mediated by the subtle, once fluid and seamless concrete. Fehn's work is perhaps most characterised by the relationship he builds to landscape, and the way this informs the making of place. Inculcated within this paradigmatic element is a deep understanding of and drawing from the particularity of site.

In essence Villa Busk is elemental. It is possibly the closest that man can dwell within the landscape, a distillation of the nature of dwelling into primal components. It is the place of earth, fire, water and air, it is the place of the Heideggerian fourfold of earth, man, sky and deities. Despite the rigour of the plan and section that resonate of Fehn's debt to Le Corbusier, despite the intensity of intention, despite the deliberate articulation of space and despite the sheer design ambition applied, Villa Busk is an essay in less being so much more. Here man is humanised in place and time.

> In relation to the natural cycle, the animal's cave is perfection, but man's sense of fulfilment involves the creation of a 'room' through the act of constructive thought. To deny man his place is to dehumanise his being.
>
> *Fjeld 1983: 47*

Like any dense literary work, Fehn's narratives are multi-layered and complex and emerge gradually upon the reading of place. His archetypal precedents that are the objects or nouns of his oeuvre are central to the plot providing structure and form, yet they in turn reveal further narratives that are concerned with the acts (the verbs) of human existence.

The stair that transports us to the lounge from the lobby is set parallel to the rock outcrop that it climbs, each step set back from the walls that frame it providing two

FIGURE 5.20 The Hearth, Villa Busk.

FIGURE 5.21 View from the Tower, Villa Busk.

parallel sloping slots that mirror the line of the rock outside, effectively allowing the landscape to penetrate the space. One has the perception that the stair is the landscape and the landscape is the stair.

The lifting of the living space mounting the rock outcrop to the west of Villa Busk is a masterstroke. Here the primal essence of the cave resonates, the hearth frames the view to the sea, the landscape and thus to the sky and the deities beyond. The hearth is the place to gather, its corner positioning inviting a particular geometry of convening within the quarter circle it prescribes yet the small blue-glazed window adjacent to the fire provides spectacular yet precise vistas of the valley below that are only available if one lies on the floor. This is the place for young eyes

FIGURE 5.22 The Bath, Villa Busk.

to reconnect to this very particular place. Around the hearth, we are invited to commune and gather, conversations to be had, lit and warmed by the fire. The throw of the light from the fire defines our conceptualisation of room or *raum* as Heidegger suggests. Outside of the light is the territory of mystery, the unknown and perhaps the subliminally fearful. Yet within light and heat we are secure within that primal cave of human existence.

In the tower we (think that we) hold dominion over all that we survey. The ability of man to rise above the horizon through building has long been a desire. It is a (perhaps inane) typology of security; from Babel to San Gimignano and beyond man has sought literal and metaphorical elevation through building towards the domain of the deities. Such ambitions are reflected in folklore and fairy tales and as in the case of Villa Busk, when the tower is the territory of young imaginations, we can be transported to the worlds of Rapunzel, knights in shining armour or indeed the poetry of William Butler Yeats:

> I pace upon the battlements and stare
> On the foundations of a house, or where
> Tree, like a sooty finger, starts from the earth;
> And send imagination forth
> Under the day's declining beam, and call
> Images and memories
> From ruin or from ancient trees,
> For I would ask a question of them all.
>
> *William Butler Yeats, 'The Tower', 1928*

The bath, in contrast, demands nakedness.

> In an interview Fehn said that the bathroom is an extension of your clothes. It is a big costume that includes waste.
>
> *Fjeld 2009: 70*

FIGURE 5.23 The View from the Living Space, Villa Busk.

In most houses such activities are separated visually and acoustically. In Villa Busk these acts are exposed to the world; not in a voyeuristic sense but rather in the subtle visual permeability of the glazed wall to the east of the bath, inviting the landscape and light to bathe with us. Early morning the space is animated with shafts of direct sunlight that cast shadow and dynamically model the space. At the close of the day, the space is devoid of direct light inviting us to adopt a more contemplative and reflective circumstance. The bath is of such capacity to facilitate communal bathing that challenges extant social and cultural mores, encouraging conversation and interaction in that most exposed of human conditions: nakedness. In the bath one is within the forest, the fully glazed east wall evaporates and one enters a primal world that is embodied within the Nordic spirit. This is ablution in its most primal and essential state.

Sitting at the dining table adjacent to the kitchen in the evening, with the south wall enclosing and the glazed north wall exposing as the light spilled out into the surrounding forests, one has a real sense of the cave in a forest clearing and that one's presencing in the world is defined by the throw of the light from the room. Beyond the throw of that light is mystery, and it was not difficult to imagine woodland spirits, residing in the darkness. Similarly, the next morning after breakfast sipping

FIGURE 5.24 The Post and Stone Detail, Villa Busk.

coffee in the high living space atop the outcrop, the wall wraps the hearth and then dissolves as the cavernous opening admits the landscape to the eye. Looking down over the inlet below from this rocky promontory one has a sense of the privilege of the shelter of the cave on high.

Thus the revealing of the narratives provides the expression of the primal values inculcated with Fehn's paradigm. The *acts* of architecture are not only facilitated but are actively encouraged through revealing the narratives by the thoughtful act of construction. The narrative is further revealed and articulated through Fehn's particular language of *techne*.

> At the core of Fehn's architectural nature in a spatial attitude that is quite different to that of [Carlo] Scarpa. His work carries a clear posture belonging to structure, structure as a screen differentiating between inside and outside, light from shadow. For Fehn it is the structure that directs the story.
>
> *Fjeld 2009: 64*

Fehn is the exemplar of Frampton's etymological narrative upon the origins of the term 'tectonic'. Fehn's paradigm is that the narratives are revealed through the poetic and simultaneously tangible acts of constructing.

In this realm perhaps the primary element of Fehn's *techne* is tectonic precision and, of this, perhaps the exemplar is Villa Busk. One only has to focus upon the articulation of the posts that support the veranda to the northern facade of the house and the stones upon which it sits. The posts are carefully carved in three dimensions following the form of the stone they sit upon. The modernist tradition would perhaps

FIGURE 5.25 The Circulation Spine, Villa Busk.

provide articulation through separation of the two elements, possibly through the insertion of a steel pin housed into both the post and the stone. In rejecting such a solution Fehn points to a hierarchy of components in that the post must be shaped to the stone, not the stone cut to the post. Here the stone representing the earth, one of Fehn's 'elements' described earlier, holds primacy. The detail also acknowledges the very nature of the materials themselves. Stone being dense is more problematic to cut and shape. Timber, however, is much more amenable to being shaped. In this one detail, we witness the narrative of Heidegger's fourfold revealed.

The concrete stair leading from the lobby up to the lounge is drawn back from the external and internal walls that hold it, allowing the external landscape of the rock outcrop to apparently enter the space perceptually, the slope of the retroussé slots mirroring the non-orthogonal quality of the landscape beyond. Inlaid in the 'meagre' concrete stair are marble slabs, which celebrate the touch of foot upon floor.

Fehn's narrative extends to structure. On the southern façade, the mass concrete wall that provides a 'built horizon', gives way to a modulated system of timber frames that articulate the floating nature of roof and facilitate clerestory glazing that simultaneously reinforces this articulation and provides mediated south light to the internal spaces.

The mass concrete wall gives way to the rock at its base, following the contours of the territory and when seen through half-closed eyes from a distance is reminiscent of wave-forms generated as the ship that is Villa Busk carves through the landscape with the rock outcrop to the east; the bow wave, the outcrop to the west; the wake.

On the northern façade, the structural frame is taken to the ground, punctuated with openings and protruding storage elements that articulate the spine of circulation, and when viewed from the inside, this structural system is resonant of the pines in the forest beyond and encourages the eye to oscillate between the domain of man and the forest of mystery.

The glazed link to the timber clad tower to the south provides structural articulation through the geometry of its framing and the tower itself articulates the constancy of floating roofs through the clerestory glazing. In changing the nature of the wall construction from concrete to timber, a sense of emphasis is created that is perhaps resonant of the heritage of the stave church.

Internally other narratives emerge. Functions of view and ventilation are disassembled in openings in the wrapping concrete walls. The caulked flooring of the bathing space is reminiscent of the caulked deck of a ship and subliminally transports us to the heritage of the Vikings and their relationship to the sea.

Yet, within this complex narrative, the palette of material is small. Concrete, stone, timber and glass with slender inlays of marble to the stair are surely an object lesson to all aspiring architects. This is not architecture of excess, this is not architecture of superlatives; this is architecture of restraint and precision and all the more profound for its modesty.

Villa Busk is also an exemplar in Fehn's unique approach in 'building the site'; drawing from the particular qualities the site holds. Here I borrow from Richard Leplastrier's design method and teachings. He suggests that 'first comes the landscape'[1]

FIGURE 5.26 Ventilation and View Disaggregated, Villa Busk.

FIGURE 5.27 Bathing Space, Villa Busk.

in his approach to architecture and that his first tactic is to 'draw from the site'. He uses such analogies as 'drawing from the source', and drawing from the well', to reinforce his point. Fehn used similar attitudes in revealing to us the particular nature of particular place. At Villa Sparre, the rock promontory is amplified by the house that floats over it, at the School for Deaf Children the landscape is intensified by the clustered disposition of built form, and at Villa Busk, I would argue that the landscape is gathered, completed and revealed by the house.

The primary tactic is the conjoining of the two significant rock outcrops in the linear disposition of the plan and section. This ensures that the building is 'held' by the landscape in that its extent is defined by the natural phenomena of this place. The second tactic is in the purposeful disposition of the tower, which defines the site to the south and holds the bank as it tumbles down the valley towards the stream. The third and most subtle tactic is the dynamic positioning of the path of entry to the house that one discovers only upon entry is aligned to the heart of the house. The fourth tactic is that of dissipation; the dissipation of constructed form at the east and west ends of the house where in both instances, the rigour of wall gives way to glass, and the landscape is invited in by the eye.

Another dimension of Fehn's tectonic tendencies is his attention to light and acoustics. Decisions regarding orientation are the lowest hanging fruit for the architect in that such decisions are usually benign in terms of cost implications, and are ignored at our peril.

FIGURE 5.28 Conjunction of Concrete and Stone.

In Villa Busk the east–west orientation of the linear plan-form informs the placement of space; the bath to capture morning light, the living space to gather west light, the clerestory glazing above the concrete wall to the south admits mediated south light, and softer non-directional light from the north is admitted by the largely glazed wall to the north façade. These purposeful design tactics make for a dynamically lit interior within which one can chart human existence across the space-time continuum.

In addition the glazed walls to the north, east and west façades allow internal light at night to leak into the surrounding landscape providing an ethereal experience for the occupants, taking us back to the narrative of the clearing within the Nordic forest.

> We do not dwell because we have built, but we build and have built because we dwell, that is, because we are dwellers.
>
> *Heidegger 1971: 148*

At the core of human existence, and by implication architecture, is the primal need to dwell. For Heidegger dwelling was a poetic act; it is only we that hold the capacity to remove its poetic resonance. Furthermore, it is clear in Heidegger's paradigm that the *act* of dwelling (the verb) sits ahead of the *object* of dwelling (the noun).

Above all, Fehn was occupied by the *acts* of human existence and sought through the action of design to manifest primal spaces that facilitated those acts in a poetic manner, through which man reconnects with existential self. Nowhere is such ambition more present than at Villa Busk. Yet at many levels Villa Busk sits in counterpoint to the apparent concerns of much contemporary architecture.

> Being active confrontations and encounters, all basic architectural events have a verb-form rather than noun-form. Architecture is essentially an art of actions not forms.
>
> *Pallasmaa 2005: 319*

In conclusion I would suggest that young Anthony would feel very much at home in Villa Busk. This is the den, the cave, the forest, the rock-pool and as day gives way to night and the fire blazes in the hearth; the first room.

Note

1 Drawn from the author's own contemporaneous notes from Leplastrier's lecture at the Third International Utzon Symposium and Workshop held at the Dar El Bacha Palace, Marrakech, Morocco, April 2012.

References

Fjeld, P. O. 1983. *Sverre Fehn: Thoughts of Construction*. New York: Rizzoli International Publications Inc.

Fjeld, P. O. 2009. *Sverre Fehn: The Pattern of Thoughts*. New York: Monacelli Press.

Heidegger, M. 1971. *Poetry, Language, Thought*, tr. A. Hofstadter. New York: Harper & Row.

Helsing Almaas, I. 2009. He Won't Let Us Off that Easily: An Attempt to Understand Sverre Fehn. Retrieved 19 February 2017 from http://architecturenorway.no/stories/other-stories/iha-on-fehn-2009.

Holl, S. 2007. *Anchoring*. New York: Princetown Architectural Press.

Norberg-Schulz, C. 1985. *The Concept of Dwelling: On the Way to Figurative Architecture*. New York: Rizzoli International Publications.

Oliver, P. 2007. *Dwellings*. London: Phaidon Press.

Online Etymology Dictionary. Undated. Primitive. Retrieved 1 July 2016 from www.etymonline.com/index.php?allowed_in_frame=0&search=primitive.

Pallasmaa, J. 2005. *Encounters: Juhani Pallasmaa Architectural Essays*, ed. P. MacKeith. Helsinki: Rakennustieto Oy.

Rudofsky, B. 1964. *Architecture without Architects*. London: Academy Editions.

Sennett, R. 2008. *Craftsmanship*. London: Penguin Books.

Yeats, W. B. 1928. The Tower. In *The Tower*. London: Macmillan & Co.

Zumthor, P. 2006. *Thinking Architecture*. Basel: Birkhäu.

6

OF COMMONALITIES, DISTINCTIONS AND SPECULATIONS

> How the artist formulates his or her own expressions is singular, since they are a reflection of the artists personality; but common to all is the manipulation of intuition.
>
> *Fjeld 2009: 107*

This final chapter explores the common elements that sit within the paradigms of Aalto, Utzon and Fehn, and also examines the paradigmatic constituents that make each architect distinct. The chapter concludes, as is appropriate to the theoretical underpinning of the study, by speculating upon the influence of our three protagonists on contemporary architecture and the potential held to influence our discipline in the future.

Of Commonality – Of Arche

Given the heritage of humane Nordic modernism discussed within Chapter 1, it is perhaps of little surprise that there are commonalities between the paradigms of Aalto, Utzon and Fehn. Indeed were we to speculate further, we may discover these commonalities extend to the precedents of this particular heritage, as they are, for our protagonists, what we might describe as 'core' shared values.

Permeability is an embedded a priori condition that sat within Aalto, Utzon and Fehn. The term itself infers that there are both inward flows and outward flows possible and the use of the term is purposeful in that regard as such oscillations of direction characterise Aalto, Utzon and Fehn. In terms of 'inward flows' through this thin permeable veil: without that permeability our protagonists would not have seen beyond surface appearances and revealed the things themselves; as Heidegger enjoins; 'the thingness of things'. The primary focus of these inward flows was differently accented in each of our three architects. For Aalto, he was acutely aware of the cultural, political and economic shifts within his epoch. For Utzon, it was focused to be permeable to external influence whether that was through travel, a deep awareness of nature or indeed his ability to understand the 'placeness of place'. Fehn was permeable to landscape and the power of mythology embedded in place. He embraced such narratives and they became the initiator of his tectonic response.

The 'outward flows' for Aalto, Utzon and Fehn had conceptual commonality. Each reinterpreted that which they detected in built form. The incremental development and increasing sophistications of Aalto's canon of work, the poetic response to place with Utzon's portfolio and the gathering of landscape and anchoring to place, that in turn revealed place within Fehn's catalogue, are each testament to 'outward flows'.

A further common element of this permeability was understanding of and reinterpretation of what we might terms archetypal precedent.

Archetypal precedent is a transparently common value within each of the three paradigms. Using travel as a means of revealing the thingness of things, Aalto, Utzon, and Fehn journeyed variously to both shared and distinct destinations. All of these chosen locations, however, were places of cultural density and significance. One common destination for Aalto, Utzon and Fehn was Morocco and that is significant.

In Morocco, even to this day, if we are prepared to leave the tourist pathways and explore more adventurously, we are able to discover peoples acting in essentially the same way that their ancestors have acted over thousands of years. If we dust off the patina of the tourist veneer present in some of these locations, look below the surface of that which appears to us, and focus upon the things themselves, there is much to discover.

We might reveal the embodied wisdom, handed down from generation to generation, that is concerned with making place. Why do we make place here, rather than there? What is the nature of place; what are our ambitions? How do we manifest deeply held cultural, social and spiritual values in the act of making place? With what do we make place? How is place sustained?

Furthermore we may reveal larger-scale relations; to the landscape beyond the place itself and within a more existential sense, relations to the cosmos and of course within such a level of comprehension, to deities beyond. Here we might appreciate Heidegger's conceptualisation of the fourfold evident within the big landscapes of locations such as the High Atlas Mountains.

We may also reveal to ourselves within these questions the potential of the concept of archetype; something that is itself of the origin yet may through a deep understanding be capable of reinterpretation within other contexts. My sense is that these archetypes exist at a range of scales. Perhaps the largest scale is that of the settlement; how societal, cultural, spiritual, political and economic values shape and layer our communities in space and time. How and why within settlements we make

FIGURE 6.1 Ait Benhaddou.

places to commune, to gather, to celebrate, to mourn and to worship. Yet in counterpoint we make place to retreat, to divest ourselves of others and to be held in the embrace of privacy; if so fortunate, to dwell poetically. This is the next level of archetype: the dwelling.

Yet the dwelling, like the settlement, is constructed of layers of meaning that again are also informed by embodied societal, cultural, spiritual, political and economic values. In ancient hill villages such as Ait Benhaddou in the High Atlas Mountains, we reveal the layering of space to ensure privacy for the intimate acts of dwelling. We reveal the courtyard as the mediator of many things; climate certainly, but also the mediator of public and private domains, territories of humans and animals and mediation between that of the mundane and that which is prized and valued. Within the dwelling we reveal how domesticity confronts the world. In Ait Benhaddou, seemingly endless external walls with only minimal opportunities for humans to penetrate boldly manifest that confrontation. Here the public and private territories are clearly defined and we are in no doubt if we transgress.

Within the archetype of dwelling we are also exposed to the acts of dwelling and what it is those acts require of place if we are to dwell poetically. The hearth that allows us to cook is also the giver of light and heat and provides both an implicit and explicit invitation to gather. When with others, we have a further invitation: to gather in silence, or in conversation, or song, or as is more likely, often a combination of them all. The bed-space: a place to sleep, to rest, to be in repose, to love, to procreate and a place to dream. Bathing space: a place to bathe, again perhaps to dream, a place to ablute, to cleanse and a place in which to immerse. Kitchen: a place to cook, a place

FIGURE 6.2 Ait Benhaddou Detail.

to eat, a place to look out, and in the courtyard, a place to look up, a place to connect outside of ourselves to all that which lies beyond.

The archetypal precedents are many and varied. As previously discussed, Utzon, for example, found the precedent of plateau in the Mayan temples of Mexico. The plateau provides the opportunity for transcendence into an otherness. In its origins in Mexico, that otherness was ascension towards the realm of the deities, cloaked in ritual and with spiritual intent. In China, Utzon revealed to himself the floating roof, apparently, at least in perceptual terms, transcending the best efforts of gravity. These two elements were conjoined to make Utzon's masterpiece, the Sydney Opera House, but each element was reinterpreted and re-appropriated within the particular contexts of programme, typology, climate, place, and culture that the project prescribed.

It is this ability to be reinterpreted and re-appropriated that makes the recourse to archetypal precedent so potent. The precedent that begins as archetypal and in that sense fixed and immutable, through a process of re-appropriation takes on a form and purpose of its own, and is thus dynamic, fluid and largely non-prescriptive in its potential re-application.

Landscape and place is the third core value shared by Aalto, Utzon and Fehn. The landscapes of each of their homelands have distinctly differing qualities yet there remains common attention within our three protagonists towards the potential that landscape provides in revealing and making place.

> The site of a building is more than a mere ingredient in its conception. It is its physical and metaphysical foundation.
>
> *Holl 1989: 9*

Here Holl articulates a central component of the paradigm of Aalto, Utzon and Fehn. The conceptualisation of site as being the foundation upon which design responses are built. Thus we may imagine conceiving of site as '*chora*', the receptacle of becoming, and where the as yet unimagined might be revealed.

FIGURE 6.3 Ait Benhaddou Landscape.

> We often talked about the first step in the development of an architectonic project. You had to see the site, the context, but then it had to rest. The architecture had to develop a character of its own before it met the site again – at that point the site had matured, the thoughts had gained a distance and a fresh discussion could begin.
>
> *Lie 2009*

Of course such attention is not confined to extant landscape conditions but is also attentive to the potential of building the landscape; the Jyväskylä City Theatre project (Aalto), the Sydney Opera House project (Utzon) and the Villa Busk project (Fehn) are each testament to the potential of building landscape to simultaneously make place and reveal place. It may seem paradoxical yet that very act of making landscape gathers and reveals the existing landscape conditions to us.

Aalto, Utzon and Fehn were each sensitised to the subtleties of existing landscape conditions and able to respond poetically in the forming of place.

The acts of architecture were a consistent preoccupation for Aalto, Utzon and Fehn. In the School for Deaf Children we witness Fehn's understanding of fundamental acts of human existence that is extended here in his understanding of the particular needs of deaf children. For them, visual connections are everything and thus spatial organisations and inter-relationships are designed to facilitate these visual relationships.

> 'The architect has to recognise your physical size,' Fehn continues. 'You cannot accept a point of view that says the structure has to stand and wait, expecting you to grow and reach twenty-one years of age before you fit into the world. … No pedagogy can reach the child if the architecture does not recognise the child's dimensions.'
>
> *Fuchs-Mikac and Brodey 2009*

At Can Lis, Utzon designed a place to dwell that is primal in the sense it invites us to rediscover our primitive inner selves. The hearth invites us to gather, the

FIGURE 6.4 The 'Great Spot' – Can Lis.

aedicule beds are reminiscent of the primal acts of sleeping within the cave, the seemingly carved openings that provide a view to the horizon resonate of the cave-mouth. For Aalto such preoccupations extend to embrace the idea of ritual. The raising of the level of the Council Chamber at Saynatsalo invites a procession upwards towards the *idea* of democracy.

Utzon also invites us in the Can Lis project to engage with the temporal dimensions of architecture. Moving our bodies in space and time we are able to seek sun or shade, coolness or heat, here one has a sense that particular spaces hold particular qualities at particular times of the day, or particular times within the seasons. This is time, space and architecture made manifest.

> [Architecture] demands a good healthy common-sense understanding of life. An understanding of walking, standing, sitting and lying comfortably, of enjoying the sun, the shade, the water on our bodies, the earth and all the less easily defined sense impressions. A desire for well-being must be fundamental to all architecture if we are to achieve harmony between the spaces we create and the activities to be undertaken in them.
>
> *Utzon in Weston 2002: 11*

Aalto, Utzon and Fehn use primal elements to reveal to us our primal selves. The hearth, whether it is the courtyard hearth of the Experimental House, the hearth in Can Lis or Villa Busk each transport us towards our inner selves, our embodied understanding of the primitive acts of dwelling. The hearths remove us from the everyday and invite us back to the clearing in the forest where, as day gives way to night, the fire is lit and the first room is created; the throw of the light defining the extent of that space.

In the Villa Busk project Fehn defines the linear extent of the house at one end with the hearth, and at the other end, the bath. Set into the floor so that when immersed eye level is just above floor level, we can gaze out to the rock and woodland beyond separated from the outside by the lightest veil of glass. This is the rock pool, the mountain stream or the woodland pond. The embodied understanding of our three protagonists of the primitive human acts of architecture, allows the poetry of dwelling to be revealed to us.

> Man has moved into the cave. The animal stands outside, and it is sad, because it has been robbed of its cave. Later, the cave man moves out and transforms nature into culture; he shapes the rock into a block of stone. The stone gives him a dimension with which to build. With the block comes architecture.
>
> *Lie 2009*

Embodied memory is the fifth paradigmatic element common to Aalto, Utzon and Fehn. For Aalto, that may mean the memories of his formative years in the forest and lakes of Jyväskylä, or the internalised memories of his travels to the classical sites of the South. For Utzon, it might manifest in those huge steel hulls in his father's shipyard in Aalborg, or the hunting, fishing and sailing adventures of his childhood. Fehn inhabited the world of collective embodied memory, grounded in the

FIGURE 6.5 The Bath, Villa Busk.

landscape conditions that surrounded him. Memories of the forest, the clearing, the lake, the fire and in differing manifestations, memories we would all recognise.

We all, of course, hold such embodied memories; the gift held by our three protagonists, whether intuitively or consciously, was to be able to draw upon them.

One concept that represents the *arche* and *techne* of Aalto, Utzon, and Fehn is *craftsmanship*, and here I draw from Richard Sennett, who describes it as:

> … an enduring, basic human impulse, the desire to do a job well for its own sake. Craftsmanship cuts a far wider swath than skilled manual labour; it serves the computer programmer, the doctor and the artist … In all of these domains, craftsmanship focuses upon objective standards, on the thing itself.
>
> *Sennett 2008: 9*

Sennett ascribes to the term craftsmanship qualities beyond merely executing a task adequately and suggests that it is the act and process that connects head and hand, in that it is a considered process. In conjoining head and hand the process bridges the concepts of *Arche,* and *Techne,* and is thus implicit rather than explicit in the individual paradigms of Aalto, Utzon and Fehn.

At its best, of course, craftsmanship holds poetic potential, and we may here reflect upon great works of art and architecture, Japanese lacquerware or handcrafted furniture by George Nakashima. I contend that Aalto, Utzon and Fehn were each craftsmen both in the imagining and execution of their individual architectural endeavour, and within Chapters 3–5 the nature of that individual craftsmanship is described.

Of Commonality – Of Techne

Building the site is a primary tactic used consistently by Aalto, Utzon and Fehn. Drawing upon the particular qualities of each place, the narratives of projects were developed. In the Experimental House project Aalto simultaneously builds the site in providing a ritualised approach to the courtyard with the hearth at its centre, and literally builds from the site in the disposition of the substructure logs that span between the rock outcrops to the guest wing. In Can Lis, Utzon developed the narrative of conceptualising of the dwelling as an archetypal settlement and the spatial articulation followed. We are thus transported to the ancient Mediterranean fishing village through a number of precise morphological dispositions that respond to the nature of that particular place. In the Villa Busk project, Fehn's tactic of building the site by bridging between the two rock outcrops, gathers the site. By these precise tactics Aalto, Utzon and Fehn each reveal the essence of place to us.

Tectonic precision is the second *techne* tactic that is common to our protagonists. For Aalto and Fehn this is given expression spanning the whole range of architectural endeavour. It is for Aalto from door handle as the handshake of the building, to the special bricks that allow a static material to become fluid. For Fehn it is the bespoke furniture that populates the School for Deaf Children to the stereotomic mass that

FIGURE 6.6 The Harbour Village.

embraces Villa Busk. For Utzon such precision is given clear expression within the rigour of process. The resolution of the ribbed shell-forms of the Opera House provide a pragmatic response to a complex challenge, informed as they were by the structures of nature and relentless prototyping and experimentation. Such precision, delivered across all scales, from the scale of hand to the scale of landscape or urban context, signifies and reveals intimate and embedded sensibilities of the acts of architecture within Aalto, Utzon and Fehn.

Material and light are the elements that reveal place and form. Aalto acknowledges the particular qualities and sources of light in the Nordic world and positions openings low accordingly to harvest the reflected light from the snow in (for example) the Aalto Museum. Equally, in the Saynatsalo project he is aware of the potential held by clerestory openings to illuminate the democratic process.

Utzon was aware of the potential of light upon material to uplift human experience and in the Bagsvaerd Kirke project, to encourage us to commune with the deities. In contrast, with Can Lis, the direct, somewhat harsh, light of the Balearics is harvested dramatically to model space, form and material.

Fehn, like Aalto, employs the clerestory to animate space and reveal material qualities within (for example) Villa Busk; the role of ventilation is often removed from the window, inviting us to re-evaluate our understanding of that opening as the purveyor of light.

Yet these commonalities are balanced by distinctive paradigmatic elements that characterise our protagonist's unique design methodologies.

Of Distinctions – Of Arche

Aalto acknowledged the power of playfulness in the creative process in imagining the as yet unimagined. His playfulness manifested itself in experimentation and testing; processes all evident within the Experimental House project. Such experimentation is evident at all scales of his work; from the rattan wrapper on the door handles of Saynatsalo that mediates between skin and door, to the fan-like trusses of the council chamber that give expression to the forces of gravity.

Utzon was, as were Aalto and Fehn, attuned to the acts of architecture, which he exhibited consistently through the facilitation of the acts of ritual. In Bagsvaerd he encourages the faithful to promenade beneath the deities, in Can Lis the ritual acts of the ancients are revealed to us in space and time and in the Sydney Opera House project we are encouraged to leave behind the ordinariness of everyday existence, as we ascend to the surface of the plateau upon which the extraordinary is revealed to us.

Fehn's distinction is revealed within his narratives in his work that project us to the world of pre-history, of legend and myth. There is a primacy within these narratives that capture and expose to us our shared and embodied sense of 'being-in-the-world'. The narratives expose us to the core elements of our existence, the horizon, the hearth, the cave, which are manifested consistently in built-form. Yet, despite the universal embodiment of such narratives, paradoxically, when given tangible expression in place, they reveal the particular essence of place to us.

Aalto and Fehn were architects of restraint. Not in the Meisian sense of 'less is more', but in making precise decisions regarding material choice and the conscious realisation that working with a restrained palette facilitated materials to be expressed in counterpoint to each other and to signify, in a semiotic sense, spatial and organisation hierarchies and functions. Villa Mairea for Aalto and Villa Busk for Fehn are perhaps the zeniths of the exhibition of such restraint; where limited material palettes provide a tectonic conversation between form and function.

We cannot discuss Utzon's contribution without giving expression to his principle of additive architecture. This pre-disposition to an additive response was evident at all scales of Utzon's design response, from the macro-scale of the morphology of the Kingo and Fredensborg housing projects and the Jeddah Stadium through to the design for the structural system of the roofs on the Sydney opera House project to the tectonic resolution of the Espansiva Housing system and the Utstep furniture project. Such a pre-disposition embraced the industrialised production processes that were emerging in parallel, in a manner that celebrated the potential in the developments in new technology. We will see such enthusiasm remain within the contemporary architects that extend the heritage of Aalto, Utzon and Fehn to our current age and beyond, later in this chapter.

Fehn's particular distinction is in his ability to reveal narratives through tectonic response. Perhaps Villa Busk described in the preceding chapter represents the zenith of this skill but it is evident throughout his whole portfolio. In the Hedmark Museum project such a capacity spans all scales of his endeavour from the concept

FIGURE 6.7 Tectonic Expression with Limited Material Palette.

that the new insertions within the existing barn are celebrated as such that extends to the precision in detailing the 'furniture' on which the exhibits are mounted.

These distinctions are not of course absolute; they are perhaps differently nuanced within each of our three protagonists: it is the particular amplification of these tendencies within the response of each of our protagonists that suggests the qualities of distinction that are set out above.

Of Speculations

The nature of this study has of course been predominantly historic as our protagonists are sadly no longer of the world, but it would be negligent not to speculate upon the heritage that remains and to examine the engagement with this 'new tradition' that is manifested within contemporary architectural thought and praxis.

Given that Aalto, Utzon and Fehn were located within a very particular Nordic context we may expect to see this heritage extended within this particular physical location and indeed it is; but I will also suggest that the paradigms of Aalto, Utzon and Fehn are also extended to my own context the UK, and will through the examination of three practices of my detailed acquaintance discuss the extension of these paradigms within contemporary praxis.

The Snøhetta practice provides an exemplar of the extension of the tradition described within this study, extending the heritage of Aalto, Utzon and Fehn within our contemporary context. Established in Oslo, Norway, in 1989, after winning the International Design Competition for the Alexandria Library in Egypt, the practice has grown to have 130 employees, and offices in Oslo, Innsbruck, New York and San Francisco.

Snøhetta simultaneously embrace the traditions of craft and the new traditions of technology and oscillate between these binary and analogue territories in the development and delivery of design. Such an engagement represents an extension of the attitudes of Utzon (for example) who embraced the emerging technologies of his time yet remained a proponent of the particular Nordic craft tradition.

Examination of Snøhetta's work will focus upon two key projects: the Norwegian National Opera and Ballet, Oslo (2000–2008) and the Tverrfjellhytta Norwegian Wild Reindeer Pavilion, Hjerkinn, Douvre, Norway (2009–2011). Although of significantly different scales, each project represents an exemplar in the projection of the paradigms of Aalto, Utzon and Fehn within a contemporary context.

The Norwegian National Opera and Ballet was won in an international design competition held in 1989. Snøhetta's entry was 'characterised by the Jury as having strongly identifiable themes that tie the building into its culture and location while also presenting an unusual and unique expression that was in many ways new and innovative' (Snøhetta 2015: 266).

Here we see 'built landscape' in the manner of Utzon's Sydney Opera House, but unlike that project the 'fifth elevation' (the roof) in Oslo is a place of human occupation where we can promenade across the apparently glacial forms that eventually slide into the water at the base, profoundly resonating of the wild and inhospitable landscape that Fehn spoke of.

> The building is as much landscape as architecture and thus fosters the public awareness and engagement with the arts.
>
> *Snøhetta 2015: 266*

FIGURE 6.8 Oslo Opera House.

FIGURE 6.9 Performance Space.

Internally, the performance space is held like a precious gem frozen within the glacier; that is, through precise tectonic articulation set at counterpoint to its surroundings, providing a clear sense of hierarchy. This relationship between landscape and place is reinforced at every level of design; even the coat racks appear somewhat reminiscent of the birch forests so prevalent within Nordic landscapes.

In contrast to the monumental scale of Sydney Opera House, the Norwegian Wild Reindeer Pavilion exhibits similar ambitions to connect landscape and place. Set at an elevation of 1,250 metres in the Douvrefjell National Park, the pavilion overlooks the mountain Snøhetta, from which the office takes its name. Described by the practice as a 'keyless structure', the project was designed as a place that mediated climate and provided a place within which National Park Guides could speak to school parties and others of the unique flora and fauna of this spectacular landscape. As Snøhetta describe the project, 'Natural, cultural and mythical landscapes form the basis of the architectural idea' (Snøhetta 2015: 265).

This is the narrative of Fehn: the revealing of the mythological within the landscape. Here is also a sense of dwelling poetically at its most primal, within this place so inhospitable to man, the cave and the fire separated from the landscape and climate by only the thinnest veil of glazing to the 'mouth' of the cave. Here also is tectonic precision and engagement with the opportunities that emerging technology

FIGURE 6.10 The Forest of Coats.

FIGURE 6.11 Reindeer Pavilion.

provides. The pre-rusted Corten steel that wraps the enclosure improves with age, and the colouration itself is resonant of the heathers within the landscape. The fluid timber seating that characterises the interior and directs the view to the hearth and the landscape beyond, was formed using 3D modelling and robotic milling machines.

This sense of narrative is reinforced in Snøhetta's own commentary upon their work:

> The projects exemplify our common attitudes rather than being complete solutions. They are samples in a string of contextual examinations rather than masterpieces. They are associative rather than symbolic. They are comments rather than statements. *Every story told is a shared experience of contemporary conditions set with a given frame.*
>
> *Snøhetta 2017; emphasis original*

And in these words we divine attitudes of modesty and humility that would resonate with Aalto, Utzon and Fehn.

The practice today is a multi-disciplinary organisation that encompasses architecture, interior design, landscape design and branding design. Snøhetta extend the paradigms of Aalto, Utzon and Fehn in the development and implementation of particular structures and methodologies of working. When interrogating these practices one gains the impression of an organisation that is 'democratic' in nature and 'permeable' by design.

Of course any organisation of the scale and reach of Snøhetta demands a structural hierarchy, yet one has a sense that in the development of project teams, facilities that encourage communal dining, as witnessed in the Oslo office I visited, and an atmosphere of collective betterment, that the structure of Snøhetta is responsive to the generous cultural mores of the Nordic world; the place of the genesis of the practice.

These principles that Aalto might recognise as 'cultural attunement' are further extended through attitudes we may describe as being permeable. Snøhetta is a multi-disciplinary practice, but it is clearly an *inter-disciplinary* practice in its day-to-day operation. Design teams are formed, predicated upon the particular needs of the project that represent this model of inter-disciplinary working. Snøhetta uses a process of 'transpositioning' where group members are invited to:

> ... break from their professional role and switch perspectives with others in the group. By releasing ourselves from disciplinary conventions for a short period of time, we can foster a greater sense of possibility, free ourselves from habitual thinking, and build empathy for others involved in the process.
>
> *Snøhetta 2017*

Such a methodology demonstrates democratic purpose, in that no discipline is regarded as being more important than any other, and exhibits permeability in an attitude of openness to new practices and inter-disciplinary working.

Snøhetta develops and amplifies this attitude of permeability in the sharing of such attitudes and practices through the dissemination of research. First published in 2012, the book *Ideas Work* (Carlsen et al. 2012) explores creative working practices in such diverse disciplines as oil exploration, banking and architecture within a structure that celebrates inclusivity and inter-disciplinary working.

Of similar scale to Snøhetta's Reindeer Pavilion, but of a radically different function, is the Kampii Chapel (2010), Helsinki, Finland, designed by Kimmo Lintula, Niko Sirola and Mikko Summanen of K2S Architects. Financed by local parishes and the Helsinki Social Services Department, the chapel is designed as a non-denominational space that affords peace and the opportunity for meditation and inner contemplation. Located at the edge of Narinkkatori Square in Helsinki at the entrance to the Kampii Shopping Centre, the chapel is an essay in harnessing the particular qualities of Nordic light and a precise tectonic response utilising a limited material palette.

Entry is made through a space that mediates between the chapel and shopping centre through which you pass to the chapel beyond. The chapel is orientated at an oblique angle to the entrance and the external façade is clad in spruce planking that glistens jewel-like in the Helsinki sun. Internally the 11.5-metre-high space is clad in alder, the complex geometry resolved by a cutting process that apparently involved nanotechnology; again, resonant of the attitudes of Utzon in engaging with appropriate emerging technology. Top-lit light cascades down the wall surfaces revealing the nature of material and drawing one's eyes upwards to the mysteries that lay above us. Within this space we might reflect upon similar atmospheres of peace,

FIGURE 6.12 Kampii Chapel.

calm and inner reflection evoked within Utzon's Bagsvaerd Kirke project, albeit within a radically different architectonic form.

We see this resonance in other sacral spaces within Finland in projects such as the St Henry's Ecumenical Art Chapel, 2005, Turku, Finland, designed by Matti and Pirjo Sanaksenaho of Helsinki. Sitting high above eye level upon approach this copper clad inverse hull-shape appears monumental yet, upon entry this sense gives-way to a sense of a more modest scale; a linear space modulated by structural arches; one could be inside the whale here, bones exposed. The eye is drawn to the light entering from beside and above the altar. Here perhaps is sacral architecture at its barest; an essay in form, material and light gifting space for prayer and meditation.

While the extension of the paradigms of Aalto, Utzon and Fehn may be somewhat predictable and even expected within the Nordic context of contemporary architecture, what is perhaps less expected is the migration and subsequent reinterpretation of the paradigms within other geographical locations that are, by implication, within different cultural contexts.

One such example is within the UK, designed in the 1960s by architect Peter Aldington, in the Buckinghamshire village of Haddenham. This modest grouping of three dwellings has since become regarded as 'exceptional and influential examples of modern architecture' (Brown 2010: 15). The project comprises three dwellings, each of courtyard typology and configuration, located within a mature garden. The houses – the Turn, Middle Turn and Turn End – are testament to Aldington's maxim that 'To make a building well assumes an understanding of people – to build otherwise is degrading' (Brown 2010: 19). Peter Aldington and his wife Margaret remain the residents of Turn End to this day.

FIGURE 6.13 St Henry's Chapel.

FIGURE 6.14 Turn End, Buckinghamshire.

FIGURE 6.15 Peter Aldington, January 2016.

The three houses have three elements in common: living space that opens to the courtyard space, a centrally placed dining space and kitchen that forms the 'hub' of the house, and more secluded sleeping spaces. The houses have relatively small floor areas, but the use of partitions that are not full-height combined with exploitation of the volume provide a sense of space far beyond that which the footprint suggests.

In tectonic terms the sense of space is enhanced by the use of a limited palette of materials that provides coherence between space and allows spaces to 'bleed' into adjacent space. All three houses are considered as dwelling in landscape; Turn End particularly holds an apparently seamless relationship with the external space beyond the dwelling. The construction is rugged and simple, fair-faced concrete block walls painted white internally, while externally the walls are clad in rough cast render, again painted white, that resonates of the chalk-wall construction heritage of the village, thus anchoring the project in the particularity of place. The title of the book that describes the project and from which I make reference here is purposeful: *A Garden and Three Houses*. This is a landscape in which houses dwell rather than 'houses with gardens'.

> The historian and critic Dan Cruikshank visited Turn End in October 1996 for a 'Masterclass' article for the journal of the Royal Institute of British Architects: his verdict was that 'these buildings remain an object lesson to all architects'.
>
> *Brown 2010: 15*

It would be all too easy to draw direct parallels to Utzon's own courtyard housing projects such as the Kingo (1958) and Fredensborg (1959) projects, in suggesting that Turn End was influenced by such projects. Aldington was clear in conversation with me that he did not visit the Nordic world until long after the houses were completed, but one senses some kind of osmotic influence at work here; informed by the contemporary atmospheres prevalent within the period.

FIGURE 6.16 Turn End.

However, one detects a clear sense of the paradigm of Aalto, Utzon and Fehn being extended in this project; the courtyard typology, manipulation of space and form, manipulation of light and material, a sense of anchoring to place, and engagement with landscape, combine here to form an essay in the potential provided by such paradigms.

Such influence clearly extends into contemporary practice in the UK. In this examination I have chosen three practices that I have intimate knowledge of. This knowledge is of both their design process and output. This provides an immersive perspective from which to weave the paradigmatic threads that our three protagonists provide within current and future architectural endeavour. The practices are each relatively small in scale, the largest being a team of six (plus Otto the dog), but each demonstrate the extension of the paradigms of Aalto, Utzon and Fehn within a contemporary UK context.

PAD Studio is located in the small coastal town of Lymington, within the New Forest National Park, on the south coast of the UK. Opened in 2005, the practice has built a reputation for the delivery of high quality, innovative architecture that is anchored within landscape and place, delivered with tectonic precision that, as with the earlier examples of Snøhetta, K2S, Matti and Pirjo Sanaksenaho, and Peter Aldington, projects the Nordic paradigms of Aalto, Utzon and Fehn into contemporary British architectural practice.

The New Forest provides a very particular landscape context that PAD consistently 'draw from' in their projects. With its origins as a Royal Hunting Forest, the woodland was largely decimated when the timber was extracted en

FIGURE 6.17 Thrifty Beeches.

Source: Nigel Rigden

masse to supply the exponential expansion of shipbuilding in the Elizabethan era. The New Forest is now characterised by open heathland, clusters of remaining forestation, and a coastal fringe to the Solent and English Channel beyond. The National Park provides a strategic landscape 'gap' between the urban settlements of Southampton to the east, and Bournemouth and Poole to the west. The forest is to this day grazed by ponies and cattle that are owned by 'commoners' who hold grazing rights across the forest that are handed down from generation to generation. It is clear that these factors coalesce within the New Forest National Park to provide a unique landscape condition.

Yet of course, paradoxically such a unique landscape and habitat provides a challenging context in which to design contemporary architecture, governed as it is by additional regulation in the form of planning control designed to minimise and control development. Such a context often within the UK leads a design response that is a pastiche of the original building forms and typologies; a position in counterpoint to the ethos of PAD Studio.

As the founding director Wendy Perring wrote:

> At PAD we are constantly searching for meaning. I believe that as a studio we share a commonality in that we look to the landscape? We believe that meaning exists in every place.
>
> *Wendy Perring, personal communication, 2017*

PAD exposes this meaning of place through narratives that Fehn would recognise, weaving the tangible and intangible 'presencing of place' at the outset of the design process. Wendy Perring continues:

> We [PAD] try to make sense of the meaning, to interpret it correctly. I always think that the site 'speaks' to us ... but we need to let it? To do this we must

> spend time on the site, we must absorb it; we must feel it. We must listen to the site. To understand what it is saying to us and to organize the 'shelter' that we are placing within it in a way that helps the site to have a voice and say 'Do you understand me a little better now … did you notice this about me before?' I hope, as we continue to do this, that the buildings we design will have a sense of connectedness with the site.
>
> *Wendy Perring, personal communication, 2017*

Through this ethos of connecting to place, PAD provides an antidote to the condition of absence that Basso laments when speaking of the discipline of anthropology:

> Missing is a desire to fathom the various and variable perspectives from which people know their landscapes, the self-invested viewpoints from which (to borrow Isak Dinesen's felicitous image) they embrace the countryside and the embrace is returned. Missing is an interest in how men and women dwell.
>
> *Basso 1996: 106*

The 'Thrifty Beeches' New Forest house project comprises a house and guest wing on an 18-acre site, adjacent to ancient woodland and heath, and is an exemplar

FIGURE 6.18 Thrifty Beeches 'Sedimentary' Wall.

FIGURE 6.19 Thrifty Beeches Sleeping Space.

of contemporary re-interpretation of the primal acts of dwelling. Here, the site is 'gathered' by the spine wall, the hearth disposed adjacent to the large glazed openings that overlook the natural swimming pool, all resonating of the woodland pool viewed from the security of the cave. In a manner redolent of the Danish landscape, the house 'hunkers down' in this place; an earth berm to the north of the site, constructed from the material excavated to form the pool, provides a tangible sense of place anchored in landscape. This connectedness to place is the foundation of PAD's design process, but such a depth and breadth of understanding similarly extends to the client:

> We are interested in our clients; they are all unique and different people who dream of dwelling in different ways. We try to engage with them, especially during the brief forming period, and to encourage them to speculate upon how they live. We hope that we are good listeners, and that we do not try to make a dwelling or home that does not suit the personality of a client, or the personality of a place.
>
> *Wendy Perring, personal communication, 2017*

Ricky Evans, an associate architect at PAD, is transparent in articulating the relationship of the work of the practice to the heritage of Aalto, Utzon and Fehn:

> In a constant search for unearthing a deeper connection with the world and a hunt for the root of one's 'being in the world' something was discovered in the work of Fehn, Aalto and Utzon. Fehn revealed a primordial connection with landscape and vision of material. While Utzon demonstrated how making and material become the structure to a poetic narrative. They are fluidly bound in a composition played out as we experience, as well dwell. The tectonic composition manipulates nature; light, sound, gravity and air to

> draw us closer to our condition, to reveal the world in a way we could not experience without it. It is integral to understanding place and our position in that given place.
>
> *Ricky Evans, personal communication, 2017*

This influence also reflects the tectonic pre-disposition of our three protagonists demonstrated within the work of PAD. In the 'Thrifty Beeches' house the clearly articulated spine wall is the organising element of the project that extends externally to gather the landscape in a way similar to Fehn's Villa Busk project. As Wendy Perring confirms:

> The spine wall is not only the retainer of the earth excavated from the ground, but it becomes the container into which the rooms are inserted. The wall defines the arrival experience, it is bold in form and it shields the view, focusing the gaze and the route. The wall unites, and it guides. It is also of the site. Whilst the original intent was to make the wall with the soil from the site, the reality proved harder to make authentic, but the idea of this connection is retained and the imprint of the place is captured upon the board-marked face. The result is much more than an object that supports the roof; the wall is an architectural device that roots the dwelling to the site.
>
> *Wendy Perring, personal communication, 2017*

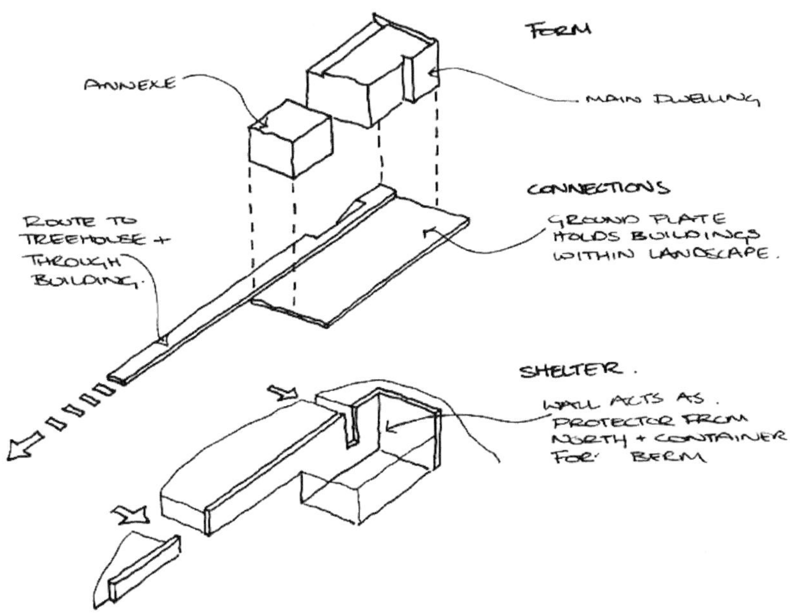

FIGURE 6.20 Concept Sketch, Thrifty Beeches.

Source: PAD Studios

This concrete spine wall appears as layers of sediment; the boards that formed the shuttering were cut from trees felled on the site, and thus the imprint of the timber is the memory of the trees that once stood in this place. Incidentally, the boards were cleaned after use and now clad an outbuilding on the site and the memory of the trees is thus amplified.

Darren Bray, the technical director at PAD, is clear as to the tectonic ambitions held by PAD:

> I believe that PAD strive to embody the role of master craftsman in its truest sense in understanding, of building and constructing, as described by Gottfried Semper, where here the qualities of making are set as being inherent in the constructional act. PAD seeks to elevate the level of making through an obsession in tectonic detailing.
>
> *Darren Bray, personal communication, 2017*

However, within such ambitions exists modesty; a level of humility that acknowledges the legacy of others in informing these pre-dispositions, that is resonant of parallel sensibilities consistently uncovered within the Nordic world. Darren Bray continues:

> Having been the apprentice to a skilled master [architect Stan Bolt – who in turn worked with Peter Aldington], educated in the truest understanding of how materials are crafted into architectural detail, through making, weaving, jointing, framing and placing on the earth. It is my understanding that by achieving a resolution in our work at PAD, we are able to reveal a tectonic resolution of our architecture.
>
> *Darren Bray, personal communication, 2017*

A more recent recruit to the PAD team, Collette Raine, encapsulates the demeanour and disposition of PAD in relation to Aalto, Utzon and Fehn succinctly as her voice brings our correspondence to a close:

> Further to the earlier commentaries, and I believe underlying of all our observations, is an intertwining thread that joins the underpinning of PAD with the works of Aalto, Fehn and Utzon, honesty and humanism. A focus on working with and drawing from the essence of the place (site) to create a form (architecture) of human scale and senses.
>
> *Collette Raine, personal communication, 2017*

Perhaps these attitudes are exemplified within the Water Tower project, a historic tower, now no longer used for its original purpose; an adjunct to a substantial historic New Forest House. PAD embarked upon a process of 'paring-back' the accretions that the tower had collected over time until the essence of 'towerness' was revealed. Upon this revelation, PAD proposed a number of discrete interventions: a projecting window opening that gathers the light in the manner of a camera lens, a sculptural spiral stair that sits in elegant counterpoint to the stereotomic orthogonal

FIGURE 6.21 Tower.

Source: Nigel Rigden

FIGURE 6.22 Tower Stair.

Source: Nigel Rigden

form of the tower. This is a place of retreat and repose that harvests the spectacular views from high level of the New Forest landscape.

In this project two further extensions of paradigmatic elements are exposed: *narrative* that would resonate with Fehn, and a sense of *serious playfulness* that would resonate with Aalto. The narrative is that the client requested a space in which to bathe on the top floor of the tower and the space should be of such power, that it would draw him up three flights of stairs. This was interpreted by PAD in a playful parti of a golden metal thread winding through the tower, drawing the client ever upward across three floors.

As Wendy Perring explains:

> The journey begins at the entrance in the form of the new metal lined front door – a heavy and dignified statement of arrival, delivering a reassuring weightiness. Above the entrance door the metal frame of the camera lens window provides a sense of the thread continuing. As you climb upwards, the metal thread is woven around the new window, which frames the forest view. The thread then culminates in the new beautifully constructed ribbon like stair that lends an air of drama and arrival at the top floor of the tower, which holds a spa-like retreat for the client to escape to.
>
> *Wendy Perring, personal communication, 2017*

PAD clearly shares, exhibits and extends elements of the paradigms of Aalto, Utzon and Fehn; particularly in their sensitivity to landscape and place which, when combined with their sophisticated tectonic resolution, results in humane modern architecture anchored to the beautiful context of the New Forest National Park.

Like Snøhetta, PAD also exhibits attitudes that are both democratic and permeable. A (relatively) small office comprising six architects, the office is 'horizontal' in design; there are no separate cellular offices for the Directors, and no separate meeting room, which ensures all conversations are enacted within shared space providing transparency and openness in working practice.

PAD are by demeanour a collaborative organisation with, by their own admission, a strong ethical compass. In the correspondence with me that forms the basis of the commentary above, each member of the PAD team had a voice; each provided an individual commentary that reflects both their personal and collective contribution to PAD through this process of collaborative working.

They also collaborate with contractors, artisans, peer professionals, community groups and engage fully with contemporary architectural discourse through active membership of professional organisations, award panels and local authority design panels.

They perceive their client relationships in that spirit of a collaborative and equitable process. This permeability is given expression also in PAD's openness to share their own practice processes with other practitioners and they have effectively mentored a number of young practitioners in the formation of embryonic design practices. In addition, all members of PAD teach, and through teaching they feel they learn, and this openness to ideas and influences characterises PAD, in the manner that Aalto would understand in being attuned to the zeitgeist.

PAD are consistently immersed in processes of reflection upon what it is they do and why. This reflection takes many forms and is embedded as individual and collective practice. From this process emerged the PAD Manifesto – conceived of as a 'work in progress'. This reflection seeks to provide fidelity in the understanding of PAD, its relationship to the thoughts of architecture in a manner that Fehn would recognise:

> Fidelity to objectives and to methods, tenacity, the courage to repeat characterise Fehn's thinking and his architecture, signalling his thoroughly Nordic character and profound ethical concern.
>
> *Norberg-Schulz and Postiglione 1997: 59*

We cannot leave the narrative of PAD without reference to the poetic qualities that inhabits all of their work. The influences and pre-dispositions coalesce and manifest themselves within poetic atmospheres that inhabit the PAD portfolio. The sediment concrete wall of the New Forest House embraces the visitor upon arrival, guides them to the door and onwards to the stair that washes the floor below in light. The essence of that wall in terms of its material quality, its nature as sediment and its embrace and gathering of the site are each revealed by light. The Water Tower is the signifier in the landscape that Fehn would recognise and upon entry is revealed as being of the landscape which is increasingly revealed as we ascend

FIGURE 6.23 Sedimentary Spine Wall.

Source: Nigel Rigden

towards what is one of the most intimate of human acts of dwelling; to bathe, naked, high above the landscape.

Similar values of democracy and permeability exhibited by PAD are evident in the Simon Astridge Architecture Workshop (SAAW), albeit within a very different physical location. Situated in North London, the SAAW context is exclusively urban within one of the most vibrant, diverse and eclectic cities on Earth.

Conceived of as a 'workshop' since inception in 2011, the relatively small practice of three architects is considered as an open and democratic organisation:

> I see SAAW as a flock of geese flying in formation. When the lead goose tires or is otherwise distracted, a goose from behind comes up to take over the lead, to face and deflect the headwinds. The workshop therefore functions as a flock.
>
> *Simon Astridge, personal communication, November 2016*

The concept of workshop is inextricably linked with a spirit of collaboration that also resonates within PAD. However, in SAAW the collaborations are predominantly focused upon alliances with artisans, artists and makers with whom the Workshop work: in various ways depending upon the nature of the project. This permeability that is exhibited in differing ways by Snøhetta, PAD and SAAW extends the Nordic paradigm and is perhaps representative of our current epoch that is characterised by fluidity, horizontality and velocity in the exchange of ideas, knowledge and, on occasions, wisdom.

> We are an assemblage of skilled architects, designers and crafts-people who contribute through a collaborative process, in the delivery of our projects. It is these people, their wisdom, their material knowledge, their working processes and dedication that defines the Workshop. We believe in making, imagining, listening, learning, and empowering the Workshop members, our collaborators and clients.
>
> *Simon Astridge, personal communication, January 2017*

In the examination of the 'plywood house', which draws its name from the material that now characterises it, the project is a remodelling of a Victorian terraced house in Balham, southwest London, and is testament to the paradigmatic element of Aalto and Fehn to transcend scales of architectural endeavour. As Simon Astridge records:

> Sheets of 18mm birch faced plywood were used as floors and walls and ceilings of one entire level of a Victorian house. This was to create warmth, lightness and shadow to the upper sanctuary of a master bedspace area for sleeping, dressing and bathing. The same material and thickness was also used as a laminated glu-lam structure in the ground floor extension roof. The exact same thickness and material was used to make furniture, a pantry and drawers for a kitchen island and a 100mm deep photo gallery shelf with a routed V groove made to rest pictures. The new staircase to the new master sanctuary was made of plywood. The structural strength in the final u-shaped winding stair is the plywood itself.
>
> *Simon Astridge, personal communication, January 2017*

FIGURE 6.24 Plywood House Rear Elevation.

Source: Nicholas Worlsey

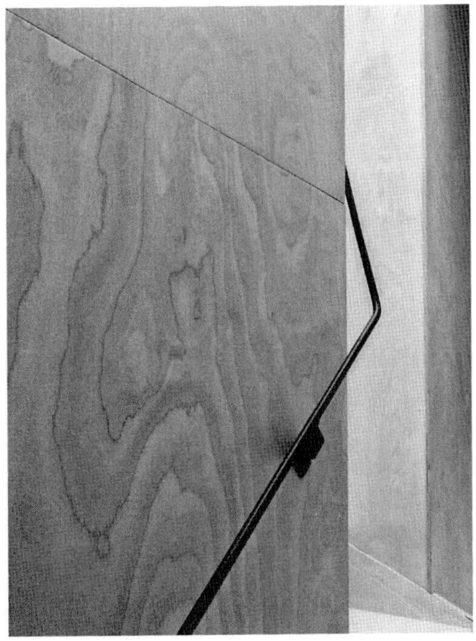

FIGURE 6.25 Saw Plywood Detail.

Source: Nicholas Worlsey

In this project we also witness the heritage of Aalto, Utzon and Fehn in the delivery of tectonic precision; junctions meticulously detailed; and materials set in counterpoint. Each material amplifying the presence of the other developed and delivered through a process of collaboration with artisans and makers: each master craftspersons in their chosen field. As those details coalesce and are perceived in combination, they reveal the opportunity to dwell poetically.

SAAW, like Aalto, Utzon and Fehn, are pre-occupied by the *acts* of architecture:

> The plywood house aims at returning to the things themselves and the fundamental acts of dwelling. Spaces were specifically designed around verbs and not nouns. The acts of gathering, reading, communing occur with in the living spaces. The acts of ascending, robing, unrobing, bathing, and sleeping are revealed in the private quarters. A floating snug was placed in the rear concrete kitchen extension wall, and glazed on the outside wall for a view of the intimate garden space. The cantilevered snug was sized specifically for mother and child to read together.
>
> *Simon Astridge, personal communication, January 2017*

These acts of architecture are revealed through a limited palette of materials that would resonate with Aalto, Utzon and Fehn:

> Concrete, stone, brick, plywood and the sky were the five new materials inserted into the Plywood House Victorian fabric. Concrete on walls and floors, brick on walls and floors, plywood on walls, floors, ceilings, stone in wet zones and the sky penetrating everywhere.
>
> *Simon Astridge, personal communication, January 2017*

FIGURE 6.26 Plywood Detail.

Source: Nicholas Worlsey

FIGURE 6.27 SAAW Concrete Samples.

Source: Nicholas Worlsey

In this attitude of restraint in material palette that Aalto and Fehn (particularly) would recognise, each chosen material is amplified in its presencing: its being-in-the-world, exposing the 'thingness of thing' to us whether that be mass, density, shadow, light, or simply an invitation 'to be.'

These material choices are for SAAW not arbitrary or wilful acts but are themselves revealed through processes of testing and experimentation that are, in a way that Aalto would empathise with, the product of 'serious playfulness'. Simon Astridge, in correspondence, suggests that for the Workshop, concrete is their equivalent of Aalto's brick experiments within the Experimental House project:

> Aalto's prototyping of brick for use in non-standard construction, is reminiscent of the Workshop's development of a range of prototyping 14 pigmented concrete samples used throughout their projects. Samples and colours and textures and hues, were inspired by the Conservation Area brick colours of London. This means that the Workshop has developed a series of pigmented concrete samples that can be used during discussions with planning authorities for permissions and with contractors for pricing. The Workshop's tectonic engagement within the endeavour of architecture results in the use of these samples throughout their work.
>
> *Simon Astridge, personal communication, January 2017*

SAAW were commissioned by a London supplier of Bulthaup Kitchens to extend their existing showroom, forming a new basement area in Putney conceived of as a wine cellar for wine tasting events, client presentations and parties. Here again we see SAAWs pre-disposition to use a limited material palette to great effect within a profoundly stereotomic act of making place.

As SAAW articulate on their website:

> The concept revolved around revealing the lightness of light, the darkness of dark and the stoneness of stone. The palette of materials chosen for the space were purposefully used to absorb natural levels of illuminance. Matt

> black concrete wall panels, matt black metalwork staircase made by Martin (the metalworker) and matt black timber and kitchen panels from Bulthaup.
>
> *SAAW 2015*

SAAW consider themselves as 'conductors' of orchestras that comprise clients, artisans, artists, and makers, each of whom are chosen on the basis of the particular demands of particular projects. However, SAAW are also of the view that such processes do not exist within a vacuum and that they are constantly influenced by the zeitgeist that surrounds them.

Climbing upon the shoulders of Aalto, Utzon and Fehn, SAAW is similarly permeable to new influences and ideas informing their work. In conversation with SAAW, the Workshop members were clear that most of their inspiration does not originate in the field of Architecture. Drawing from such diverse influences as music, art, literature, poetry, cuisine and counter-culture, all members of SAAW are inquisitive and believe in the idiom that 'culture is their currency and ideas are their cash'. Following the paths of our three protagonists they travel to cultures which are not their own; to locations of 'cultural density' is a central element of the SAAW ethos:

> Simon travels extensively and all Workshop members undertake summer cultural trips together to invigorate and to create a cultural discourse. In the summer of 2016, the Workshop travelled to the northern lakes of Italy, where we rented a villa on the banks of Lake Iseo. This lake was the location of Christo and Jean-Claude's masterpiece; The Floating Piers. The shimmering and breathing orange fabric was constantly being repaired and was temporal for 2 weeks only. It was to this day the most powerful piece of art my body has experienced.
>
> *Simon Astridge, personal communication, January 2017*

FIGURE 6.28 Putney Cellar.

Source: Nicholas Worlsey

FIGURE 6.29 Putney Cellar Stairs.

Source: Nicholas Worlsey

FIGURE 6.30 Putney Cellar Wine Rack.

Source: Nicholas Worlsey

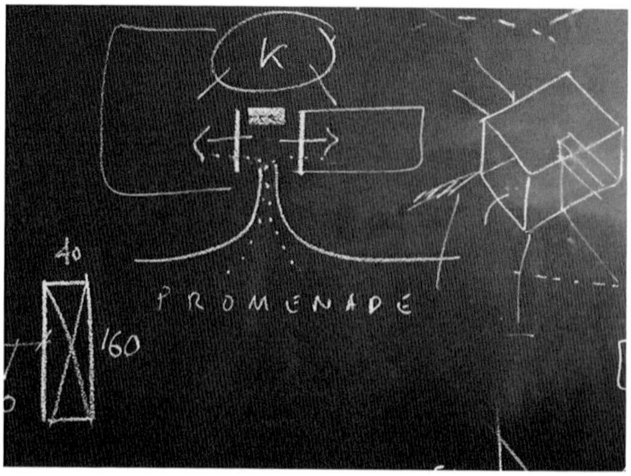

FIGURE 6.31 PCA Sketch Wall.

These complex and diverse influences coalesce within the poetic qualities of SAAW's oeuvre. The Putney cellar is celebrating the absence of light that is in direct contrast to the plywood house that celebrates the play of light upon material, inviting a tactile response. The stereotomic mass of the cellar walls are the stone to the feather of the birch-face of the plywood house. Yet although each material is meagre (at least in the sense of lacking in ostentation), the tectonic precision of SAAW ensures that the essential qualities of the material are revealed to us and within that revelation each material becomes radiant.

The attitudes of permeability evident within SAAW, are also evident in the work of Paul Cashin Architects (PCA), a small practice located in Winchester, Hampshire. This relatively young practice that was formed in 2012 is establishing a reputation for high quality architecture in urban, sub-urban and rural contexts. The principal, Paul Cashin, is clear as to the legacy he builds upon:

> I hope to bring forward lessons from Aalto's work in our own practice. Perhaps by creating a house at the bottom of the hill instead of at the top, rooting it into the landscape …
>
> *Paul Cashin, personal communication, January 2017*

Like PAD and SAAW, Paul Cashin is pre-occupied with the *acts* of architecture, drawing upon the paradigms of Aalto, Utzon and Fehn. When writing of a current project these acts are translated into signifiers of the primal nature of dwelling. He writes:

> The reason my Clients acquired the house is to replace the existing dwelling with a bespoke house of their own requirements, influenced by their own travel experiences in Scandinavia. Within their brief they encouraged moments where 'pools of light' and 'nooks of darkness' occur within the spaces of the house. Currently we have proposed these moments to happen along a procession that encircles the main loving space where a log-burning

> hearth will be placed. The principle is to look within the house for meaningful positions in which to sit, lie … dwell.
>
> *Paul Cashin, personal communication, January 2017*

Yet such primal ambitions are layered with the poetic qualities of human existence exemplified by the PCA entry into the International Yeats Design Competition, in Innisfree, Ireland. PCA designed a journey of narrative, where the landscape so loved by Yeats was incrementally revealed to the visitor through a series of landscape interventions that were conceived of as gentle incisions of the surface of the Earth.

PCA are equally preoccupied with matters of landscape and tectonic authenticity. When writing of his experience of Aalto's Experimental House, Paul Cashin recalls:

> Aalto's focus is on a space immediately in front of the main living and sleeping rooms. This space, of the hearth, the courtyard, and the surrounding tectonic examples of brick construction, carries greater implicit meaning to the inhabitant who knows that dwelling 'within' the landscape …
>
> *Paul Cashin, personal communication, January 2017*

FIGURE 6.32 PCA Innisfree Competition Entry.

Source: Paul Cashin Architects

FIGURE 6.33 PCA Le Touquet House.

Source: Paul Cashin Architects

This approach of appropriate tectonic resolution within particular landscape conditions is exemplified by the PCA Le Touquet (2) project on the northern coast of France. In the manner of Snøhetta's Reindeer Pavilion the garden walls and thresholds are formed from pre-weather steel that wraps around the house and defends against the saline environment. The house, clad in birch, appears as a defended place of retreat, held within this shifting landscape by the elements of steel. The extrusion of the steel out across the site in elements such as steps, anchors house to place and that sense of anchoring will only increase as the sands of time incrementally cover the steel.

The PCA website acknowledges and celebrates the nature of place, the idea of revealing landscape and the influences upon the practice:

> We think it is paramount for contemporary design to consider the nature of a place before we commit to any proposal which may change that place forever. We see the landscape as a precursor to dwelling.
>
> *PCA undated*

It continues:

> We also imagine spaces as atmospheres, contrasting and complementing each other, attempting to foster a 'sense of place' within any architectural proposition. Our approach draws from examples of the contemporary architecture found in Scandinavia, Switzerland, Japan, and America, but all the while rooted in the rural vernacular found most commonly in the UK.
>
> *PCA undated*

With few projects yet completed, it is impossible as yet to judge the poetic quality of place designed by the practice, but all images of projects are evocative and atmospheric that represent poetic ambition that will become manifest as the practice develops.

However, the heritage of Aalto, Utzon and Fehn extends beyond the shores of the UK and mainland Europe, crossing the Atlantic and being evident in the work of such proponents as Rick Joy and Steven Holl.

Steven Holl (1947–) is a New York-based architect, with offices in Beijing and San Francisco, educated at the University of Washington and the Architectural Association (AA), London. He currently holds a tenured academic position at the University of Columbia, USA.

Holl acknowledges the heritage of his intellectual position that draws directly from the writings of Merleau-Ponty and Juhani Pallasmaa: 'Phenomenology concerns the study of essences; architecture has the potential to put essences back into existence' (Holl 1996: 11).

Holl's primary tactic in the manifestation of these essences is the interrogation of the essential qualities of site that anchors the work to the place. As he articulates:

> With each project the firm explores new ways to integrate an organizing idea with the programmatic and functional essence of a building. Rather than imposing a style upon different sites and climates, or pursued irrespective of program, the unique character of a program and a site becomes the starting point for an architectural idea.
>
> *Holl undated*

He continues:

> While anchoring each work in its specific site and circumstance, Steven Holl Architects endeavours to obtain a deeper beginning in the experience of time, space, light and materials. The phenomena of the space of a room, the sunlight entering through a window, and the colour and reflection of materials on a wall and floor all have integral relationships.
>
> *Holl undated*

Like Aalto, Utzon and Fehn, Holl is open to diverse influences, which informs his work; in the Stretto House project (1989–1991) he draws upon the structure of Bella Bartok's *Music for Strings, Percussion and Celeste* to inform the parti and ordering of the house. He sees the project as 'a series of spatial dams with an aqueous space flowing through them' (Holl 1989: 150). And, in the manner in which Bartok redistributed the orchestra, providing adjacencies of tone rather than adjacencies of instrumental typologies, as is usually the case. Yet, in contrast, in the material sense, the project draws directly upon the Texas vernacular of concrete block and corrugated metal that anchors house to place.

However, it is the Kiasma project (1992–1998) in Helsinki that perhaps exemplifies Holl's intellectual relationship to the paradigms of our three protagonists most clearly. This museum of contemporary art was won by Holl in an international competition

FIGURE 6.34 Kiasma.

FIGURE 6.35 Kiasma Weaving.

in 1988: Holl used the pseudonym 'Chiasma'; a term drawn from ancient Greek that denotes a crossing and in current parlance refers to the crossing of optic fibres in the brain that allows the visual cortex to receive the same hemispheric visual field from both eyes. *Kiasma* is the Finnish translation of 'chiasma'.

The site is surrounded by iconic urban architecture: to the west, is the Finnish Parliament Building, to the east, Saarinen's railway station, and to the north, Aalto's Finlandia. Drawing upon this unique set of conditions, Holl uses the parti to weave Kiasma to its particular context. As he writes:

> The concept of Kiasma involves the building's mass intertwining with the geometry of the city and landscape which are reflected in the shape of the building. An implicit cultural line curves to link the building to Finlandia Hall while it also engages a 'natural line' connecting to the back landscape and Töölö Bay.
>
> *Holl undated*

The Kiasma occurs in the interweaving of programme, urban context predicated upon precise and differing spatial dispositions that coalesce around a spinal route that lifts the visitor through space and time. This sense of spatial articulation and processional route is amplified by Holl's use of natural light deep within the plan, in addition to that emitted indirectly above the external walls; the primary curved form of the building designed to reflect the sun path at latitude 60° north.

Holl exhibits similar abilities to transcend scales of architectural endeavour as our three protagonists; the door handles that represent the handshake of Kiasma etched with the memory of the thousands of human hands that have touched them, the light fittings that interweave space, the handrails that invite ascent all combine in a tactile provocation to us, evoking our desire to move through space.

This is a place of encounter, with light, shadow, art, and through those encounters a further encounter: with our own innermost being. However, Kiasma is largely devoid of what is perhaps Holl's most significant contribution that largely eluded Aalto, Utzon and Fehn: his ability to use colour to great effect. The story of modernism, that of course includes Nordic humane modernism, is largely a 'narrative of white'. Bringing together light and colour Holl extends the modern paradigm in a manner reminiscent of the artist James Turrell.

Holl has an international portfolio of projects that demonstrate permeability in the possibility for the translation of phenomenological ideas in cultural contexts that are not Holl's own, founded upon the desire to understand and reveal the essence of place, wherever that place might be. This is not the application of style to place, in order to make a signature building that we might recognise (for example) in the work of the late Zaha Hadid, but rather demonstrates a design narrative founded upon ideas of spatial archaeology alluded to earlier in this study. At its best, permeability encourages flows in two directions: inwards and outwards. It is this quality of permeability that releases the poetry into the world and perhaps today, more than ever, we need the poets.

Heidegger posed the question, *what is the role of the poet in destitute times?* And today, that question is most apposite. We are within a post-truth, Trump and Brexit world in which information flows ever faster, more horizontally and fluidly and apparently with little control. Commentators are identifying the demise of the nation-state and we see in a variety of constructs oppositional forces at play: democracy and authoritarianism, truth and alternative truth, human rights and discrimination, order and disorder, homogenisation and retribalisation, globalisation and localism; the list appears almost without end. In addition we identify flux in the world: refugees and economic migrants, climate change, sea-level rise, the dissipation of institutions, the rise of networks and widespread distrust of the political class.

Yet, in response, we apparently seek to counterbalance all this uncertainty and anxiety with things outside of ourselves; consumer spending continues to rise and underpins much of the Western economy, and individual debt apparently spirals ever-upward perhaps in an attempt, as the Romans suggested, to purchase the 'bread and circuses' that will distract us just enough, for just long enough.

Thomas Friedman (2016) suggests that we are within an epoch of disconnection; where the pace and volume of developments in the world exceed even the exponential growth defined by 'Moore's law':[1]

> The three largest forces on the planet – technology, globalization and climate change – are all accelerating at once. As a result, so many aspects of our societies, workplaces, and geopolitics are being reshaped and need to be reimagined.
>
> *Friedman 2016: 4*

FIGURE 6.36 Kiasma Stair.

Friedman continues, 'In such a time, opting to pause and reflect, rather than panic or withdraw is a necessity. It is not a luxury or a distraction' (Friedman 2016: 4).

However, evidence suggests that pauses are not being taken and in fact the antithesis of such a position is emerging. With the prospect of the evaporation of our ability to control or at least engage with such exponential change, Friedman suggests that we increasingly disconnect, seeking solace in a diverse range of distractions that are the 'bread and circuses' of our own times; reality TV, substance abuse, pornography (in all of its forms), exotic holidays which inevitably evaporate upon rejoining the everyday, buying more, buying bigger, buying newer are all, by definition, thirst that can never be sated as there is always something 'more, bigger, newer' to be bought.

As Marx and Engels prophesied in 1848:

> All fixed fast-frozen relations, with their train of ancient and venerable prejudices and opinions are swept away, all new-formed ones become antiquated before they can ossify. All that is solid melts into air, all that is holy is profaned, and man is at last compelled to face with sober senses, his real conditions of life, and his relations with his kind.
>
> *Marx and Engels 1967: 7*

The external distractions to which we resort to divert our attention from these uncertainties, are of course a mere bagatelle; these are the flickering shadows on the wall of Plato's cave, when measured against the essence of what it is to be human and to dwell (poetically) on the earth under the sight of the deities. We are in destitute times. Perhaps, it is the role of the poet in desperate times to reveal our selves to our selves, our outer selves to our inner selves, and of course vice versa.

The *genre* of the poetry is largely inconsequential; whether it is Leonard Cohen suggesting that 'First we take Manhattan', or perhaps Rilke telling the young poet to 'search inside himself', or Brancusi who gives us essence, or Rothko, who takes us beyond mere earthly existence to the realm of the metaphysical. Yet …

My own *primary* source of poetry lies within architecture and my embodied need in that regard is to be moved; moved from the mundane acts of 'mere building' towards the profound realm of 'dwelling'. And such is the common denominator of Aalto, Utzon and Fehn; each had the capacity to reveal 'the things' to us as poets always do, rather than to merely present that which immediately appears. These revelations are themselves born of ways of seeing embodied within Aalto, Utzon and Fehn. Certainly such qualities were informed by their particular Nordic heritage, but there is something universal in the qualities revealed that resonates within all of us if we are prepared to go beyond that which appears.

Revelations such as what it is to sleep, to love, to arise, to be in repose, to prepare food, to dine, to bathe are all held within the Heideggerian concept of dwelling poetically. In counterpoint to the mere bagatelle of our consumerist culture where we seek things externally, within this phenomenological paradigm we seek things internally; we refer to our 'inner self' and that inner self responds. The joy of this inner self is that within a world of flux, fluidity and disconnection it provides relative stability as it represents the core of our whole self. It is this relative stability that provides counterpoint to the instability described by Friedman, Marx and Engels.

This idea of counterpoint is well known within the world of music; the rhythm and weight of the bass line at counterpoint to the lightness and fay-like qualities of the harmony; percussion in counterpoint to flute, Eric Clapton's riffs to Ginger Baker's drums. Counterpoint is not, however, exclusive; it merely presents a rather oppositional position that paradoxically reveals the whole to us. Without the combination of the counterpoints of Bruce, Baker and Clapton, there would have been no Cream.

Implicit within this book is a narrative that there may, within the context of architectural endeavour, be value in a phenomenological approach. A response that acknowledges the primal conditions of man, the primal qualities of what it is to dwell poetically and to see beyond appearances; to reveal the thingness of things. However, such methods require intentionality and a degree of self-discipline; we are surround by superficial claims upon our consciousness, and the plethora of architectural images (for example) that are available to us today actively subvert and distract.

The paradox of course in our world of rapid change is that such an approach involves a process of 'going back' to the origin of things as did Aalto, Utzon and Fehn. And implicit within that process of returning to the origin of things is that development of a 'personal permeability' that allows such origins to be recognised, observed, speculated-upon, and perhaps eventually, within the spirit of our three protagonists, reinterpreted within our contemporary world as a counterpoint to conditions of flux.

This position does not represent an attempt or desire to overturn our world: that, given the momentum and velocity of contemporary culture, political, economic and social flows, would be a vacuous ambition. Rather it intends to present an alternative – a counterpoint – that through reflection upon the heritage provided by Aalto, Utzon and Fehn, and extended by those discussed above within this chapter, might signify a route into the future, for architecture of greater substance and significance. In conclusion, I will end with the words of Jørn Utzon, the genesis of this book:

> But to elicit our unconscious reactions until they become conscious to us ought to be our starting point. By rehearsing our ability to grasp these differences and their effect upon us, by being in contact with our surroundings, we find our way into architecture's innermost being.
>
> *Jørn Utzon in Weston 2002: 10*

Note

1 Intel co-founder Gordon Moore postulated in 1965 that the speed and power of microchips would double every year, which he later adjusted to every two years, and such a pattern of exponential growth has been proven to be roughly correct over the last 50 years.

References

Basso, K. 1996. *Wisdom Sits in Places*. Albuquerque, NM: University of New Mexico Press.

Brown, J. 2010. *A Garden and Three Houses*. Aylesbury: Turn End Charitable Trust.

Carlsen, R., Clegg, S. and Gjersvik, R. 2012. *Ideas Work*. Oslo: Cappelen Damm.

Fjeld, P. O. 2009. *Sverre Fehn: The Patterns of Thoughts*. New York: Monacelli Press.

Friedman, T. 2016. *Thank You for Being Late: An Optimist's Guide to Thriving in an Age of Accelerations*. London: Random House.

Fuchs-Mikac, N. and Brodey, I. 2009. Skådalen School, Oslo, 1969–1975. Retrieved 22 January 2017 from www.architecturenorway.no/stories/other- stories/skadalen-fuchs-mikac 2009.

Holl, S. 1989. *Anchoring*. New York: Princetown Architectural Press.

Holl, S. 1996. *Intertwining*. New York: Princetown Architectural Press.

Holl, S. Undated. Philosophy. Retrieved 8 February 2017 from www.stevenholl.com/philosophy.

Lie, T. 2009. The Word Thief: An Interview with Per Olaf Fjeld. Retrieved 22 January 2017 from www.architecturenorway.no//stories/people-stories/fjeld-on-fehn-09.

Marx, K. and Engels, F. 1967. *The Communist Manifesto*. London: Penguin Books.

Norberg-Schulz, C. and Postiglione, G. 1997. *Sverre Fehn: Works, Projects, Writings 1949–1996*. New York: Monacelli Press.

PCA. Undated. Approach. Retrieved 5 February 2017 from www.paulcashinarchitects.co.uk/contemporary-modern-chartered-architects-winchester-hampshire/approach.

SAAW. 2015. Wine Cellar: South London, 2015. Retrieved 13 September 2017 from http://simonastridge.com/project/wine-cellar.

Sennett, R. 2008. *Craftsmanship*. London: Penguin Books.

Snøhetta. 2015. *Snøhetta: People, Process, Projects*. Oslo: Forgalet Press.

Snøhetta. 2017. Transpositioning. Retrieved 28 January 2017 from http://snohetta.com/process/transpositioning.

Weston, R. 2002. *Utzon: Inspiration – Vision – Architecture*. Hellerup: Blondal.

INDEX

Entries in *italics* denote images.